assistance at various times, especially to the late Sir James H. Ramsay, Bart., of Banff, who placed at my disposal his valuable historical library, and to the Rev. T. Holme for reading some of the proof-sheets. My thanks are also due to the librarians of the Advocates' Library, Edinburgh; the Rylands' Library, Manchester; and especially to Dr. John Sampson of the Tate Library in the University of Liverpool; as well as to the Librarian of my own University and the British Museum authorities. Moreover, I must pay a tribute to the unfailing patience and courtesy of the advisers, readers, and compositors of the Clarendon Press.

A. J. M.

CONTENTS

LANFRANC

Oxford University Press

London Edinburgh Glasgow Copenhagen
New York Toronto Melbourne Cape Town
Bombay Calcutta Madras Shanghai

Humphrey Milford Publisher to the University

LANFRANC

A STUDY OF HIS LIFE WORK & WRITING

BY

A. J. MACDONALD, M.A.
His Majesty's Indian Service. Madras Establishment
Formerly Vicar of S. Luke, Liverpool
Formerly Exhibitioner of Trinity College, Cambridge

OXFORD UNIVERSITY PRESS
LONDON : HUMPHREY MILFORD
1926

Printed in England
At the Oxford University Press
By John Johnson
Printer to the University

PREFACE

THE absence of any 'Life of Lanfranc' in English encouraged me to undertake the present biography. In French there are only two short studies, those of M. de Crozals and the Abbé Longuemare, which are, moreover, deficient in their treatment of Lanfranc's English pontificate. My obligations to them are acknowledged in the foot-notes. In German there is nothing save the monograph of Prof. Boehmer on the forgery question. While paying my tribute to the great learning and ingenious imagination of Prof. Boehmer, I have not been able to accept his conclusion that Lanfranc was the forger of the documents. It seems to me to be the result of the skilled marshalling of points of evidence which are not always inwardly related to each other, and which belong to different categories. I am aware that Boehmer's conclusions have been accepted by most English writers, but Maitland was doubtful, and so I felt that the question was not closed. I do not claim to have discovered the forger, but I do claim to have set up a reasonable defence of Lanfranc, and to that extent to have cleared his name. As the book has been written for the general reader as well as for the student, the examination of Boehmer's evidence and the presentation of my own case have been placed in the Appendices. Moreover, unfortunately, the stringent demands for compression which are made to-day have prevented me from treating this problem with the fullness that its importance requires.

The sources for Lanfranc's life are scattered, in spite of the collection made by Dr. J. A. Giles in his *Opera Lanfranci* (Oxford, 1844), a collection which has been reprinted in Migne, *Pat. Lat.* cl. Giles printed the Letters, Benedictine Constitutions, Commentaries on S. Paul, and the 'De Corpore et Sanguine Domini' of Lanfranc, together with some other fragments mentioned in Appendix III of this book. He also printed Milo's *Vita Lanfranci*, but this has been largely displaced by the appearance of Dean Armitage Robinson's edition of Gilbert Crispin's *Life of Herluin* (Cambridge University Press, 1911) from which Milo drew most of his material for the early career of Lanfranc. But Milo is still valuable for small points unrecorded by Gilbert. The other leading Norman authority, Orderic Vitalis, has been consulted in the edition of Le Prevost (1845).

The chief English sources, with the exception of the Saxon Chronicle (Plummer, 1892) and Florence of Worcester (English Historical Society), have been consulted in the Rolls edition, and I have not thought it necessary always to make this known in the footnotes. They include the writings of William of Malmesbury, Eadmer, Matthew Paris, Symeon of Durham, Walsingham, Gervase, &c., and they may be easily identified in the Rolls series. For one or two of Lanfranc's letters I have given Dean Hook's translation, though only rarely. I am indebted to the late Mr. W. H. Stevenson, of S. John's College, Oxford, who submitted the first three chapters to a searching criticism shortly before his death at the end of last year; and to a number of friends for

I

EARLY LIFE

THE last Italian king, until the days of Victor Emmanuel, was crowned at Pavia in the year 1002.[1] But it was to a sorry eminence that Arduin, the Margrave of Ivrea, had raised himself by seizing the Lombard crown. Even in Lombardy some of the bishops, headed by Leo of Vercelli, maintained the German interest against the Lombard king. In Rome he possessed not a vestige of tangible authority. The city was torn by the rival factions of Count Crescentius and of the house of Tusculum, each bidding, like the partisans of Lombardy, for the aid of the new German king, Henry II. The Papacy was both the pawn tossed to and fro between these rival houses and the tool of the German kings who came across the Alps seeking imperial honours from its hands. In the south, Saracen and Greek, Lombard and Norman, struggled with each other for supremacy. Italy was torn by the factions, some political, some dynastic, some racial, which sprang into being after the dissolution of the Ostrogothic power. Neither Lombard nor German nor Pope had so far been able to restore to her a semblance of unity.

Into this welter of intrigue and utter decay of morals and religion Lanfranc was born, soon after 1000, at Pavia.[2] His

[1] Gregorovius, *History of Rome in the Middle Ages*, iv, Pt. I, p. 4 (Eng. trans., A. Hamilton).

[2] The date of his birth is unknown. He appears to have left Italy about 1036 (cf. infra, p. 8, n. 3). Before he entered Bec he felt 'worn out in body and mind' (Milo, 3). If we may accept this statement, he can hardly have made this complaint before he was approaching middle life. Thus his birth should be dated c. 1000. Milo, 2, says that his father died when he was 'in primaeva aetate'. His father can hardly have died much later than 1015, otherwise Lanfranc, who was a child at the time, would not have been on the verge of middle life by 1036.

Some further help, though still only of a conjectural nature, is forthcoming from a passage in Orderic, iv. 6 (ii, p. 209), copied by Milo (13). Orderic says that while still young (adolescentulus orator) Lanfranc vanquished the older advocates of Pavia, and continues

parents, Haribald and Roza, belonged to the same city,[1] and occupied a position of some standing.[2] His father belonged to a senatorial family.[3] The qualification for senatorial rank in an Italian town during the eleventh century was the possession of real property, which entitled the owner to a voice in the government of the city. If to this qualification was added a judicial office, the status was roughly equivalent to that of an alderman in later times. At Rome itself the senator no longer possessed the rank and prestige of the days of the Republic, or even of the later Empire. Thus, although Lanfranc's father was of senatorial rank, he did not belong to the class of great landowners from whom Arduin sprang, and who influenced so largely the destinies of the North Italian towns in the eleventh century.

The childhood of Lanfranc was passed amid political disturbance. Two years after Arduin became king, Henry II of Germany entered Pavia and assumed the Lombard crown, while Arduin retired to his Alpine strongholds. In 1013 Henry appeared again, and Arduin fled to Ivrea. In 1015 the German faction compelled the Lombard king to become a Benedictine monk at Fructuaria, where he died.[4]

'in ipsa aetate sententias promere statuit quas gratanter jurisperiti aut judices aut praetores civitatis acceptabant'. If 'ipsa aetate' means 'in age itself' or 'at a ripe age', then circa 1000 is not too early for his birth-date.

[1] Gervase, ii, p. 364, a secondary authority.

[2] Ord. iv. 6 (ii, p. 209), Milo, 1: nobili parentela ortus. Robt. of Torigny (Rolls, *Chronicles of Stephen, Henry II and Richard I*, vol. iv), p. 30: nobili genere natus. Cf. Milo, 1: Parentes ejus . . . magni et honorabiles habentur inter suos concives. Longuemare, *Lanfranc* (1902), p. 3 (quoting Stephen Marinus, *Imagines Beccariae Gentis* (Ticino, 1598), p. 24): 'Il était de l'illustre famille des Beccaria, célèbre dans la Haute-Italie pour sa munificence et ses goûts artistiques.' On the other hand, Malmes., *G. P.*, p. 37: 'non adeo abjecta et obscura progenie oriundus erat.' Gervase, ii, p. 363: civibus egregiis, et honesta conditione.

[3] Milo, 1: pater ejus de ordine illorum qui jura et leges civitatis asservabant fuit. Robt. of Torigny, p. 30: de senatorum Paviae nobili genere natus.

[4] Gregorovius, iv, Pt. I, p. 24.

In the midst of these troubles the boy's father died.[1] He may have been killed in one of the faction fights common at Pavia. The paternal office and dignity were not allowed to pass to Lanfranc. But he found means sufficient to enable him to follow the example of other young men of Pavia, and to take up the study of law;[2] and his decision to study at one or more of the great schools of northern Italy in itself affords an adequate explanation for his departure from Pavia at this time.[3]

He had already received a thorough grounding in the Latin language.[4] But while the Latin of his mature years is the composition of a scholar, the extent of his classical knowledge is obscure. In his extant works there are few allusions to classical authors.[5] The study of Latin literature was not neglected in Italy at the time,[6] but intellectual life was most active in the department of law.

The Lombard lawyers of the eleventh century divided their attention between the old Lombard dooms and Roman law. The Pavian lawyers, especially, 'had been harmonizing,

[1] Milo, 2: 'in primaeva aetate patre orbatus'.

[2] Ord. iv. 6 (ii, p. 209); Milo, 2.

[3] Milo, 1: relicta civitate amore discendi ad studia litterarum perrexit. De Crozals, *Lanfranc* (Paris, 1877), p. 8, says that Lanfranc left Pavia because no teaching on law was to be had there, but at that time the Pavian lawyers were engaged codifying the Lombard laws (Pollock and Maitland, *Hist. of Eng. Law*, 1895, i, p. 55), and some teaching must have been going on.

[4] Will. of Poitiers, Duchesne, 194 B; Ord. iv. 6 (ii, p. 209); Milo, 13; Malmes., *G. P.*, p. 37; Robt. of Torigny, p. 30.

[5] Cf. Epis. XXXVI. He deliberately avoided classical studies in later years. Modern writers have assumed that he possessed a knowledge of Greek. The only ground for this assumption is a passage in Gilbert Crispin, *Vita Herluini*, p. 95 (Armitage Robinson): 'Ortus Italia quidam vir erat, quem Latinitas, in antiquum ab eo restituta scientiae statum, tota supremum debito cum amore et honore agnoscit magistrum, nomine Lanfrancus; ipsa quoque in liberalibus studiis magistra gentium Graecia discipulos illius libenter audiebat et admirabatur.' But this is a rhetorical statement drawing attention to the recognition accorded by both branches of the world of letters to Lanfranc's influence.

[6] Lane Poole, *Illustrations of Med. Thought and Learning* (1920), p. 71 f.

digesting and modernizing the ancient statutes of the Lombard kings.'[1] To this extent their studies were Teutonic, and the strong German faction, which included many churchmen like Heribert of Milan and Leo of Vercelli, may have received support from the lawyers, though it is more probable that the traditional rivalry between lawyer and churchman inclined the former to rally round Arduin.

The study of Roman law also had been revived at Pavia.[2] In Italy this new study was encouraged by the German emperor, Conrad II (1024–39), who, led on by imperial ambition, gave his support, not to the Teutonic legal schools of Lombardy but to the students of Justinian at Rome. He received the imperial crown at Rome in 1027, and while there, appears to have issued the rescript which commanded that all disputes between Lombards and Romans at Rome should be tried by the canons of Roman law.[3]

We are not informed where Lanfranc spent the years of his first exile from Pavia. But the revived interest in Roman law lends support to the suggestion that part of the time was passed at Bologna.[4] According to a tale which has come down, he was responsible, with Irnerius, for the discovery of the Digest at Bologna.[5] The story cannot be accepted as evidence of any collaboration between Irnerius and Lanfranc, who had left Italy before the time of Irnerius. But he may have studied the Institutes at Bologna, and may even have conducted some researches which led finally to the achievements of Irnerius.[6]

[1] Pollock and Maitland, *Hist. of Eng. Law*, i (1895), p. 55; Maitland, *Collected Papers* (1911), p. 31 n.; cf. Vinogradoff, *Roman Law in Mediaeval Europe* (1909), p. 37 ff.

[2] Pollock and Maitland, *Hist. of Eng. Law*, i, pp. 55–6; Vinogradoff, *Roman Law in Mediaeval Europe*, Lecture II; Lane Poole, *Illustrations*, p. 73.

[3] Gregorovius, *Hist. of Rome in the Middle Ages*, iv, Pt. I, p. 38.

[4] Mabillon, *Ann. Ord. S. Ben.*, iv, p. 449, suggests that he went to Bologna.

[5] Robert of Torigny, p. 25.

[6] The study of the Digest had been revived at Bologna before the time of Irnerius (Rashdall, *Universities of Europe in the Middle Ages*, i, pp. 122–3). But it is possible that the Lanfranc referred to was not our Lanfranc; cf. *infra*, p. 7, n. 2.

After his return to Pavia, he taught grammar and dialectics,[1] but the teaching and practice of law soon became his chief occupation, and while still young he achieved a notable ascendancy over older men as a practising advocate. By the time he had reached middle life his opinions were sought by all the legal authorities of the city.[2] He became widely known as an acute and subtle lecturer and exponent of law, and gathered round him a large number of students.[3] Some of his legal discussions have been preserved. He was once lecturing in the school of the learned lawyer Bonfilius on the question of the payment of the 'quartam et antifactam'. This was the fourth part of a man's property, due to his wife, after his death, in place of her dowry. In the case discussed by Lanfranc the husband had persuaded his first wife, willingly or unwillingly, to enter a convent, and had married another woman on whom he also settled a marriage portion. Which of them, asked Lanfranc, should obtain the money if he died? The pupils replied that the first wife should receive it, because, according to a law of Lothar, she was not qualified to receive the veil. Lanfranc answered that the discussion did not really concern the first wife, but the second. However, as they had raised the point he went on to show that under the same law of Lothar her marriage was not lawful, because the law forbade the husband to put away his first wife, and if the second wife was not lawfully married she was not entitled, under the law of 'cartam morgincapt' and the Institutes, to any payment. The pupils agreed, but Lanfranc pointed out that according to the law the second wife could only be mulcted if she had over-reached the first wife, and this had not been done, because the first wife was in a convent.

[1] Porée, *Histoire de l'Abbaye du Bec*, i, p. 47, quoting *Miracula de Sancto Nicholao*, Bibl. d'Evreux, MS. Lat. 96, an early twelfth-century document.

[2] Ord. iv. 6 (ii, p. 209); Milo, 13.

[3] The *Hist. Litt. de la France*, viii, p. 261, says that Lanfranc opened his first law school at Pavia, and that he published a little treatise on law which was of great assistance to jurisconsults and magistrates. But this is very free interpretation of Milo and Orderic (cf. *supra*, n. 2). Cf. Longuemare, *Lanfranc*, p. 6: A Pavie Lanfranc eut comme collègue, dans l'enseignement du Droit, le célèbre Guido Langobardus.

Again the students agreed, but Lanfranc said that the second wife had really encroached upon the rights of the other, because the first wife had been made a nun against the law. The disciples agreed again, and Lanfranc went on to assert that while it was proved that the second woman had gone beyond the rights of the first wife, yet the law in question only mulcted a woman whose husband was still living, but in this case the husband was dead. The pupils agreed, and Lanfranc returned to the charge by reminding them that the statute was not really concerned with the question whether the husband was alive or not, but with the fact of the encroachment by one woman upon the rights of another. Still the pupils agreed, and Lanfranc said that when the law concerning encroachment was made, the statute of Lothar, which prohibited a woman from taking the veil without her husband's consent, was not in existence, so that the first wife was free to take the veil and to be separated from her husband, who was free to take another wife, and she in turn was able to receive whatever he had made over to her. But one more trap remained for the pupils. Lanfranc's final opinion was that the statute of Lothar was already in existence in the form of the canons,[1] which were drawn up before it, so that the first wife could not be separated from her husband, nor could the second one marry him, therefore she could obtain nothing after his death.[2]

On another occasion he brought up a question of inheritance. If a Lombard had daughters, and had married them before a son was born to him, and if after his death the son also died without descendants, ought the daughters to succeed to their father's inheritance according to the law? The students maintained that they should succeed. But Lanfranc explained that the law only provided for the succession of the sisters if they were married during the brother's lifetime, but in the case before them he was not living because he had not been born! [3]

[1] Canon 36, passed at a Council held by Pope Eugenius (826).

[2] Pertz, *Mon. Ger.* (Leges) iv, p. 402; cf. Vinogradoff, *Roman Law in Mediaeval Europe*, pp. 41–2.

[3] Pertz, *Mon. Ger.* (Leges) iv, p. 404.

A third proposition was made to Judge Bonfilius himself. If a man wished to establish the legality of a charter which had been declared to be a forgery, when the lawyer who had drawn it up and the witnesses were dead, how ought he to proceed? Bonfilius replied that the charter could be vindicated if twelve witnesses and two other charters were produced. Lanfranc asked whether no other course could be adopted. Bonfilius replied that nothing else could be done, but Lanfranc maintained that the practice was against the law, according to the prologue of Otto, which said that this detestable and dishonest procedure ought not to be permitted in Italy. Bonfilius left the court with shame on his face and head bent.[1]

These passages reveal the same acuteness of mind and closeness of reasoning which are characteristic of well-established utterances of Lanfranc made in later years.[2] They also illustrate the wide range of legal studies in North Italy at the time—studies which embraced the Lombard statutes, Roman law, and the canons of the Church. The older Pavian lawyers were trained mainly in the schools of Lombard law. Their knowledge of Roman law had been gained later in life in order to meet the changing conditions of the time. Lanfranc, on the other hand, had, while still a student, taken up the study of Roman Law; so that, besides his own natural ability, which would cause him to stand out prominently among his contemporaries, the freshness of his

[1] Ibid., p. 566; cf. Vinogradoff, *Roman Law in Mediaeval Europe*, pp. 40–1.

[2] Muratori, *Ant. Ital.* v, p. 521 (Editio Maj.), quoting a document in the monastery of S. Felix at Ticino, reports a case heard at Ticino in 1043, in which the Abbess of S. Felix secured the royal protection. Four 'Lanfrancs' are mentioned among members of the Court. One was the Royal Advocate, and the other three were Judices sacri Palatii. As our Lanfranc had only left Italy a few years before this date, there were at least five lawyers of the name practising about that time in Pavia, and the reports in the *Liber Papiensis* may not therefore be concerned with him. On the other hand the *Lib. Pap.* definitely assigns them to 'Archbishop' Lanfranc. Milo tells us that Pavia 'remembered him' (Milo, 13), so that the tradition would be carefully preserved. Cf. Pollock and Maitland and Vinogradoff, who assign the reports to our Lanfranc.

methods, and his practical application of the new legal teaching, were sufficient in themselves to guarantee to a vigorous lawyer of the mature age of from thirty-five to forty a pre-eminence over the older men. But suddenly his legal career was brought to an end.

In the winter of 1036 the Emperor Conrad II came to Pavia in order to deal with a rising which has been characterized as one of the earliest popular movements in Europe.[1] Two currents seem to have converged upon the stream of revolt. The smaller vassals rose against the tyranny of the big landowners, from whom they held their fiefs ; and the small freeholders joined them in a movement against the influence of the bishops, headed by Heribert of Milan. The appearance of Conrad did little to appease the trouble, and his intervention resulted in a confusion of the issues. Heribert and three other bishops refused to recognize a judgement given by the Emperor at Pavia. They were therefore imprisoned without further trial. But the action of the Emperor served only to arouse the national feeling of the Lombards. The bishops escaped to Milan, and the first of the great conflicts between Milan and the German Emperor began.[2] It is probable that during this turmoil Lanfranc decided to leave Italy.[3]

[1] H. Pabst, *De Ariberto*, ii, Berlin, 1864, quoted by Gregorovius, v, Pt. I, p. 44.

[2] Gregorovius, iv, Pt. I, pp. 43–4.

[3] Ord. v. 2 (ii, p. 306) says that in 1034 Herluin became a monk. Three years later (1037) he was ordained and made abbot. Gilbert (p. 94) says that some little time after this ('post aliquantum temporis ') Herluin left Bonneville for Bec, where he built a church and wooden cloister which collapsed one night. He was still engaged on building when Lanfranc arrived (Gilbert, p. 96). Thus, Lanfranc's arrival at Bec cannot have been much later than 1040 (cf. De Crozals, p. 40), and this would allow time for the visit to Berengar and the sojourn at Avranches. Three or four years should be assigned for this period (cf. *infra*, pp. 10–11).

Orderic says that Bec was built when Herluin was made abbot. This statement is confirmed by the old *Chronique du Bec* (Porée, 1883, p. 2). Milo, 5, says that when Lanfranc arrived at Bec, Herluin had recently been ordained. ('Abbas ex grandaevo laico nuper in clericum promotus.') But Milo has altered the original text of

Gilbert (p. 96), who refers to Herluin as 'Abbas quondam clericatus ex grandaevo laico'. So that Herluin appears to have been in orders some time before he became abbot and before Lanfranc's arrival, a suggestion which harmonizes with the rest of Gilbert's account, and with Orderic.

Porée (i, p. 43) dates the foundation of Bec 1039, and the consecration of its first church 23rd Feb. (quoting the Evreux MS. Lat. 96) in the year 1041 (quoting *Gallia Christiana*, xi, col. 218). He dates Lanfranc's arrival at Bec 1041–2 (i, p. 47), which agrees well with the date in the *Chron. Bec.* (1042). But Lanfranc must have left Italy before 1041–2 in order to allow time for the visit to Berengar, the sojourn at Avranches, and the teaching at various places. Some five or six years may well have been passed in this way, and the winter of 1036 would not have been too early for the departure from Italy. Hook, *Archbishops*, ii, p. 76, gives 1035 as the earliest date for leaving Italy.

II

AVRANCHES AND BEC

WHATEVER was the immediate occasion which caused Lanfranc to leave Italy, a complete change of motive had taken place in his mind. He had determined to abandon the law for theology, and the most famous schools of theology in Western Europe at that time were at Lyons, Rheims, Tours, Poitiers, Angers, and Chartres.[1] Attracted by reports of Berengar of Tours, Lanfranc went to him, and, concealing his identity, became his disciple. But perceiving that he could not further his own interests by remaining with Berengar, especially as his teaching appeared to be unsound, he left him and travelled through Burgundy and other parts.[2]

[1] Porée, *Hist. de l'Abbaye du Bec*, i, p. 47.

[2] Ibid., p. 69, quoting *Miracula de Sancto Nicolao.* Bibl. d'Evreux MS. Lat. F. 96. 'Audiens famam cuiusdam Berengarii Touronensis, ecclesiae archidiaconi, qui multos et prope omnes praecellibat scientia litterarum in illis partibus, venit ad eum celans omnino quis esset, subdiditque se eius discipulatui. At cum nil ibi se proficere cerneret, revera vere, ut post apparuit, intellegens non eum esse sane doctrine abcessit ab eo, et iterum per se et in Burgundia et in ceteris regionibus Gallie cepit maximas scolas tenere et magnopere per hoc cunctis innotescere et in magna admiratione esse.' This document appears to be the source of the statement in the *Chron. Bec.* 'Audiens Lanfrancus famam regionis Northomaniae quae prius Neustria dicebatur, in qua ducatum tenebat haereditario iure Willelmus . . . sciens certo relatu illic multum collapsum studium litteraturae barbaricae gentis, et intelligens providentis ima inspiratione inde se posse adipisci maiorem gloriam et plurimum quaestum, venit illic cum paucis.' Longuemare, p. 7, wrongly attributes this statement to Milo.

On the state of learning in Normandy at that time, cf. *infra*, pp. 25-6.

The statement of the Evreux MS. is preferable on the following grounds:

(*a*) It explains the attitude of Berengar to Lanfranc at the beginning of the Eucharistic controversy, and also

(*b*) the attitude of the Norman clergy to Lanfranc on the arrival of Berengar's letter.

(*c*) It is confirmed by the reports that Lanfranc met Berengar in discussion before the controversy became public (cf. *infra*, p. 43 and n.).

One tradition says that he made a short stay at Paris.[1]

Thrown back on his own resources, he opened schools which attracted students in the different places through which he passed, and began to build up a reputation for himself.[2] A nucleus for these schools was found in the company of scholars who went with him from Italy.[3] Finally he came to rest at Avranches,[4] and in the cathedral school of that city, where he stayed some time, gathered a number of students around him. The ecclesiastical authorities appear to have afforded him a welcome, for certain clerks were associated with him in the work of the schools.[5]

It is possible that his experience with Berengar prevented him from pursuing the study of theology for the time being. At Avranches doubtless he acquired facility in the Norman-French language, but his main activity must have been directed to the teaching of grammar, rhetoric, and perhaps dialectics, subjects always required at a cathedral centre as a foundation for the study of theology.[6] It is even possible that at this period his thoughts turned again to the teaching and practice of law. The presence of the Digest and Institutes in the monasteries of Normandy early in the next century suggests the influence of Lanfranc.[7]

(*d*) It was more probable that a scholar, on coming to Gaul for the first time, especially if he were a layman, would attach himself to a teacher of note like Berengar than that he should immediately try his fortune in a comparatively unknown centre like Avranches.

Gilbert, Milo, Orderic and other authorities intentionally conceal Lanfranc's early connexion with Berengar in view of the part played by Lanfranc in the controversy and because of the esteem in which he was held by the Papacy and the Church at large.

[1] Antonio Gatto, *Gym. Tic. Hist.* in Graevius, *Thes. Ant. et Hist. Ital.*, iv. Pt. ii. 28 (Leyden, 1722).

[2] Evreux MS. (Porée).

[3] Gilbert Crispin, p. 95: Milo, 2. 'Quam plures multi nominis scholares secum habens.'

[4] Milo, 2. The sojourn at Avranches is not mentioned by Gilbert.

[5] Gervase, ii, p. 364: 'Sibi associatis clericis scholas regebat.'

[6] Robert of Torigny, p. 26, says that he taught theology before going to Bec, but the statement occurs in a doubtful passage about Irnerius.

[7] But the sources make no allusion to the study of law. Longuemare, p. 8, remarks that no copies of Digest or Institutes were found

But if at one time he entertained the hope of creating in Normandy a legal reputation and practice such as he had left behind in Pavia, it was soon abandoned. The Duke was in his early teens. There was no scope for a master of legal forms before the master of arms had drilled the wild baronage into order. The interests of the Normans were divided between the military and the religious life. The Duke had now assumed the reins of government, and Lanfranc realized that the people who might expect to receive his favour were the soldier and the monk, and we need seek for no more ample motive for the change [1] which came over him soon after Herluin's foundation of Bec.[2]

Such an explanation does not necessarily place his motives upon a low plane. The possibility of a career in the Church must have been considered long ago in Italy. But those were the days of the infamous boy-Pope, Benedict IX, and of all the chicanery and knavery carried on at the papal elections by the houses of Tusculum and Crescentius. In the north of Italy the conditions were not much better. But Lanfranc was now domiciled in a country where, relatively, the condition of the Church was good, and its work stable and progressive, protected by the care of the ducal house. Even if it be granted that ambition influenced his decision, and urged him to become a churchman, his action was not insincere. There is an ambition for mere reputation, and there is an ambition to lead in usefulness. There was plenty of room for the latter motive in the Norman Church of his

at Bec. He suggests that Lanfranc may have given them away when he abandoned secular studies. (Cf. *infra*, p. 30.)

[1] Hook, *Lives of the Archbishops*, ii, p. 80 (but cf. Ramsay, *Foundations of England*, ii, p. 84), has attempted to find an explanation for this second change of life in the death of his wife. But we do not know that Lanfranc was ever married. The only evidence is a tradition at S. Albans reporting that Abbot Paul was his son (*Gesta Abbat. Monast. S. Alb.* i, p. 52. Even this does not prove that he was married, and the statement is not borne out by the other S. Albans Chroniclers, who assert that Paul was Lanfranc's nephew. Matt. Paris, *Hist. Ang.* iii, p. 172 ; *Flores Hist.* ii. 5, 21, though Paris alludes to the tradition that Paul was his son.

[2] c. 1040, cf. *supra*, p. 8, n. 3. The *Chron. Bec.* gives 1042. Longuemare, p. 11, has 1047. This is far too late.

day. Moreover, he brought to the service of the Church some forty years of experience, a ripe scholarship in secular learning, and a trained legal mind. The success of his later career showed that the ambitious layman offered no mean gifts to the cause of religion.[1]

Before he left Avranches his mind again became haunted by the idea that secular learning was useless, and he began to think of adopting the religious life.[2] He made a careful scrutiny of the monasteries in the neighbourhood,[3] and finally set out for Rouen in order to learn further particulars there. Avranches he left quietly, in the company of one young pupil.[4] The road lay through the forest of Ouche, and as night came down, the travellers reached the banks of the Rille. On the farther side they were attacked by robbers, who blindfolded them and tied them to trees, taking away their belongings. During the night Lanfranc tried to solace himself by saying the office for Lauds. This he found he could not do, and cried out, 'Oh! Lord, I have spent so much time in gaining knowledge, and have worn away both

[1] The story of a late English writer (*Henry of Knighton*, Rolls, i, p. 89) recounts a legend of this period. One day, while walking up and down on the banks of the Seine, deep in thought on the doctrine of the Trinity, he noticed a boy scooping up water from the river and emptying it into a ditch. Lanfranc asked what he was doing. The boy replied that he was trying to pour all the water of the river into the ditch. 'You will never be able to do it,' said Lanfranc, and the shrewd boy answered, 'nor will you be able to do by thinking that which is in your mind'. The boy disappeared and the scholar gave up trying 'to scrutinize the majesty of God further lest he should be overpowered', and immediately entered the monastery of Bec. But this story is apocryphal. It is told of Alan of Lille to explain why he became a monk at Citeaux (Migne, *P. L.* ccx, col. 37). It has been attributed to Augustine by Thomas of Cantimpratensis (Johannes Gallensis), *Liber Apum*, ii, cap. xlviii, 3. (Part iii, fol. lxvi, in the edition of N. Bonaspes, published by W. Hopyl, Paris, 1516).

[2] Gilbert, p. 96; Milo, 2; Ord. iv. 6 (ii, p. 210). But Malmes., *G. P.*, p. 38, attributes his conversion to the effect of theological study, yet he does not appear to have studied theology before reaching Bec, except for a short period under Berengar.

[3] Malmes., *G. P.*, p. 38.

[4] *Chron. Bec.*

body and mind in the study of secular letters, but up to the present I have not learned how to pray to thee or how to say the office for Lauds. Deliver me from this trouble, and with thy help I will amend my life, and will so arrange it that I may not only serve thee, but know how to serve thee.' When the morning light began to come through the gloom of the trees, he heard some travellers grumbling as they passed along. He called to them, and after they had recovered from their surprise, they came and cut him and his companion loose, and led them back on to the road. He inquired of them the way to the nearest monastery, and followed a direction leading along the banks of the Rille to the monastery of Bec.[1]

The story of the attack in the wood of Ouche falls quite naturally into the sequence of events. It cannot be regarded

[1] Milo, 3, and *Chron. Bec.* The reference to the travelling companion comes from the *Chron. Bec.* This account has been embellished with more legendary details. They were bound naked to two trees. Their bonds were loosed so soon as Lanfranc had made his vow. This story does not appear in Gilbert. Armitage Robinson (p. 59) considers that it ' thus loses what has hitherto appeared to be its most important attestation '. But Gilbert was not writing a life of Lanfranc. He therefore omits all legendary matter from his brief notes of Lanfranc. But on pp. 100–1, Gilbert gives at length the legend of Herluin's crossing the Channel, a story, in turn, omitted by Milo, who was not writing a life of Herluin.

In later years, when the story was told, it was adorned by adding a tale which had come down from Gregory the Great. A certain holy man named Libertin was once attacked by Lombards who made off with his horse. He called them back and gave them the whip which they had left behind. Then he began to pray. When the robbers reached the river Volturno they found themselves unable to cross, and realized that they suffered this inconvenience because of the violence which they had offered to the servant of God. They turned back, restored the stolen animal, and assisted Libertin to mount before leaving him.

Chron. Bec. The Bec writer incorporates the tale into the story of the attack in the wood of Ouche. Lanfranc remembered this story when the robbers first went off. He thereupon followed and offered his cloak, which they had left behind, hoping for treatment similar to that which Libertin experienced. But he was then bound naked to a tree. This was because, unlike Libertin, his own motive was not pure.

as the cause of his conversion,[1] though it appears to have been the means of directing him to Bec. Doubtless Lanfranc made a vow on this occasion, a vow which was faithfully kept in later years. But conversions such as that which caused him to enter the monastery at Bec are quiet processes, though they may be completed by a striking incident like the robbery on the banks of the Rille.

Bec [2] was situated on a small river in the vale of Brionne. It was shut in by thickly-wooded hills. The trees afforded ample supplies of timber for all human requirements, and the stream gave excellent water. But in contrast with the natural beauty of this woodland retreat, the monastic buildings were mean and squalid. Some time before Lanfranc's arrival, the roof of the dormitory had been blown off at night, and the wall of the cloister and its wooden pillars had fallen down. The Abbot had succeeded in rebuilding the cloister with stone, and on Lanfranc's arrival was still engaged upon the reconstruction of the rude buildings. He was erecting a furnace, assisted by the monks, and was working with his own hands.[3]

When Lanfranc approached the Abbot, saying, 'God give you salvation,' the Abbot recognized his nationality and replied, 'God bless you, are you a Lombard?' 'I am,' said he. 'What do you want?' replied the Abbot. 'I want to become a monk,' said Lanfranc. The Abbot then ordered a monk named Roger, who was working close at hand, to bring the book of rules. Having read it through, Lanfranc said that with the help of God he would willingly keep them.

[1] As alleged by Milo, 3, and *Chron. Bec.*, and followed by most writers since.

[2] Gilbert, p. 94, and *Chron. Bec.*—so named after a little river which was called a 'bec'. These references were missed by Charma, *Notice Biographique* (Paris, Caen, 1849), p. 39, and Hook, *Archbishops*, ii, p. 83, who give long explanations. The campaign of 1918 was ended by the Artillery of the 15th Scottish Division at Rebecq-Rognon, 20 m. SW. of Brussels. In the neighbourhood are Clabecq, Lembecq, and Wisbecq, all villages on small rivers. Lembeck (*sic*) is also the name of a small stream.

[3] Gilbert, p. 96. Malmes., *G. P.*, p. 38, says that he was prepared for baking bread—his hands covered with dust.

On hearing this, and after ascertaining his identity, the Abbot granted his request. Lanfranc prostrated himself on the ground and kissed his feet, and became filled with a great veneration and love for the humility of spirit shown by the Abbot, and for the dignity of his address.[1] The friendship between the two men lasted long after their pathways had separated, and was only severed by the death of the Abbot (1078).

The founder of the humble little community which afterwards became, partly through Lanfranc's influence, the rich and famous abbey of Bec, was Herluin, who was born about 994.[2] He was a descendant of the Danes who had conquered Normandy, and his mother was a near kinswoman of the Duke of Flanders. He was brought up at the court of Gilbert, Count of Brionne, where he became expert in the use of arms. His fearless spirit and handsome person made him a favourite with the leading houses of Normandy and with Duke Robert I.

At the age of thirty-seven[3] Herluin began to turn his mind towards the religious life. His decision was made finally during a skirmish between the knights of Gilbert and the Count of Ponthieu. While flying for his life Herluin vowed that if he escaped he would devote the rest of his life to God.[4] A request to be put in possession of his property was refused by Duke Gilbert. After a while he abandoned the practice of arms, put on mean raiment, and allowed his hair and beard to grow. Whole nights were spent praying in the castle chapel, but he did not permit himself to be absent in the morning from the Duke's table, where he took only bread and water and often had to submit

[1] Milo, 4; an addition to Gilbert. The Evreux MS. (Porée, i, pp. 49–50) has different details. Lanfranc tried to kiss Herluin's feet, but the Abbot only allowed him his hand. Then Lanfranc, quitting his cloak, went to work with Herluin and the brothers. When the time for work ended, Herluin consulted the monks, who agreed that Lanfranc should join them.

[2] Ord. v, 2 (ii, p. 306), who states that in 1034 Herluin became a monk. Cf. the old Annals of Bec (Porée, *Chronique du Bec*, 1883, p. 1).

[3] Gilbert, p. 88.

[4] Ord. iii. 1 (ii, p. 13).

to the gibes of the other knights. Sometimes he was sent to a neighbouring castle riding upon an ass, and his miserable appearance provoked either pity or mirth in those who saw him. At last Gilbert surrendered his property, and Herluin built a small monastery, on the manor of Bonneville, labouring at the work himself. By night, although now forty years of age, he began to master the elements of grammar.[1] In order to ascertain the details of monastic routine he visited the monasteries of the neighbourhood. But his experiences would have broken the spirit of most men. On one occasion he approached the gate of a monastery 'as though it were the gate of Paradise', but on entering into the courtyard he was struck on the neck by the porter, who dragged him by the hair back to the gate. At the following Christmas he arrived at a monastery of even greater reputation, just as the brethren were going on a festive procession. He saw the monks smiling ostentatiously to the lay-people, pluming themselves on having their decorations better arranged, showing them off, and then racing for the doorway in a disorderly crowd. One monk, on being jostled by another, thrust him aside with a blow of his fist and felled him to the ground with another blow on the mouth. But in the same house Herluin discovered that not all the monks were tinged with what Gilbert Crispin[2] calls 'Norman barbarism', for in the oratory, at midnight, long after all the others had retired, he saw a monk alternately kneeling and prostrating himself on the ground till dawn.

After his return to Bonneville he was consecrated Abbot by Herbert, Bishop of Lisieux, and introduced the regular Benedictine rule into the little community. When the morning office was finished in church, the Abbot, with a sower's bag or basket suspended from his neck, or carrying a rake or hoe, went forth at the head of all the monks into the fields to work there until the end of the day. Some cleared away the briars and weeds, some sprinkled manure, which they had carried on their shoulders, some hoed, while the rest carried things to and fro, and no one ate his bread in idleness. At

[1] Gilbert, p. 91.

[2] Ibid., p. 92.

the hours for saying the service, all came back to the church together. Their daily food consisted of wheaten bread with vegetables, salt, and water. The water was muddy, because there was no stream nearer than two miles. They called it a gift from Heaven when they had better bread, or cheese, or some other eatable. All inclination to murmuring was checked by the example and bearing of the Abbot. He was the first at work and the last to leave it. He was always at work.

In this busy, happy community Herluin was joined by his noble mother. She dedicated her lands to God, and undertook the work of a maidservant in the monastery, washing the clothes of the brothers, and doing whatever she was told with extreme carefulness. The chronicler goes on, in his simple way, to relate how one day, while the lady was baking bread, the huts of the monks caught fire. A message was brought to Herluin saying that his mother was burned to death. 'Thanks be to Thee, O God, that while she was serving Thee, the fire took my mother,' he said with tears in his eyes. But it was a false report, for the lady was not harmed.

The inconvenience of the situation of Bonneville, especially its isolation in the country, caused Herluin to transfer his community to Bec.[1] More difficulties had to be overcome before the property became his, but after protracted negotiations with Count Gilbert the transfer was effected, and the wooden buildings which Lanfranc found him replacing with stone were erected.[2]

Such was the primitive community, and such was the simple-hearted soldier-monk with whom Lanfranc now allied himself. The story of Herluin gives details of what must have been the experience of many Norman and English monks in those days. The monastic houses were recruited partly from the number of quiet or timid or studious or religious youths who showed little or no capacity or desire

[1] Robt. of Torigny in a late recension of Jum. (vi. 9) says the monks were compelled to drink muddy water. There was no spring nearer than two miles.

[2] Gilbert, p. 94, from which the whole account is taken.

for the life of the camp and castle. They were recruited also from the ranks of the knights and squires who had spent their early manhood in arms, but who then turned to the religious houses as a refuge from the brutality and coarseness of a rough age; or who came as penitents, when the sins of youth were no longer attractive, but were recalled as accusing memories, demanding expiation before the day of life should close. To many men of Herluin's disposition, active and accustomed to bodily exercise, but with the desire for goodness firmly rooted in their hearts, the quiet life of the primitive Benedictine rule, with its days of healthy occupation in the fields broken by quiet intervals of worship in the chapel, and its hours of quiet study, must have made a strong appeal. It was in marked contrast with the splendid if severe round of religious duties, divided between choir and cloister and refectory, which appears in the Benedictine rules [1] drawn up by Lanfranc in later years. The monk of Herluin's day who lived on into the later period must have been dazzled by the richness of religious ceremonial under the new régime; but he must have gazed back wistfully to that earlier period of Norman monasticism, when the main duty of life [2] was the quiet work of the fields, performed out in the sunshine or the rain, amid the smell of the newly-turned sod or newly-mown hay, followed by quiet study at evening-tide. Yet the change was inevitable. Even Herluin's system failed to keep out evils which nearly drove him to despair.[3] It was not sufficient to isolate the brothers in a country district. It was not sufficient to tire their bodies by day and their minds by night. The primitive fierceness of the Norman blood needed to be made captive before it could be trusted profitably to do its work. Feudalism may have existed among other races, but its complicated yet efficient organization was especially suited to the needs

[1] Cf. Lanfranc, *Decreta pro Ordine S. Benedicti*, infra, pp. 153–71.

[2] In the original Rule of S. Benedict (xlviii), labour in the fields was the monk's chief occupation. Benedict's rule was drawn up for a community of laymen. Herluin's community was organized on similar lines; cf. G. G. Coulton, *Five Centuries of Religion*, i, p. 211.

[3] See pp. 23–4 and 23 n.

of the Norman nature. The genius of the Norman perceived its own needs and the remedy, and this saved him from becoming a mere freebooter, and made him much more than a conqueror. So also in the monastery. The system of Cluny was the counterpart in religion of feudalism in civil life. The transition from Herluin's book of rules to Lanfranc's Constitutions [1] was inevitable if monasticism was to be saved from a Sodom and Gomorrah far worse than the hidden chambers behind the baron's stern walls.

At the right moment for Herluin's community and the good man's peace of mind, the trained, well-read stranger appeared, possessed of an experience of life different in form but similar in result to Herluin's; a man like himself, dissatisfied with the world and its prospects, but, unlike himself, not stirred by the zealot's mystic fire and enthusiasm. Yet this seeming deficiency constituted Lanfranc's best qualification for Bec and for monasticism. There was much of the fanatic in the Norman, and it led him to excess as well as to achievement. What the Norman needed in administration as well as in religion was the cool head and calculating statesmanship of the more cosmopolitan and more evenly-balanced Italian, who had not yet become what he was to become in the later Middle Ages. There was still something of Roman strength and Roman urbanity in him, made mobile by the strong dash of Teutonic blood which flowed in Lombard veins. Hence for many years to come Italy supplied servants, but also masters to the Normans, whose great achievement next to conquest was the choice of men of another race, whom they brought in to help them to govern their conquests. Whatever Bec achieved in later years it owed to Lanfranc, just as England owed the rescue of Saxon Christianity from decay to the order and vigour of the new religious system introduced by the great Archbishop.

On the other hand, Lanfranc owed much to Bec, as every Italian who came westward owed much to the Norman and Teutonic institutions. If the Italian perfected the religious system of the Middle Ages, none the less he usually received the initial impulse from the Teuton. Cluny and Henry III of Germany played the leading part in the beginnings of

[1] *Decreta pro Ordine S. Benedicti.*

reform. Without them the work of Leo IX would have been impossible. Lanfranc, like Anselm, received his religious training in Normandy. At the quiet retreat of the professed brothers at Bec the ambition of both men was captured and harnessed for the service of the Church and religion. In the routine of the common life of the monastery the individualism of Italian ambition became impressed with the spirit of corporate public service characteristic of the community life, and of that feudalism in which the Church was to find her setting and her opportunity, though also, in the end, her ruin.

Lanfranc's appearance before the bakehouse door at Bec marked an epoch in his life greater than the departure from Pavia, and an epoch in the life of the Normans as great as the seizure of England. We should have heard nothing of Lanfranc to-day, beyond some casual reference to his legal eminence, unless he had become a Churchman, just as it is doubtful whether the Conqueror could have made good the retention of his spoils without the support of the clever Archbishop who not only won for him the Saxon Church, but probably showed him the way to apply feudalism in a new form—ecclesiastical feudalism—to England.

Lanfranc found at Bec a refuge suited to his temperament and experience. He came as a layman with a mind formed by the habits of thought of a layman, and while it was too late for him to become a thoroughly professional ecclesiastic, he found a quiet retreat in which he might begin the serious study of theology. Herluin regarded his coming as an answer to his own prayers.[1] The Abbot was often absent from the cloister for long periods, purchasing necessities of life, or selling some of the produce of the community, or engaged on legal business. Although Lanfranc was not yet promoted to any office in the monastery, Herluin could trust to his influence to assist in maintaining order while he was absent on these journeys.

The newcomer was unable to take any part in the work of the fields.[2] Three years he spent mainly in the cloister, quietly fulfilling the pledge made to God in the wood of Ouche, learning the daily and nightly offices of the Church,

[1] Milo, 5. [2] Malmes., *G. P.*, p. 38.

and studying closely the sacred writings.[1] He was devoted to the Abbot, with all the deference of an experienced scholarly man towards the ex-soldier of handsome person, high principles, and simple faith. Herluin was illiterate, but his comments on passages of Scripture possessed the freshness and directness which unlearned people often show. On one occasion, after the Abbot had been giving instruction, Lanfranc is reported to have said, 'When I listen to that layman I don't know what to say, except that the Spirit breathes where it listeth.'[2]

The secret of his identity was known only to Herluin and to one or two others to whom Lanfranc confined his conversation.[3] This is illustrated by another story, which also confirms the report of his humble submission to the rules of the community. We are told that he was unwilling to read the Gospel in Church unless the precentor had first heard him read the passage. One day, when it was his turn to read during the meal in the refectory, he pronounced the word 'docēre' with the correct quantity. The Prior, who was an illiterate man, corrected him, and ordered him to say 'docĕre'. Lanfranc at once complied,[4] knowing, says the writer, that obedience was due rather to Christ than to Donatus,[5] and that there was no crime in mispronouncing a syllable, but that it was a crime against God not to obey an order.[6]

It is improbable that Lanfranc undertook any teaching during this period. The Prior would scarcely have rebuked him if he had been recognized as a teacher in the monastery. Moreover, he needed these years of seclusion in order to lay the foundation of his own theological learning. But he had to learn one of the most common lessons of life. It is impossible to find anywhere an occupation or retreat where everything conduces to peace and happiness, and nothing arises to disturb the quiet indulgence of individual tastes, or the quiet development of individual gifts. The primitive simplicity of life at Bec should have created for the little community an existence disciplined but happy. But he had

[1] Milo, 4. [2] Milo, 6. [3] Ibid.

[4] Or was this his method of teaching them good Latin?

[5] Donatus the grammarian. [6] Milo, 6.

not been there long before the conduct of some of the brothers, perhaps of a majority, began to trouble him, just as it had troubled the good Herluin before his arrival. The monks were unlettered men, and the religious life had so far made little impression upon them. They were lazy. Their morals were bad. The rules of the house were openly broken.[1] They became jealous of Lanfranc. They suspected that he would soon be elevated over their heads. He, in turn, was wearied by their loose and unruly conversation, and began to think of leaving the monastery to take up a hermit's life. To provide an opportunity for leaving Bec he simulated a sickness of the stomach, and asked the gardener, Fulchran, to bring him every day the roots of a certain thistle, which he said would cure him of his illness. His plan was to leave Bec at night. But, according to the story, Herluin was warned in a dream. A clever boy named Hugo, the son of Aldric of Sanvarville, the Abbot's nephew, had recently died. One night he appeared before Herluin, robed in white. 'What do you want, my son? How are you?' said Herluin, not in the least disturbed. 'I am quite well, good Father, for through God's mercy, and your intercession, I am delivered from all torments, but God sent me to tell you, that if you don't take care, you won't have master Lanfranc with you long.' 'Why, son?' said the Abbot. 'Because,' replied the boy, 'he wants to be a hermit, and he is arranging to leave the monastery, since the morals and life of the brothers do not please him. Take care what you do therefore, because it is not good that he should leave you.'

The Abbot was astonished and passed the rest of the night in prayer. On the next morning, so soon as the hour for conversation had arrived,[2] he took Lanfranc aside, and made him sit down with him alone. Herluin was greatly distressed. He could not, at first, speak, and tears coursed down his cheeks. Lanfranc implored him to make known the cause of the trouble. After a time the Abbot broke out with the words, 'Alas! with what a calamity God threatens me! Alas! I have lost my counsellor and my helper! Many a time have I besought God with deep groans and tears, that

[1] Gilbert, p. 95. An ugly story of moral depravity is recorded.

[2] After the meeting in the chapter house.

of the divine mercy He would send to me a man like you, by whose advice and assistance I might improve this place, and train the monks in habits pleasing to God. And, brother Lanfranc, when you came, I thought my prayers were heard. I was thinking of transferring my burden to you. I did hope that you would undertake the weight of all my load. And now, I don't know for what reason, but you want to leave me for some other business, and go to live in the woods.'

When Lanfranc perceived that the plans, which he thought were secured, had been detected, he threw himself at the Abbot's feet, and humbly asked to be informed how they had been discovered. Then Herluin gently told [1] him about the vision or dream. Lanfranc was amazed. He prostrated himself and confessed all his plans and desires. He begged for and received forgiveness, and promised never to leave the Abbot, but always to obey his commands. Soon after this incident, as quickly as he could arrange matters, Herluin nominated him Prior of Bec, and handed over to him the spiritual direction of the monastery.[2]

After the appointment of Lanfranc as Prior [3] we read of no more trouble at Bec. The superior personality and wider experience of the Italian lawyer made themselves felt so soon as an executive power was conferred on him.

[1] *Blanda voce.*

[2] Milo, 8. According to Milo, Lanfranc repeated the story to a monk named William, who wrote it down and sent it to Bec after Lanfranc's death. Lanfranc desired that it should not be repeated until then. It is possible that Lanfranc was partly influenced in his attempt to leave Bec by the arrival of old students from Avranches and new scholars seeking his instruction (Milo, 6). In Milo's sequence these begin to arrive before the event related above. But Lanfranc remained, according to Milo's previous statement, three years incognito, until he became Prior. The jealousy of the monks would have been repressed if the distinguished visitors, referred to by Milo, had begun to arrive in the earlier period. The story of Lanfranc's attempt to leave Bec is accepted by Boehmer, *Die Fälschungen Erzbischof Lanfranks von Canterbury* (Leipzig, 1902), p. 127.

[3] This occurred 1043–5, taking 1040–2 as the time of Lanfranc's arrival at Bec (cf. *supra*, p. 8, n. 3). Milo, 6, says that he remained three years quietly at Bec, and then records his promotion to the office of Prior (Milo, 8).

III

PRIOR OF BEC

WORK IN THE SCHOOLS

THE chroniclers are unanimous in ascribing the revival of Latin scholarship in Normandy to Lanfranc. But their statements must be received with discrimination. Orderic, as usual, exaggerates. He says that Lanfranc was the first teacher to give instruction to the Normans in literature.[1] If this means that scholarship did not become productive, that no written work began to appear until Lanfranc came to Normandy, we may accept the statement. But in the context he implies that before the arrival of Lanfranc the Normans were altogether illiterate. This is obviously an exaggeration. Under the influence of William of Dijon and the Cluniac monks, learning had been reviving for more than a generation. Whereas in 1001 William of Dijon had found only four decayed abbeys in Normandy, and not a single clerk who could read Latin, by 1066 twenty-six great monasteries had been founded, with flourishing schools attached to them. At least fifteen of these houses had been founded or refounded when Lanfranc arrived in the duchy.[2] Even his eulogists drop hints of the true state of affairs. Among the visitors to Lanfranc at Bec were many 'famous masters of Latin'.[3] When Thierri became Abbot of the restored S. Evroult (1050) he took with him Gunfrid, Reginald and Fulk, and other 'skilled grammarians'.[4] These statements are influenced by the desire to heap credit on Lanfranc and Thierri, but the rapid movement of students towards Bec proves the existence of a wide-spread desire for learning which must have received its inspiration from earlier days. Lanfranc's influence on

[1] Ord. iv. 6 (ii, p. 210).

[2] Boehmer, *Kirche und Staat in England und in der Normandie* (Leipzig, 1899), pp. 5–7, 18–27; Porée, *Hist. de l'Abbaye du Bec*, i, pp. 15–29; Heurtevent, *Durand de Troarn* (Paris, 1912), pp. 23–5.

[3] Gilbert, p. 97.

[4] Ord. iii. 2 (ii, p. 20).

the revival of letters in Normandy was exerted mainly through his organization of the famous schools at Bec and Caen. As a competent grammarian he was one of a line of scholars who, beginning with William of Dijon, laid the foundation of that Norman scholarship which burst into creative power in the days of his successor Anselm.

Students from all quarters now began to come to Bec. The sudden disappearance of Lanfranc from Avranches may have caused the members of the cathedral school to realize that a great master had been in their midst and they had not taken advantage of his lectures. From Avranches, doubtless, came some of his new pupils at Bec. Perhaps the fact that he was now in orders supplied something formerly wanting in his credentials. As a foreigner and a layman he had the aspect of an adventurer. As a Churchman and monk, and now as Prior, he was a highly accredited member of a society which looked only to the clergy for scholarship and liberal knowledge. From Normandy, Gascony, Brittany, Flanders, Germany and Italy, came the most eager students of the age until, it has been estimated, the community under him at Bec reached the number of two hundred brothers.[1]

Among the students who became famous later in life were Pope Alexander II; Anselm and Theobald, Archbishops of Canterbury; Guitmond, Archbishop of Aversa; William, Archbishop of Rouen; Ivo, Bishop of Chartres, the great Canonist; Ernest, Gundulf and Ernulf, Bishops of Rochester; Gilbert Crispin, Abbot of Westminster, and author of the life of Herluin; Henry, Prior of Canterbury, to whom Lanfranc addressed the Benedictine Constitutions; Paul, his nephew, Abbot of S. Albans; and William of Merseberg.[2] Among other pupils of less distinction were another nephew

[1] Longuemare, *Lanfranc*, p. 44.

[2] The list includes Turold, Bp. of Bayeux; Fulk, Bp. of Beauvais; Richard and Geoffrey, Bps. of Evreux; William, Abt. of Cormeille (cf. *supra*, p. 24 n.); Ravel, Abt. of Battle; Michael and Vincent, Abts. of Préaux; Roger and Geoffrey, Abts. of Jumièges; Bernard and Robert, Abts. of S. Michael de Monte; Robert, Abt. of S. Evroult; Nicholas, Prior of Rochester; Hamelin, Prior of S. Albans; John of Bouleia, and John Ribald of Cerisy (Milo, 21; D'Achery in Migne, cl, cols. 18 and 89; *Hist. Litt. de la France*, viii. 276).

and namesake [1] of Lanfranc, who became Abbot of S. Wandrille; two chaplains of the Emperor Henry IV, and two nephews of Pope Nicholas II.[2] Bec became the seminary from which the leading ecclesiastics of England and Normandy were promoted, and its students passed out into France, Germany, and Italy, wherever the work of Church reform was destined to flourish.

The schools at Bec, as in all Benedictine houses, possessed a department for boys [3] as well as for older students and advanced scholars. All branches of education received attention, including the instruction of boys in the elements of knowledge; the training of professed monks in theology, and perhaps in medicine and law; training for works of research and scholarship, such as the writing of history and biography and the compilation of theological treatises. In addition, a regular part of the life of some members of the community was the copying of manuscripts and the correction of biblical and patristic texts.

The curriculum in the junior schools was based upon the 'seven liberal arts', consisting of the trivium and quadrivium, which correspond roughly with arts and science of modern days. The subjects of the trivium were grammar, rhetoric and dialectics; of the quadrivium, arithmetic, geometry, astronomy and music.

The foundation of all study was grammar, and the textbooks in use were Priscian, Donatus, Aulus Gellius, Macrobius, Martianus Capella and Cassiodorus. Rhetoric, or the art of speaking, was studied from the works of Cicero, Quintilian, Priscian, Cassiodorus, Isidore of Seville and Alcuin. Grammar and rhetoric also comprised the study of poetical and historical works, but whereas a number of historical authors appear to have been available—Suetonius, Josephus, Orosius, Hegesippus, Eusebius of Caesarea, Sidonius (Epistles),

[1] Lanfranc, Epis. XLIX.

[2] Nicholas II, Epis. XXX (Migne, cxliii). The date is fixed by the Pontificate of Nicholas (1059–62).

[3] Cf. Lanfranc, *Decreta pro Ord. S. Ben.* xvii, xxi. On the schools of Bec, cf. Porée, *Hist. de l'Abbaye du Bec*, i, pp. 95–103; Longuemare, *Lanfranc*, pp. 49–59; De Crozals, *Lanfranc*, pp. 51–5.

Eutropius, Trogus-Pompeius, Prosper and Gregory of Tours—only one poet was to be found in the library at Bec early in the twelfth century.[1] The books read for dialectics were Cicero and Seneca. Aristotle, Plato and other Greek writers were known only through the Latin translations of Porphyry, Boethius, Martianus Capella, and Chalcidius.[2] Dialectics formed the basis for the study of theology, and while Lanfranc professed to distrust dialectics as an aid to the interpretation of doctrine,[3] his own works were based on dialectical methods, and until Anselm introduced a more philosophical treatment into the schools of Bec, no other method for theology was in use.

The quadrivium of necessity played a smaller part in the education of a monk. Arithmetic was regarded as a mystical science and was confined almost entirely to the interpretation of the calendar, and particularly for ascertaining the festal and ferial days.[4] Isidore of Seville, Macrobius and anonymous works were the text-books in use. A text-book of Gilbert was used for elementary instruction in geometry.[5] Music, which was distinguished from singing ('cantus'), was studied in relation to arithmetic and astronomy, and especially as a conclusion to the study of rhetoric. But attention was paid to the laws of harmony and acoustics.[6] The writings of Macrobius, Boethius, Donatus, Bede, Alcuin and Odo of Cluny were available. For astronomy the works of Isidore as well as anonymous writers were in use. Most of the anonymous works or text-books so frequently mentioned in the catalogue were drawn up by Benedictine instructors in the schools.[7]

[1] Porée, i, p. 96, notes the absence of Virgil from the list and quotes a letter of Anselm (i. 55) as evidence that Virgil was not studied at Bec.

[2] De Crozals, *Lanfranc*, p. 54.

[3] Lanfranc, *De Corpore*, vii.

[4] Porée, i, p. 98.

[5] Porée, i, p. 99, thinks that Gilbert on geometry refers to Gerbert's work. This writer was Pope Sylvester II. Porée draws attention to the elaborate practical geometry used by church and cathedral builders.

[6] Ibid., p. 97.

[7] The writers mentioned in the text are taken from the catalogue of Bec published by Ravaisson, *Rapports sur les Bibliothèques de l'Ouest* (Paris, 1841), pp. 375–95. Cf. *Catal. des MSS. Biblio.*

During his early days at Bec, Lanfranc lectured on grammar and the classical subjects.[1] The formation of the curriculum may have been his work, but before leaving Bec he gave up teaching secular subjects. There is a letter addressed to him by William of Bamberg, congratulating him upon having concentrated attention in his lectures upon the lives of the saints.[2] The Bec library included several works of Augustine, Jerome, Ambrose, Origen, Gregory the

Publiques de France, T. ii, pp. 385 ff. ; Becker, *Catalogi Bibliothecarum Antiq.* (Bonn, 1885) ; Migne, cl, cols. 771–8. The catalogue comprises two lists, the first containing 161 volumes belonging to the early part of the twelfth century, the second drawn up by Robert de Torigny when Bec received 113 books from a bequest of 140 volumes made by Philippe d'Harcourt, Bishop of Evreux, who died in 1164. (Cf. Armitage Robinson, *Gilbert Crispin*, pp. 52–3 ; Porée, i, p. 92 ; De Lisle, *Chron. de Robert de Torigny*, ii, p. xix.) No works from the second list have been quoted in the text, and it is probable that not all the books mentioned in the first list were at Bec in Lanfranc's time. In some cases the works of more than one writer were bound up in the same volume. In addition to the works mentioned in the text, all of which may have been in the library in Lanfranc's day, the catalogue includes the Tripartite History, the Lives of Herluin (Gilbert Crispin) and Anselm, the Chronicles of Prosper and Siegbert, an interesting volume containing the History of the Normans to the death of Henry I, the History of Charles the Great, the History of Alexander the Great, together with his letters to Aristotle on the situation of India, the History of the Kings of France from their departure from Sigambria to the death of Louis the Child, the History of the Kings of Great Britain to the coming of the Angles (Geoffrey of Monmouth, no doubt the MS. shown in 1139 to Henry of Huntingdon by Robert of Torigny) and extracts from Gildas ; another volume containing the History of France by Gregory of Tours, the History of the Capture of Jerusalem by the Crusaders, by Baldric, Archbishop [*sic*] of Dol ; another volume containing the Expedition to Jerusalem up to 1126 by Fulcher of Chartres ; History of the English, by Henry of Huntingdon (?) ; works by Burchard of Worms, Ivo of Chartres, Gilbert de la Porée, Peter Lombard (*Sententiae*), Hermes Trimegistus, as well as collections of Papal Decrees, Canons, and Benedictine Charters. Only a few of these works remain ; they are in the Bibliothèque Nationale.

[1] Lanfranc, Epis. III.

[2] Longuemare, *Lanfranc*, p. 52 ; De Crozals, *Lanfranc*, p. 55, but Lanfranc (Epis. III) says that he instructed the relations and friends of Alexander II in religious and secular knowledge.

Great and Isidore, and single volumes by Tertullian, Cyprian, Athanasius, Basil, Gregory of Nyssa, Eusebius of Caesarea, Chrysostom, Cassian, Fulgentius, Hegesippus, Ephraem, Dionysius the Areopagite, Gregory of Tours, the 'Shepherd' of Hermas, and the works of Rabanus Maurus. English writers included Bede, Alcuin, and the *Regularis Concordia*.[1] Many of these books had been collected by Lanfranc.[2] They supply some indication of the sources of his own theological knowledge. In his commentary on the Epistles of S. Paul, the greater number of the quotations are taken from Augustine and Ambrose. While there are frequent allusions to the Bible in these commentaries, and especially to the Old Testament, it is strange that the catalogue contains no references to the Bible or to devotional works or liturgies. Nor does it mention the lives of the saints with the exception of lives of S. Nicholas and S. Neot. The Abbé Longuemare points out that it is curious that not a single work on law is mentioned, whereas many copies of the Digest and Institutes of Justinian are found in the lists of other abbeys, dating from this period, and particularly in those of Jumièges and S. Michael.[3] But in a list of books at Bec made by Robert of Torigny about 1150,[4] copies of the Digest, Institutes and Codex of Justinian are mentioned. It is possible that their absence from the earlier list was due to the influence of Lanfranc, who did not wish to trouble his monks with a study which he had definitely abandoned.[5] Although there is no evidence for the teaching of medicine at Bec, a dispensary existed there, and a knowledge of simple pharmacopeia was part of the training of some of the monks,[6] so that medicine cannot have been entirely neglected.

As the community grew in numbers and in fame, through

[1] On the *Regularis Concordia*, cf. Armitage Robinson, *The Times of S. Dunstan*, pp. 143–58.

[2] De Crozals, *Lanfranc*, p. 67, says he collected fifty.

[3] *Lanfranc*, pp. 57–8, but cf. p. 69, where he says that legal studies were always held in honour at Bec, &c.

[4] Migne, cl., cols. 779–81.

[5] But cf. Pollock and Maitland, *Hist. of Eng. Law*, i, p. 55, for Lanfranc's influence on the study of law in Normandy.

[6] Porée, *Hist. de l'Abbaye du Bec*, i, p. 101.

the lectures of Lanfranc, so it grew in material prosperity. Among the constant stream of visitors to Bec were clergy, young nobles, 'well-known' Latin scholars and powerful lay-folk, all of whom came to make offerings because of their respect for Lanfranc.[1] Their benefactions took the form of grants both of land and movables.[2] The five years between 1045 and 1050 constituted the formative period for Bec. During that time its fortunes were founded, its numbers were built up, its famous schools were established. So also for Lanfranc that period was decisive. It established his reputation as the leading teacher of the West. Whatever he had lost by leaving Pavia was then regained. The law was exchanged for theology, and although his knowledge of theology never equalled his practical skill in law, yet in that age of backward learning his theological attainments were by no means small. But his chief fame in the record of Western learning will remain, as the chroniclers all agree, in the work which he did in the schoolrooms of Bec, training a host of able Latin scholars and writers to take their part not only in the learned circles of monastic life, where an easy Latin style was essential, but in the world of political life, which was then just opening for the churchmen of Europe.

During the second part of his career at Bec (1050–62) he was not able to give the same undivided attention to the cloister or lecture-room. He began to be involved by events on a wider theatre.[3] Perhaps his chief contribution, though an indirect one, to the cause of learning during that period, lay in the care and attention he devoted to Anselm, his successor as Prior of Bec, and the brightest light of scholarship and creative thought of the age. Anselm arrived at Bec about the year 1059.[4] At a preliminary visit he perceived in

[1] Gilbert, p. 97. [2] Ibid., p. 97.

[3] In 1049 he appears to have been present at the Council of Rheims; cf. *infra*, pp. 41, 43-4.

[4] Anselm took the cowl in 1060 at the age of 27. Twelve years before this date (1048) he was lying sick in Italy. Then some time was spent in gay life in Italy. After this he wandered for three years through France and Burgundy. He probably arrived at Bec, where he passed the winter before 1060, after Lanfranc's return from Rome in 1059.

Lanfranc a man of no ordinary ability, and decided to enrol himself among his students. After a short time he was admitted to terms of closer intimacy than the other members of the community. While Lanfranc supervised his reading he appointed him to undertake some of the teaching in the school. But the severity of his studies, and the fatigues of monastic life, the cold, the fastings and the vigils, threw him into a state of mental depression. He had a genuine desire for the religious life, but his thoughts were filled with a mild jealousy of Lanfranc. He feared that he would never be able to shine in close proximity with the Prior. But he conquered these thoughts and decided to remain at Bec.[1] However, he was still troubled by the question of a definite vocation. He consulted Lanfranc, who declined to offer any opinion, but agreed to go with him to consult Maurilius, the Archbishop of Rouen. Maurilius had no difficulty in making a decision. He advised Anselm to adopt the monastic life and to remain at Bec. Anselm then took the cowl at the age of twenty-seven.[2]

Some time before 1050, Lanfranc formed a connexion with the monastery of S. Evroult which continued to engage his attention from time to time in later years. Eminent among the great founders of monastic houses was the family of Grand-Mesnil. William, son of Giroie,[3] a member of that house, gave the lands of the decayed house of S. Evroult to Bec, when he joined the community as a monk. Lanfranc was sent to take charge of the new property and to begin the work of restoration. S. Evroult was in a serious state of decay. The walls of the church were in ruins, covered with ivy and infested with rats and mice.[4] The services of the church were no longer conducted. Only two old monks,

[1] Eadmer, *Vita Anselmi,* i. 5.

[2] Ibid. i. 6. The story has a further interest in showing that Anselm was probably allowed a longer novitiate than was usually permitted. But the delay may have been due to a free use of the rule by Lanfranc, or to special indulgence shown by him to a novice of exceptional ability.

[3] William, son of Giroie, had been blinded and mutilated by William Talvas, son of William of Belesme. Ord. iii. 2 (ii, p. 15).

[4] Milo, 7; Ord. iii. 2 (ii, p. 16).

Restould and Ingran by name, inhabited the place. They were living in extreme poverty. Lanfranc was accompanied by three other monks from Bec, to assist in reviving the religious life of the decayed house.[1] One day, when returning to S. Evroult from Bec, he took with him a cat, wrapped in a cloth, and tied behind him on the saddle. On the road he was joined by a friendly traveller, who suddenly heard the cat's 'Mew!', and began to look around to see where the noise was. He noticed the bundle tied behind Lanfranc, and asked what it contained. Lanfranc replied: 'We are infested with rats and mice, so I am taking a cat to keep them away.'[2]

In the year 1050 S. Evroult was completely refounded by Hugh and Robert, the nephews of William of Giroie.[3] The monks of Bec withdrew, and their house was compensated by the gift of the lands of La Roussière.[4] Duke William granted the new foundation a charter[5] and invested Thierri, the first Abbot, with the pastoral staff.[6] Robert of Grand-Mesnil, one of the founders, joined the community and became Prior of S. Evroult, but quarrelled with Thierri, who was entirely devoted to the religious life and appears to have neglected the secular welfare of the monastery. The dispute was carried on for some years until the Abbot resigned his office to the Duke, who appointed Maurilius, Archbishop of Rouen, to conduct an inquiry. In 1056 Maurilius took with him his Chancellor Fulbert, Hugh Bishop of Lisieux, Ansfrid Abbot of Préaux, and Lanfranc, and spent the Feast of S. Peter at S. Evroult, when Thierri was reinstated as Abbot and Robert was ordered to obey him.[7] By 1061,

[1] Ord. iii. 2 (ii, p. 16).

[2] Milo, 7. Dr. W. Hunt in the *D. N. B.* fixes the date of this incident 'about 1049'. But the connexion between Bec and S. Evroult was severed in 1050, after being maintained for 'some time'. Ord. iii. 2 (ii, p. 18). Milo places the incident before his account of Lanfranc's elevation to the office of Prior, but this is too early. It would throw the incident back into the period of his three years' seclusion.

[3] Ord. iii. 2 (ii, p. 17).

[4] Ord. iii. 2 (ii, p. 17).

[5] Ord. iii. 2 (ii, p. 39)

[6] Ord. iii. 2 (ii, p. 18).

[7] Ord. iii. 3 (ii, p. 63).

Robert, who was then Abbot,[1] had quarrelled with the Duke, and went to Rome to lay his case before Pope Nicholas II. On the advice of Lanfranc and Ansfrid, the Duke nominated Osbern, the Prior of Cormeille, and sent him to Maurilius to be consecrated Abbot of S. Evroult.[2] The new-comer was not cordially received, for when the deposition of Robert was confirmed, the Prior Mainer, disregarding the appointment of Osbern, went to Lanfranc to secure another abbot. Lanfranc was greatly offended, although Mainer had originally made his monastic profession to him, and rebuked him so strongly that Mainer withdrew from S. Evroult and joined a community at Cluny.[3] But in 1066 Mainer was made Abbot of S. Evroult, by Duke William, on the day that Lanfranc was formally invested with Caen,[4] when the quarrel with Lanfranc was also composed and the latter sent Mainer a present of twenty pounds of English money and two marks of gold.[5]

Meeting with Duke William

In 1053 William married Matilda, who was within the degrees prohibited by the Church, and Normandy was placed under an interdict by the Papacy. The ban cannot have been strictly enforced, for clerical discipline at that time was not rigid, and some of the clergy had committed a much worse offence by having wives themselves. But a good deal of gossip was going on, and Lanfranc became involved. It was the age of the Cluniac reform movement within the Church. There were two main themes in the reforming programme—the suppression of simony and clerical marriage. The uncompromising attitude of the Church, under the guidance of the Archdeacon Hildebrand at Rome, towards the marriage of priests, was bound to reflect itself in the attitude of churchmen towards the marriage of laymen. Lanfranc's new role as a convert to the religious life made him at first a ready supporter of the

[1] Elected 1059. Ord. iii. 4 (ii, p. 68).
[2] Ord. iii. 6 (ii, p. 82).
[3] Ord. iii. 5 (ii, p. 86).
[4] Ord. iii. 12 (ii, p. 125).
[5] Cf. *infra*, p. 190.

reforms, more especially as he was a disciplinarian by nature as well as by choice. Although he did not in later years press even the ecclesiastical claims of the new movement to their logical conclusion, after the manner of the Roman churchmen, yet at this period he seems to have expressed some strong views on the question of William's marriage, which were reported to the Duke.[1]

Both Gilbert Crispin and Milo place the quarrel between Lanfranc and the Duke after William had taken Lanfranc into his confidence as an adviser upon secular and religious matters. But this we cannot credit. Lanfranc was too shrewd a man to offend such an overlord as William, once he had made his acquaintance and had received marks of his confidence. Moreover, William was not the man to allow a petty offence to interfere in his relations with a man of Lanfranc's character and gifts, once he had realized his value to himself. The quarrel was just such a dispute as often arises between strong and able men before they have realized their common identity of interest.[2]

A prime mover in the attempt to get rid of Lanfranc was Herfast, the Duke's chaplain. William was not so short-sighted as to think that he could altogether ignore the attitude of the leading churchmen in a country like Normandy, where the clergy exercised a strong influence upon public opinion. On learning that Lanfranc was among those who disapproved of his marriage, he sent Herfast with a splendid retinue to Bec in order to convert the Prior to his interests.[3] William's choice of an intermediary was

[1] Milo, 10, followed by *Chron Bec.*, anno 1060 (not in Robt. of Torigny).

[2] The meeting probably took place before the 29th June 1056, the date when Lanfranc went on William's commission to settle the affairs of S. Evroult (cf. *supra*, p. 33). It is possible that William had made a first acquaintance with Lanfranc when campaigning near Bec against Guy of Burgundy, before 1050 (cf. Porée, i, p. 58).

[3] We are not told that this was the object of Herfast's visit, but it is difficult to account for the dispatch of the pompous cavalcade to Bec on any other grounds, unless we are to accept Milo's suggestion that Lanfranc was already a counsellor of the Duke, or the statement of Malmesbury (*G. P*, p. 150) that Herfast, a man of small intellect

unfortunate. Herfast did not possess the first qualification of a courtier—correctness of accent and charm of address. The Prior saw at once that the royal chaplain 'knew nearly nothing', and he determined to turn the whole situation into a joke. He placed an alphabet[1] in the Chaplain's hand and asked him to read it aloud, avoiding his wrath by the grace of his own Italian facetiousness.[2] But Herfast returned to William in high dudgeon, stirred up his resentment against the Prior, and persuaded him to order Lanfranc to leave Normandy.[3]

Whether we can accept this story or not, Gilbert says that mischief was made between William and Lanfranc 'by the accusations of informers', and that in consequence the Duke, being vehemently embittered against him, gave orders that he should be turned out of the monastery, and banished from the country. Herfast had spoken with effect, for even this peremptory order was not sufficient to cool the Duke's anger. William ordered the farm of Parque, belonging to Bec, to be burned. The order was carried out, and Lanfranc perceived that it was time to move. 'So he who was all the joy and solace' of the brothers departed, and 'high grief remained'.[4] Lanfranc made a sorry figure on a lame horse, accompanied by only one servant, who went on foot; for in spite of the benefactions already made to Bec, the house was still poor.

From Gilbert's statement it seems that Lanfranc obeyed the Duke's order promptly, but the blazing buildings of Parque probably had more to do with the Prior's haste than the Duke's order. Even so, it does not appear that he took the shortest route out of Normandy, for he met the Duke on the road. Was he going to Rouen to plead his case? If so, the mind of the old lawyer must have been ablaze with zeal, for if they were all illiterate at the court like Herfast he could promise himself an easy victory. He met the Duke and

and only partly educated, who had a reputation for learning, was attracted by the fame of Lanfranc, and so came to visit him with great pomp.

[1] *Abecedarium.*

[2] *Expediendum.*

[3] Malmes., *G. P.*, p. 150.

[4] Gilbert, p. 97.

saluted him, his lame nag bobbing its nose to the ground at every step. Conscious of his innocence, says Gilbert, he was not unhopeful of the result, if an opportunity for speaking were given to him. We should say that he was conscious rather of his legal and debating skill. At first, the Duke refused to notice him, but 'by the action of divine clemency' he quickly thought better of it, and looking upon Lanfranc with commiseration, made a kindly motion to him to come forward and speak. William was obviously impressed by Lanfranc's personality,[1] and, making use of his own quick appreciation of a likely collaborator, seized the opportunity for trying his man. Lanfranc's ready wit at one turn settled the dispute, and cast the spell of a lifelong friendship over William. 'At thy order, I turn my steps from your duchy, hindered by this useless quadruped. Give me a better horse so that I may fulfil your order.' With an outburst of laughter the Duke replied, 'Who ever demands a reward from an offended judge, before the crime alleged has been expiated?' Then Lanfranc let his persuasive eloquence have play, and 'by the aid of God' soon carried his case to the desired conclusion. Thus by means of a joke he turned aside the hostility which had been brought to a head, if not originally created, by a jest.

We are not told whether Lanfranc and William discussed there and then, or at a later date, the delicate question of the marriage. But in either case William could regard Lanfranc's attitude to the marriage as forced upon him by his status as a churchman, and if Lanfranc was attracted to the Cluniac idea by temperament and choice, he was too much the layman by training and outlook to let that scruple stand in the way of an understanding with William.

Lanfranc had won no mere verbal victory. His lawyer-like skill had secured all the requirements of his position. The Duke received his plea with marked favour. He promised that he would not allow any accusation in future to involve Lanfranc. Bec was to be reimbursed for its devastated property with more than it had lost, and the reconciliation concluded with the exchange of embraces.

[1] Malmes., *G. P.*, p. 38: 'Ex dignitate frontispitii.'

The servant rushed back to Bec with the news. The tears of the brothers were turned into a Te Deum, which they sang, not once, but 'with heart and voice' for the rest of the day! The Abbot refused to believe the news until Lanfranc arrived. The joy of the community was increased when it became known that complete restitution for the devastated property was to be made, and especially when William confirmed the abbey in the possession of its lands.[1]

The irruption of Conrad into Italy in 1036, the robbery in the woods of Ouche in 1042, and now the sudden meeting with Duke William—all threatened Lanfranc with ruin, but ended in a marked development of his career. He was, through all his life, the favoured child of fortune, although an adventurer so far as his plans were concerned. But in all the long series of fortunate accidents which accompanied his steps, none turned out so well as the meeting with William on the Rouen road when he rode the lame nag, for the event proved that there was something more than phrase-making in the description of his relations with the Duke handed down by William of Poitiers. According to that well-informed writer, the Conqueror cultivated Lanfranc's friendship, because he merited reverence and honour by reason of his practical capacity, or because of his mature knowledge of theology, or his singular devotion to the monastic life. He entrusted to him the schemes of his mind and the special care of all the ecclesiastical affairs of Normandy, because, says Poitiers, the watchful care of such a man promised no small security for his dearest wishes, for to the very great authority of wisdom was added the prerogative of holiness.[2]

The compact with William was ratified when Lanfranc made his second journey to Rome[3] to attend the Lateran Synod held by Nicholas II in 1059. Lanfranc's business was mainly concerned with the Duke's affair, but before that came up he was compelled to take part in the case of Berengar. Yet so well did he acquit himself on behalf of the

[1] Gilbert, p. 98.
[2] William of Poitiers (Duchesne, 194 B; Migne, cxlix, col. 1241).
[3] Cf. *infra*, p. 44, for the first journey.

papal interest in that matter, that he won an easy victory for William afterwards. He pointed out that the Pope's interdict only bore heavily upon those who had not united William and Matilda, and who could not disunite them, for since the Duke had married the girl, he was not willing, by any arrangement, to give her up.[1] Nicholas admitted the force of this argument, and granted dispensation for the marriage, on condition that the Duke and his wife should build two religious houses,[2] one for men and one for women, where the divine offices might be observed day and night for the salvation of the souls of the ducal pair. After the return of Lanfranc, the papal order was obeyed.

Lanfranc meanwhile resumed his duties at Bec without delay. Pupils had continued to arrive at the monastery, and the number of the professed brethren continued to grow. The primitive buildings erected by Herluin had long ceased to be adequate for the growing community. The monks were cramped for space.[3] The situation of the house had proved inconvenient and unhealthy. The Prior approached Herluin with the suggestion that more commodious buildings should be erected on another site.[4] But the Abbot was now old and was becoming inefficient through the infirmities of age. The fear of the upheaval which the work would entail was sufficient to alarm him. Lanfranc drew attention to the damp, unhealthy site, but all his persuasions failed to move Herluin to give his consent. Lanfranc is reported to have

[1] Milo, 10. Cf. *Chron. Bec.*

[2] And four hospitals. Cf. *Roman de Rou*, 9665 (Freeman, *N. C.*, iii, p. 107, n. 1.)

[3] Gilbert, p. 98.

[4] Dean Hook (*Archbishops*, ii, p. 87) without any authority gives 1046 as the date. Dr. Hunt (*D. N. B.*) suggests 'about 1058', but Lanfranc would scarcely have undertaken the work before his journey to Rome. The date is indicated by Gilbert, p. 99, who says that three years later, before the new buildings were finished, Lanfranc went to Caen. This was in 1063, and so the new work was commenced about 1060, after Lanfranc's return from Italy. Cf. *infra*, p. 56. I find that this date is accepted by Porée, i, p. 66. Robt. of Torigny, p. 41, writing under the year 1077, says that the new buildings were commenced sixteen years before (1061).

remarked in despair to certain people of standing, 'The lord Abbot wastes his time and labour in this marshy place, nor will he believe me when I say that he should cease from working here, and begin another building in a more healthy situation. May God Almighty create such an impediment that he will listen to me and cease expending his labour upon this unhealthy spot.'[1]

Not only was the community cramped for space, but the damp was rapidly destroying the earlier buildings, which were originally erected in a rude and hasty manner by amateurs. Even before Lanfranc's arrival at Bec, one night during a storm of wind the roof of the dormitory was blown off, and a newly-erected cloister fell down.[2] Shortly after Lanfranc's conversation with the nobles, the right wing of the presbytery, or Abbot's quarters, came down, uncovering the oratory and the altar of S. Benedict. Lanfranc seized the opportunity, when he was consoling the disturbed and anxious Abbot, to urge him again to remove the monastery to a different site. Herluin gave way and began the new work on a much more healthy and suitable spot, building on a more magnificent plan and relying not only on his private resources, which were small, but also upon the gifts of others, brought by his faith and trust in God. Lanfranc assisted by reopening his school, and by handing over the proceeds to the Abbot, for the building fund.[3] The work was hindered for a short time when Lanfranc became Abbot of Caen, but then it went forward rapidly, assisted by his gifts and advice.[4]

[1] Milo, 11.
[2] Gilbert, p. 94.
[3] Milo, 11.
[4] Gilbert, p. 99.

IV

CONTROVERSY WITH BERENGAR

On the 3rd October 1049, Leo IX held at Rheims one of his great reforming councils. At this council it was declared that the Bishop of Rome alone possessed the right to the title of Apostolic Primate of the Catholic Church. Simony and clerical marriage were condemned, and the right to make elections to ecclesiastical offices was declared to be the privilege of clergy and people, and not of individual lay patrons. One of the numerous body of ecclesiastics attending the council was the Prior of Bec. To Lanfranc, who had only a few years before received ecclesiastical office, the topics discussed and decreed were of absorbing interest, especially because of his knowledge of the undisciplined state of the smaller Norman monasteries and parochial clergy. But his interest in the proceedings and conclusions of the synod was disturbed by the receipt of a summons to accompany the Pope to Rome for the Lenten Council of 1050. The cause of this summons was not, apparently, made known to him, and he was not enlightened until a clerk from Rheims, at the command of Leo IX, read out before the Roman Council a letter addressed by Berengar of Tours to the Prior of Bec.[1]

The seeds of the controversy were sown in Carolingian times. The school of Alcuin of York carried over to the Continent the classical tradition and liberal studies which had been founded in England by Theodore, and continued by Bede. The Irish monks, whose influence extended far and wide throughout the empire of Charles, maintained their independence not only against monastic and episcopal organization, but sometimes, drawing upon Greek theology, gave offence to more strict upholders of the received theology of the Western Church. They preserved the classical spirit, with its love of poetry and delight in literature for its own sake. Even Greek was not neglected by them.[2]

[1] Lanfranc, *De Corpore et Sanguine Domini*, iv.

[2] Lane Poole, *Illustrations* (1920), pp. 8–23.

At the beginning of the ninth century the reaction from the teaching of the traditional scholars of the Church broke forth into revolt in the writings of Claudius of Turin and Agobard of Lyons, who protested against the spread of formalism in worship; [1] and a philosophical foundation was given to the reaction when John the Scot based his system upon a revived Neo-Platonism, and adopted rather the method of dialectics than the appeal to authority as the *modus operandi* of theological teaching.[2]

The influence of John the Scot made itself apparent in the writings of Ratramnus, a theologian who criticized the works of his master Paschasius Radbert, a contemporary of John the Scot. Ratramnus maintained that the bread and wine of the Eucharist, after consecration, did not become the body and blood of Christ in an actual or material sense as Radbert had taught, but only in a spiritual sense. The change was secret and spiritual, and manifest only to the eye of faith, although an objective influence was exerted upon the soul, which received a communication of the Divine Logos.[3]

Some time before 1040 Berengar developed the teaching of Ratramnus and John the Scot, by laying greater emphasis upon the 'tropical' or figurative nature of the consecrated elements.[4] While a pupil in the school of Fulbert at Chartres, who lectured on the teaching of Paschasius Radbert, and confuted the teaching of Ratramnus, Berengar had defended Ratramnus, and after a time was compelled to leave Chartres. He gathered round him a number of pupils

[1] Lane Poole, *Illustrations*, pp. 25–44.

[2] Ibid., p. 47.

[3] Neander, *Hist. of the Christian Religion and Church*, vi, pp. 303–4. On the antecedents of the controversy, cf. the admirable account of Heurtevent, *Durand de Troarn* (Paris, 1912), pp. 165–99.

[4] Harnack, *History of Dogma*, vi. 48 ff.; cf. *De Sacra Coena* (Neander, 1834), pp. 83, 163–91, 197, &c. But Berengar did not deny the real or spiritual presence; cf. pp. 51–7, 66–7, 113, 136, 145, 160, 194, 233, &c.; cf. Heurtevent, pp. 200–16. It is uncertain whether Berengar used a work of John the Scot which has since been lost, or the work of Ratramnus which has been frequently assigned to John the Scot.

at the Cathedral school of Tours, where Lanfranc, who had recently left Pavia, attended his lectures. The astute Italian, although at that date not learned in theology, realized the discrepancy between the teaching of Berengar on the Eucharist and that which was rapidly becoming the accepted doctrine of the Church. He left Berengar with some precipitancy, though not before some discussion had taken place between them in the Schools.[1] But Berengar did not forget the impression made upon him by the personality and gifts of Lanfranc. In 1049 he sent a letter to the Prior of the new and growing school at Bec, couched in friendly terms, and addressed to 'Brother Lanfranc'. He had heard, he said, from Ingalran of Chartres that Lanfranc rejected the teaching of John the Scot on the Sacrament of the Altar. He suggested that Lanfranc was not well versed in Scripture, but expressed a desire to hear from him. He said that if Lanfranc rejected the teaching of John the Scot, he must also regard as heretical the writings of Ambrose, Jerome, Augustine, and others.[2]

Lanfranc had left for Rheims when the letter reached Bec. The bearer delivered it to certain clerks who, against all ecclesiastical usage, read it and showed it to the other clergy. The letter was sent on to Rheims, where it was shown to the Pope, but was withheld from Lanfranc. From Lanfranc's statement [3] and from that of Siegbert of Gembloux [4] we learn that its contents fixed suspicion on Lanfranc's own orthodoxy. The cause of this suspicion has hitherto remained

[1] Bibl. d'Evreux Lat. MSS. 96. Cf. *supra*, p. 10. The early writers are almost entirely silent on this early connexion between Lanfranc and Berengar, and if the Benedictine editors knew of it they also deliberately remained silent in view of Lanfranc's reputation as an orthodox doctor of the Church. Guitmond of Aversa, who wrote a work against Berengar, entitled *De Corpore et Sanguine Domini*, mentions that Lanfranc had vanquished Berengar before the dispute broke out (Migne, cxlix, col. 1428). This statement appears to be behind the tradition of Henry of Knighton (i, p. 90), a late writer, who says that discussions had taken place between Lanfranc and Berengar in the Schools (quando in scolis militavimus).

[2] Migne, cl, col. 63.

[3] *De Corpore*, iv; Milo, 10

[4] Neander, Preface to Berengar, *De Sacra Coena* (1834), p. 3.

unexplained, but it becomes clear from Lanfranc's early connexion with Berengar.[1] It is possible that when at Tours, Lanfranc's views, even if ostensibly opposed to those of Berengar, showed some leaning towards them. Possibly also the jealousy of some of the monks at Bec, who had already given trouble to Lanfranc, began the stir among the northern clergy.[2] Berengar certainly writes as to an old friend, and the letter indicates that formal discussions had taken place between them, and the mere fact that the two men had met may have caused the French clergy to regard Lanfranc as an adherent of Berengar. The letter contains nothing upon which a definite charge against Lanfranc could be made, but it does suggest surprise, on the part of Berengar, that Lanfranc's views were so different from his own—a surprise which would have been natural if Lanfranc had already shown some leaning to Berengar's position. At the same time the official suspicion of Lanfranc may have been no more than a reasonable doubt of the orthodoxy of a priest who had taken orders late in life, and who was obviously deficient in theological knowledge. Leo IX ordered the letter to be brought to Rome, and to be read by a clerk from Rheims at the Lenten Synod, to which Lanfranc had been summoned, and there for the first time he was made aware of the letter. But once again, a most unfortunate situation was completely transformed by his dexterous handling. Without much difficulty he was able to clear himself before the Roman court, and to secure a prominent part in the later stages of the controversy. Describing the proceedings at the Roman council, he says, 'I rose; what I felt, I said; what I said, I proved; what I proved was pleasing to all, and displeasing to none.'[3] So, with a vigorous defence, the old lawyer of Pavia rescued himself from a difficult position which might have ruined for him all prospects of further promotion in the Church.

[1] Cf. *supra*, p. 10 and foot-note.

[2] *De Corpore*, iv.

[3] Ibid., iv. For the course of events up to 1050, cf. Heurtevent, pp. 119–59.

The case swung round against Berengar, who was condemned and excommunicated.[1] In order to give him an opportunity for making his defence, another Council was summoned to meet at Vercelli in September of the same year (1050). Although friends tried to dissuade him, Berengar determined to attend,[2] but Henry I of France imprisoned him under the sentence already promulgated against him at Rome.[3] The case was accordingly heard at Vercelli in Berengar's absence, and Lanfranc appeared as one of the protagonists on the papal side.[4] The writings of Ratramnus, John the Scot and Berengar were burned, and when one of Berengar's clerks attempted to speak on his behalf, he was arrested by the Pope's order, to save him from ill-treatment.[5]

Through the intercession of friends, Berengar secured his release after the synod of Vercelli,[6] but did not cease to press his case. His friends advised moderate action, and he agreed to refer the matter to a synod of bishops. The need for a formal discussion before a properly constituted assembly was becoming evident.[7] Confusion was being caused by the

[1] Siegbert of Gembloux (Neander, Pref. to *De Sacra Coena*, p. 4), Berengar, Epis. to Richard (Giles, Epis. II, *Op. Lanfranci*).

[2] Berengar, *De Sacra Coena*, p. 41.

[3] Berengar, Epis. to Richard (Giles). *De Sacra Coena*, pp. 42, 47.

[4] Milo, 10.

[5] Lanfranc, *De Corpore*, iv; Berengar, *De Sacra Coena*, p. 47. Berengar denies that a second clerk, who attempted to defend John the Scot's book, was one of his following, as Lanfranc alleged (*De Corpore*, iv). This was a compatriot of Lanfranc whom the Pope also ordered to be arrested to save him from attack.

[6] Neander, *Hist. of the Christian Religion and Church*, vi, p. 316.

[7] The movements of Lanfranc and Berengar during 1050–1 are obscure. Modern writers have recorded that Lanfranc attended a council at Brionne. But Lanfranc does not mention Brionne. He says that between the Councils of Rome (Lent, 1050) and Vercelli (Sept. 1050) he remained with the Pope (usque ad ipsum synodum secum remansi: *De Corpore*, iv), and Berengar does not challenge his statement, a remarkable circumstance if Lanfranc had returned to Normandy in the interval, since Berengar was on the alert for slips in Lanfranc's account, and challenges his accuracy on several other points.

On the other hand, Berengar refers to a discussion which took place

different statements which were being bandied about. Berengar complained that Lanfranc was not receiving correct

at Brionne when, he had heard, Lanfranc reported the condemnation of John the Scot by Leo IX (sicut apud Brionnum, ubi aderas tu, narrasti quibusdam, a Leone papa dampnatus est . . . Scotus—*De Sacra Coena,* p. 38; de Johanne cur conscissus fuisset, te ipsum causam consissionis quibusdam narrantem audivi—Ibid., p. 37; te ipsum narrasse quibusdam—Ibid., p. 43). (Boehmer, *Kirche und Staat,* p. 21, n. 1, points out that the last quotation is followed, in the only MS. which has survived, by the words 'me audiente', but that these words have been cancelled). John the Scot's book was not condemned by Leo IX until the Roman council of 1050, so that if Lanfranc remained with the Pope until the Council of Vercelli, this conference at Brionne could not have been held till the autumn of 1050, after his return.

The problem is complicated further by the statement of Durand of Troarn (Migne, cxlix, col. 1421), who says that Berengar came to Normandy and persuaded Duke William to hold a conference at Brionne, which took place before the Council of Vercelli, and that Berengar was defeated by the arguments of those who were present. Durand does not mention Lanfranc's presence. Moreover, his statements are not altogether trustworthy. He dates the Council of Vercelli 1053. Boehmer (*Kirche und Staat,* p. 21, n. 1) thinks that this error need not discredit the rest of his account, and accepts his statement for the conference at Brionne. Heurtevent (*Durand de Troarn,* p. 139, n. 2) overcomes the difficulty by bringing Lanfranc to Brionne between the Councils of Rome and Vercelli. But Lanfranc's statement that he remained with the Pope, which was not challenged by Berengar, surely renders this impossible. Some writers (cf. Boehmer, p. 21, n. 1, and Sudendorf, *Ber. Tur.* p. 28) suggest two Councils of Brionne, one attended by Berengar, before the Council of Vercelli, and the other attended by Lanfranc after that council.

A safer conclusion appears to be that a conference was held at Brionne after Lanfranc's return from Vercelli, when he reported the papal decision against John the Scot, as Berengar says (Hefele, *Hist. des Conciles,* iv, pt. 2, p. 1055, comes to a similar conclusion). Lanfranc does not mention this conference because it was an informal gathering for the benefit of the Norman clergy, although if Berengar had been present he would scarcely have avoided referring to the fact. Berengar's language supports this view. He does not speak of a council formally assembled, but says that he has heard that Lanfranc reported the decision of the Pope to certain people at Brionne. His language does not prove that he was himself present. Durand's report then appears to refer to this meeting,

reports of his sayings.[1] A council of bishops met at Tours (1054) [2] under the presidency of Hildebrand, and, if we may trust Berengar's own account, the astute archdeacon just missed composing the whole dispute. Berengar convinced Hildebrand that he accepted the formal doctrine of the Church, that after consecration the bread and wine became the body and blood of Christ. It was arranged that time should be given for the disturbance to die away in France, and that Berengar should then proceed to Rome, in order that the dispute might be settled finally in another council. At the demand of some of the bishops, he took an oath stating that he really believed what he said. He did this under the impression that the contents of the oath did not state the means by which the bread and wine became the body and blood of Christ, but the mere fact of the change.[3]

Lanfranc gives a different report of this meeting. He says that Berengar not only declined to defend himself, but swore to observe the accepted beliefs of the Church, which were recited before him, and promised that he would maintain them from that hour. The two accounts are, perhaps, not irreconcilable. When the different accounts

although he confuses it with an earlier excursion of Berengar into Normandy.

The tradition of a formal meeting between Lanfranc and Berengar was long maintained. The fifteenth-century writer, Henry of Knighton (i, pp. 89–90) records the attendance of Lanfranc, Herluin and Berengar at the Council of Rome. Lanfranc with difficulty persuaded Herluin to allow him to go, and at the Council only secured the Abbot's reluctant consent to speak, and so to confute Berengar. Obviously this report cannot refer to the Council of Rome, where neither Berengar nor Herluin was present. But if Lanfranc and Berengar had met at Brionne this story may embody the tradition, for, as Brionne was close to Bec, Herluin could have attended.

[1] Migne, cl, col. 66.

[2] Lanfranc, *De Corpore*, iv; Milo, 10. The writer in the *D. N. B.* repeats the old mistake of placing this council in 1055. He has been misled by Lanfranc's statement that the legates of Pope Victor were present. Leo IX died in April 1054, and Victor II was not consecrated until April 1055. Lanfranc dates back Victor's pontificate to the time of Leo's death. Berengar, therefore, rightly challenges his statement that the legates of Leo were present (*De Sacra Coena*, p. 49

[3] *De Sacra Coena*, pp. 49–53.

were written, both men were drawing upon personal recollections, and Lanfranc may easily have confused the events of the Council of Tours (1054) with those of the Lateran (1059).[1] In any case it was possible to take two views of the proceedings. Hildebrand was clearly uncertain about Berengar's heterodoxy. On the other hand, if Hildebrand supplied Berengar with a formula to which the latter agreed, Lanfranc may well have regarded this as an acceptance of the orthodox position. Moreover, Berengar may have promised to remain loyal to the compromise, as Lanfranc alleged, but without regarding himself as having surrendered his own position until another council at Rome should finally decide the question. In this, as in all similar cases where a definition can be interpreted from the realist or nominalist standpoint, opposite impressions of the conclusions and implications of a discussion may easily be carried away by the contending parties. The categories of the disputants had now become irreconcilable.

The settlement at Rome was postponed by the death of Leo IX (April 1054). Berengar consequently felt free to continue the defence of his own position as formerly. In the eyes of Lanfranc, this action naturally appeared as perjury.

In 1059 Berengar was summoned to appear before the Lateran Council at Rome, convened by Nicholas II. Lanfranc's business on that occasion was twofold. He came to obtain the removal of the papal ban on William's marriage, celebrated six years before, and although his diplomacy in that matter was a considerable achievement, yet the Council was favourably disposed towards the King's business because it was looking for the assistance of Lanfranc in the matter of Berengar.[2]

[1] *De Corpore*, iv. Lanfranc's passage reads at first sight as though Berengar was present at the previous Council of Rome (1050). But he refers to the Lateran (1059) which he had already described (*De Corpore*, ii).

[2] The leading part on the orthodox side was played by Cardinal Humbert, a more extreme upholder of advanced views, and one to whom the suspicion of Berengar's influence had not at any time been attached. Hildebrand's attitude at this Council is not clear. Some years later he was still the friend of Berengar, but in the

Lanfranc says that Berengar did not dare to defend himself at the Council. He lighted the fire and threw his own works into it, and then read and swore to an oath handed to him at his own request by Cardinal Humbert.[1] A copy of the oath was sent by Nicholas to the chief churches of Italy, Gaul and Germany, wherever the report of Berengar's teaching had reached.[2]

Even now Berengar was not vanquished. He continued to give his teaching publicly. In a 'little work',[3] which Lanfranc says he 'received for destruction', Berengar omitted to give a copy of the oath. Lanfranc alleged that the omission was made with the object of saving himself from the imputation of perjury when, after the Council, he went back upon the oath, and alleged that Berengar also said that it had proceeded from Humbert.[4] Berengar replied to this charge in his later work, the *De Sacra Coena*. He denied that he had signed the oath. He was not even asked to give his opinion, but only to take the document into his hands. This he did under fear of death, without compromising his conscience, therefore he felt justified in saying that Humbert was its author.[5] If Berengar's statement may be accepted, it shows that his treatment at the Council was not ungenerous, but it also shows that Lanfranc's charge of disingenuousness was not without foundation.

For nearly twenty years the controversy continued,[6] until the public feeling of the Church made its resentment heard in the letter of Hugh, Abbot of Cluny, to Gregory VII,

presence of the zealots at Rome he took no steps to defend him. Possibly, like Lanfranc, he regarded the renewal of Berengar's teaching after the synod of Tours as a breach of the compact then made, and therefore left him to the mercy of the Council.

[1] *De Corpore*, ii, which also gives the complete form of the oath 'Ego Berengarius,' &c.

[2] Ibid.

[3] *De Corpore*, v: 'in hoc opusculo'.

[4] Ibid,, ii.

[5] *De Sacra Coena*, pp. 25–6.

[6] Between 1050 and 1079 Berengar was anathematized by thirteen councils—Rome (four), Tours (two), and one at Brionne, Vercelli, Paris, Florence, Rouen, Angers, and Poitiers. The *Chron S. Maxentii* (Bouquet, *Rec. Hist. Gaules*, Paris, 1781, xii, p. 401) says that at the Council of Bourdeaux (1080), 'Berengarius reddidit fidei suae rationem'.

complaining of the influence of Berengar.[1] The Pope replied by sending a messenger to Cluny to place his proposals before the Abbot, and sent with him a letter, in which it is made clear that other anxieties played their part in causing him to take decisive action.[2] Berengar was summoned to Rome (1078), and Gregory tried to arrange a compromise as at Tours.[3] He refused to allow Berengar to undergo the ordeal by fire.[4]

The Council was adjourned until the next year (1079), when the whole question was reopened in the church of S. Salvator. The discussion lasted three days. Berengar gave full expression to his views, but on the third day he submitted and swore to observe another oath, which he then took, retracting all his opinions.[5] In order to settle the question finally, Gregory obtained from him a promise that he would not in future discuss the matter, save with the object of winning back some of his disciples from the teaching given to them by himself.[6] Berengar carried away with him the Pope's goodwill.[7] A general anathema was issued against all who should molest him in future,[8] and later still, the Archbishop of Tours and the Bishop of Angers were specially charged to defend him from attack.[9]

Lanfranc was not present at the councils of 1078–9, and in consequence the dispute was settled without his assistance. If the unfortunate accident had not happened to Berengar's original letter, Lanfranc might have escaped being drawn into the controversy. On questions of practical theory he

[1] Jaffé, *Mon. Greg. Reg.* v. 21.

[2] Ibid.: 'Tot enim angustiis . . . fatigamur.'

[3] Neander, *Hist. of the Christian Religion and Church*, vi. p. 330.

[4] *Hist. Litt. de la France*, viii, p. 210.

[5] Jaffé, *Mon. Greg. Reg.* vi. 17a, and Lanfranc, *De Corpore*, ii.

[6] Lanfranc, *De Corpore*, ii.

[7] De Crozals (p. 95) gives a partial and misleading account of the attitude of Gregory, and reports a legend to the effect that, as a means of ending the dispute, Gregory threw the host into a brazier of burning coal, where it remained unconsumed.

[8] Jaffé, *Mon. Greg. Reg. Epis. Coll.* 24.

[9] Ibid. 36. Berengar passed the remainder of his days after 1079 quietly near Tours, and died in 1088 (Neander, *Hist. of the Christian Religion and Church*, vi, p. 334). Malmes., *G. R.*, ii, p. 339.

was not usually dogmatical. On purely theological questions he indeed showed a more dogmatic attitude, but the letter of Berengar suggests that prior to 1050 some kind of agreement upon matters of Church doctrine had existed between them.

Before leaving Bec, Lanfranc sought to make permanent the results of his achievements at the councils of 1050, by entering into a literary contest with Berengar.[1] But whatever laurels he gathered in the councils, the palm does not fall to him on the merits of his written work. His treatise, the *De Corpore et Sanguine Domini*, is a halting, amateurish attempt to deal piecemeal with selected passages from one of Berengar's shorter works. This was doubtless a method

[1] The version of the *De Corpore et Sanguine Domini* which has come down was edited by Lanfranc after 1079. It refers to the Council of Rome in that year (§ ii). It was not written before 1059:

(*a*) It contains numerous references to the Roman Council of that year.

(*b*) It quotes sixteen passages from a 'little work' of Berengar, and among them the oath submitted to Berengar in 1059 (§ ii). Berengar's 'little work' therefore was written before 1059, and time must be allowed for it to have reached Lanfranc.

(*c*) The heated phraseology suggests that it was written while the controversy was still active.

It was not written later than 1062:

(*a*) In 1062 Lanfranc went to Caen, where his sojourn was too broken by other work to have allowed time for it there.

(*b*) Berengar's 'little work' was received by Lanfranc 'for destruction'. The latest date when the order for the destruction of Berengar's writings can have been given was 1059, and Lanfranc is not likely to have preserved the 'opusculus' for many years after that date. D'Achery (Migne, cl, col. 25) assigns the *De Corpore* to the period at Bec. He also says, on the authority of Baronius, that Lanfranc wrote a work against Berengar in 1059 which John Brompton called *Tonantem Librum* and which was entitled by Lanfranc himself *Scintillarum*. It is not clear whether D'Achery regards this work as the original of the *De Corpore*, but the tradition confirms the evidence for the writing of a work at Bec after 1059. Mabillon dates the *De Corpore* 1069. The *Hist. Litt. de la France*, viii. p. 281, assigns it to the period at Caen and says that it was a reply to Berengar's *De Sacra Coena*, but this is impossible (cf. *infra*, p. 53, n. 4). Sudendorf, *Berengarius Turonensis* (1850), p. 39, dates the *De Corpore* 1063–9.

which commended itself to an advocate pleading a case in court, but as an attempt to discuss and define philosophically the orthodox position it does not take a high place in theological literature. He protests that he avoided intentionally the dialectical method,[1] but the impression is created that he was not really capable of contending with Berengar's wider theological knowledge and more subtle mentality, and he sometimes resorts to a dialectic thrust when an opportunity for scoring a point presents itself.

He challenges Berengar's main contention that after consecration the elements did not cease to be what they were, while, at the same time, they were changed into something else. Lanfranc says that a thing cannot be changed into something else without ceasing to be what it was.[2] This was an argument which might have secured applause in a court of law, but even Lanfranc himself would not have accepted it elsewhere without qualification.

In some passages he twists Berengar's argument round to make it fit his own views. Berengar contended that just as he who said that Christ is the headstone of the corner did not do away with Christ, so, when it was said that the bread and wine are the true body and blood of Christ, they did not suggest that the bread and wine ceased to exist. Lanfranc turns the argument round by maintaining that as the illustration from the corner-stone did not make Christ a stone, so, if the body of Christ was called bread, it did not convert it into bread,[3] which was tantamount to claiming that the bread was the body of Christ before it was bread.

In nine of the twelve sections in which passages from Berengar's tract are challenged, Lanfranc was content to repeat the traditions of the Church,[4] or to express agreement with Berengar,[5] without allowing the points upon which they agreed to carry weight. No new argument which could compare with Berengar's development of the teaching of John the Scot was forthcoming, and no criticism which really went to the heart of his position was offered. In the

[1] *De Corpore*, § vii.
[2] Ibid. ix.
[3] Ibid. vi.
[4] Ibid. v, viii, xiv, xvii
[5] Ibid. x, xi, xii, xiii, xv, xvii.

latter portion of the *De Corpore* [1] he begins with an effective appeal to the hypostatic union of the Incarnation. The form of the elements remains, but their nature is changed partly by human benediction and partly by divine consecration, as in the mystery of the Incarnation. The Catholic Church does not teach that we consume the body and blood visibly.[2] But in the passages which follow [3] he slips back into the evasive treatment of the earlier part of the work.

The closing section of the tract is a rhetorical declamation against the claim that Berengar and his followers represented the true Church. It ends with the summary statement: 'Falsum est igitur quod de corpore Christi a te creditur et astruitur. Ergo vera est ejus caro, quam accepimus, et verus est sanguis quem potamus.' The judge gives his decision. If the ex-lawyer had been content with issuing judicious opinions upon the points in dispute, and had avoided the attempt to overthrow the arguments of Berengar, an attempt for which he was by training, knowledge, and intellectual capacity unqualified, a more effective criticism of his opponent might have been supplied. But these things did not really matter to the Church of those days. She was contented if her protagonists were able to mass together the traditional statements of the fathers. In an age when authority and not reason carried weight, the marshalling of received opinions counted for more than intellectual acumen or logical consistency.

Berengar's work, *De Sacra Coena*,[4] is of a different order.

[1] Ibid. xviii–xxiii. The best sections of the earlier portion are viii and xiv.

[2] Ibid. xviii–xix.

[3] Ibid. xx–xxiii.

[4] Neander (1834). It quotes many passages of Lanfranc's *De Corpore* verbatim. It was not written, therefore, before 1060–2, the date when Lanfranc's book probably appeared (cf. *supra*, p. 51 n.). It makes no reference to events recorded by Lanfranc later than 1059. Berengar therefore used Lanfranc's earlier edition, before the latter added the reference to the Council of 1079. As Berengar was then finally reconciled to the Church, it is unlikely that he wrote *De Sacra Coena* after 1079, especially as his last years were spent quietly at Tours in full communion with the Church (Malmes., *G. R.*, ii, p. 339). It bears evidence of having been written while the controversy was still hot, and appears to have been composed at intervals.

While Lanfranc's tract is confined to some thirteen thousand words, the *De Sacra Coena* runs up to two hundred and sixty-six octavo pages of printed matter, and the beginning and ending of the MS. are missing. Although written in a polemical style, it attempts a serious philosophical treatment of different aspects of the theory of the Eucharist, and though all attempts to solve the metaphysical problem of the two-nature doctrine fail, yet the attempt of Berengar fails only at the point of definition. The philosophic argument behind that point is sound and consistent with the premisses upon which it is based.

Both writers indulged in acrimonious abuse, but that was characteristic of the controversial writings of the age, and represented merely the antagonism of debate. When the controversy was well advanced, an acute divergence upon the fundamental theory of the Eucharist undoubtedly appeared. Both writers were less bound by tradition than other churchmen of the age, both had rather the scholar's than the theologian's temperament. In the confraternity of letters a compromise might have been expected in their case more confidently than if Humbert or Damiani had been originally in the lists. Berengar did not commence with any inherent hostility towards Lanfranc,[1] and in the 'little work', quoted by Lanfranc in the *De Corpore*, his criticism was levelled chiefly against Cardinal Humbert. It was not until after Lanfranc had appeared repeatedly against him, and after the *De Corpore* had come into his hands, that he delivered his grand attack upon Lanfranc in the *De Sacra Coena*.[2] On the other hand, Lanfranc had not been trained as a professional theologian. He approached theology with

In the middle of the book (Neander, pp. 165–71) the style changes from the second to the third person. Being a lengthy work (266 pp. of octavo print have been preserved) it was not quickly produced. Allowing time for Lanfranc's work to reach Berengar, in or soon after 1060, the *De Sacra Coena* probably did not appear before 1063–5. Sudendorf, *Ber. Tur*, p. 47, dates it 1063–9; Harnack, *Hist. Dog.* vi, p. 48 (Eng. Trans., McGilchrist, 1899), dates it 'about 1073'; Hefèle, *Hist. des Con.*, iv, pt. II, p. 1052, gives 1063.

[1] Cf. *supra*, p. 43.

[2] It is not certain whether Lanfranc ever saw this work.

an open mind, and did not accept wholeheartedly either the theory of papal supremacy or the practical reforms.[1] It is possible that if, while defending himself, he had shown a not unfavourable attitude to Berengar, Hildebrand would have thrown himself entirely on the side of Berengar, and a *rapprochement* of Hildebrand, Berengar and Lanfranc might have secured a place for the reform of theology and theological method in the programme of Hildebrand when he became Gregory VII. An opportunity was missed for carrying the reform movement into the region of theology. The whole course of medieval church history might have been changed. Truly, as Berengar said, 'a light had shined in the darkness and Lanfranc had comprehended it not.'[2]

The Norman and English writers claim the victory of the Church for Lanfranc.[3] But that honour must be conceded to Cardinal Humbert. Lanfranc's treatise[4] has caused later generations to accept the plaudits of his eulogists without question. But Lanfranc was placed at the bar as a defendant in the first instance. He never became more than chief witness for the prosecution, which was conducted by Humbert, with Hildebrand intermittently appearing as a kind of mild devil's advocate for Berengar. There is little evidence for the conclusion that his 'victory' over Berengar was instrumental in hastening his own promotion. More was effected for him at Rome by his friendship with Alexander II, and by the papal consideration for his influence over William; and more was gained for him in Normandy by his successful negotiation for the removal of the ban on William's marriage. The controversy with Berengar exerted little more influence upon his career than the role of a witness in a lawsuit upon the fortunes of ordinary men. The Norman and English writers exaggerate the importance of Lanfranc's literary work in the controversy. The literary defence of the orthodox position was more ably conducted by Guitmond of Aversa and Durand of Troarn.

[1] Cf. *infra*, pp. 151–2.
[2] *De Sacra Coena*, pp. 280–1.
[3] Milo, Orderic, Malmesbury (*G. R.*).
[4] Berengar's *De Sacra Coena* was discovered by Lessing before 1770.

V

THE CALL TO ENGLAND

Abbot of Caen

The Council at Rome of 1059 was fraught with larger consequences for Lanfranc than his final vindication in the dispute with Berengar. We have seen that he successfully negotiated a dispensation for William's marriage, on condition that two religious houses were built by the Duke and his wife. The new houses were erected on William's demesne land at Caen, the monastery was in due course dedicated to S. Stephen, and the nunnery to the Holy Trinity. Both communities were endowed from the revenues of the Duke and his Duchess.[1] The work was begun about 1060, but before the princely foundations were completed, William gave to S. Stephen's an abbot of princely qualities in Lanfranc (1063).[2] Indeed, it is probable that Lanfranc's hand was

[1] Milo, 10. William's grant to S. Stephen's included lands in Devon, Dorset, Somerset, Wilts, Essex and London (Migne, cl, col. 71).

[2] Orderic, v. 2 (ii, p. 307), says that Anselm succeeded Herluin as Abbot of Bec in 1078, after being Prior for fifteen years. Thus Anselm succeeded Lanfranc in 1063. Robt. of Torigny, p. 34, states that Anselm took the cowl in 1060, and became Prior after being three years without promotion. Thus Lanfranc left Bec in 1063. Gilbert, p. 99 (Milo, 11), says that Lanfranc became Abbot of Caen three years after the commencement of the new buildings at Bec, so that they were begun in 1060. As William would not have risked the displeasure of the Papacy by delaying the work at Caen, he must have commenced building in or soon after 1060.

The only difficulty is another statement in Orderic, iii. 12 (ii, p. 126), reporting that Lanfranc was appointed to Caen on the same day as the elevation of Mainer from the office of Prior to that of Abbot at S. Evroult, when William was waiting to sail on the English expedition (16th July 1066). But William would not have delayed an appointment to Caen so long. The Pope's sanction for the English expedition would not have been given without definite evidence of William's submission to the papal judgement of 1059. The later

working on Caen from the beginning. He was engaged after his return from Rome upon the rebuilding of Bec, and it is unlikely that the work at Caen was entrusted by William to any one else. The purchase of a stone quarry[1] at least indicates his interest and activity in the work at Caen soon after he became its Abbot. The Papacy also took the new house under its special care.[2] In the papal charter for the foundation it was expressly stated by Alexander II that Caen should be free from episcopal control. But the right of the bishop to intervene in cases involving moral offences was preserved, qualified by the right of appeal to the Archbishop of Rouen.[3]

date (1066) was the occasion of Lanfranc's formal investiture at Caen.

Two other incidents confirm the earlier date (1063). When William, son of Radbord, was received by Lanfranc at Caen, the building was so incomplete that William was sent to Bec to be trained for the religious life (Milo, 4). But by 1066 the work at Caen must have been so far advanced that this would not have been necessary. In 1067 Lanfranc was offered the Archbishopric of Rouen, but this offer would scarcely have been made if he had only just gone to Caen.

Longuemare (*Lanfranc*, p. 83) accepts Orderic's later date (1066) on the authority of William's Charter to Caen. He points out that William signed as 'King'. But Longuemare fails to notice that Lanfranc signs as Archbishop, so that the earliest date for the Charter is 1070, and it is valueless as evidence for the promotion to Caen. The Charter is printed in Migne, cl, col. 71.

The fact that the Charter was not issued till 1070 at the earliest, and that Caen was not formally consecrated till 1077, need not imply any undue delay in the building operations.

Longuemare is supported by Charma, *Notice Biographique*, Paris and Caen, 1849, p. 21; Hippeau, *L'Abbaye de Saint-Étienne de Caen*, Caen, 1855, p. 5: De Crozals, *Lanfranc*, Paris, 1877, p. 77, all of whom give 1066. But Porée, *Hist. de l'Abbaye du Bec*, Evreux, 1901, i, p. 118, prefers 1063, following *Hist. Litt. de la France*, viii, p. 266 (1062–3); D. Ceiller, t. xxxi (1063); and Mabillon, *Ann. Ord. S. Ben.*, iv, p. 590 (1063). Cf. Denys de Sainte-Marthe, *Gallia Christiana*, ed. Piolin, Paris, 1874, xi, col. 423 (1063–4); Du Monstier, *Neustria Pia*, p. 625 (1064).

[1] Cartul. S. Et. de Caen (Bibl. Nat.) quoted by Longuemare, p. 84.

[2] Alex. II, Epis. XX (Migne, cxlvi).

[3] Ibid., Epis. LVII, and Migne, cl, col. 72.

Lanfranc left Bec unwillingly.[1] He took with him, among other monks,[2] Radulf, who had recently assumed the habit at Bec.[3] The change was made more difficult for Lanfranc by the influx of young men who came to join the new community before facilities for instruction were ready. Among them was William, the son of Radbord, Bishop of Séez, who made his profession at Caen and was then sent to Bec to learn the monastic life, because of the imperfect condition of the buildings at Caen.[4] Later on William rejoined Lanfranc at Caen and assisted him in the lecture room.[5]

An interesting little tale of Lanfranc's relations with his pupils at Caen has been handed down. One day Gundulf, who had followed him from Bec to Caen, was sitting with two companions near Lanfranc, looking through a copy of the Gospels. The Abbot was intent upon other matters, and the three young men amused themselves by turning over the pages to find texts which might indicate which of them should become an abbot, and which a bishop. Gundulf came to the passage : 'Thou faithful and prudent servant whom the Lord has placed over His family.' Walter's finger fell on the words, 'Thou good and faithful servant, enter into the joy of thy Lord.' The third student found a passage which greatly disturbed him, but Malmesbury, who tells the tale, could not recall what it was. They were talking loudly about this passage, when Lanfranc asked the cause of their excitement, and on being informed, said that Gundulf would become a bishop, Walter an abbot, but that the third would slide back into secular life.[6] The reply attributed to Lanfranc is improbable, but the story affords evidence for the careful study of the New Testament in the schools supervised by Lanfranc. While at Bec and Caen he wrote his lengthy commentaries on the Epistles of S. Paul, and left them behind when he came to England.[7] There is some

[1] Gilbert, p. 99 ; Milo, 14. [2] *Chron. Bec.*

[3] Milo, 11. Radulf became Prior of Caen and Abbot of Battle.

[4] Milo, 11.

[5] Ord. iv. 6 (ii, p. 213). William became Prior and Abbot of Caen and Archbishop of Rouen. [6] Malmes., *G. P.*, p. 137.

[7] Anselm Lib. I, Epis. LVII (Migne, clviii).

uncertainty whether the text we possess is that written by Lanfranc, or a copy of notes taken down by one of his pupils.[1] Our copy does not contain two of Lanfranc's comments on the Epistle to the Hebrews, which are quoted by Peter Lombard.[2] But, as it has been pointed out, the existing texts differ on so many points that this objection carries little weight.[3]

The work consists of simple exegesis, together with explanatory glosses, inserted in the body of S. Paul's text, accompanied by explanatory footnotes, which contain ample quotations from the Latin fathers. The greater proportion of the quotations are taken from Augustine. The writers and subject matter of the Old Testament receive constant attention. In one place he alludes to the Hymn of Prudentius in the same context with the psalms of David.[4]

The commentaries were written for elementary students of the Bible. The explanation of the text was the main object. Doctrinal questions are seldom discussed. No opportunity for emphasizing 'proof texts' for the monastic life was allowed to pass by. Celibacy, the tonsure and asceticism generally are supported by quotations from S. Paul.[5] The short introductions to the epistles contain nothing of importance. He maintains that the Roman epistle stands first because God wished the city of Rome to possess the primacy over the whole Church. The Galatians were Greeks, the Ephesians and Colossians were Asiatics, the Philippians were Macedonians. The Pauline authorship of the Epistle to the Hebrews was maintained, but he says that S. Paul omitted his name from the address on account of his humility, in contrast with the pride of the Hebrews, and in imitation of S. John. The Epistle to the Hebrews was written in Hebrew and translated into Greek by S. Luke after the death of S. Paul.

The exegesis contains little which is of value or interest for later generations. Two points only are worth notice.

[1] Charma, *Notice Biographique*, p. 86.
[2] *Hist. Litt. de la France*, viii, p. 278.
[3] Giles, *Op. Lanfranci*, ii, p. v.
[4] Gloss on Eph. v. 9.
[5] Notes on 1 Cor. vii. 23; x. 10; xi. 10.

The difficult passage in 1 Corinthians xv, concerning baptism for the dead, is referred to the death of Christ, and the phrase 'for the dead' means 'as dead'. The faithful are baptized as dead men. The 'episcopus' must be 'the husband of one wife', meaning that he must not be bigamous.[1] Once or twice S. Paul's language is described as 'an exaggeration'.[2] The Pauline doctrines of justification and predestination cause him no trouble, and his explanation of passages in Hebrews i shows that on the doctrine of the Trinity Lanfranc's teaching was orthodox. The teaching of the contents of the Bible was the main object of the commentator, and the whole work was written under the influence of his distrust of secular letters and the methods of the philosophers. In the commentary on 1 Corinthians i and ii there are several warnings against dialectics, logic, philosophy and secular letters generally.[3]

The work in which he was engaged at Caen held out the prospect of a long period of useful and contented service which might fittingly crown a varied and active career. He desired the studious life of the cloister, or at least the sober activity of guiding the studies of young men. He possessed some of the qualities of the don in a marked degree. But the busy world of politics, both civil and ecclesiastical, continually broke into the academic peace of his life. Not only was he sent on long journeys to do the Duke's business, and to confute the intellectual opponents of the Church, but men began to cry out for his promotion, and to demand that

[1] Gloss on 1 Tim. iii. 3. [2] 2 Cor. xiii. 4; Gal. iv. 25.

[3] Lanfranc's biblical studies were continued in later years in England. He found the text very corrupt, and, according to one writer, undertook the task of correcting it in both Old and New Testaments. (Milo, 48, followed by M. Paris, *Hist. Ang.* i, p. 38; *Hist. Maj.* ii, p. 29, and *Flores Hist.* ii, p. 21.) William of Merseberg says that he wrote a commentary on the Psalms, which was seen by Trithemius (*Hist. Litt. de la France*, viii, p. 294). In the sixteenth century he was accused by a Puritan writer, Edward Brown, of having falsified the text of the New Testament (Migne, cl, col. 99). The only evidence Dr. Brown can have had at his disposal was supplied by the expansions in the text of S. Paul's epistles, which are quite clearly and ostensibly inserted as explanations.

he should give up the retired life of the cloister. From several quarters came the request that he would become either bishop or abbot of some distant see or monastery.[1] He resisted all temptations to leave Bec and Caen, but in the year 1067 he narrowly escaped being removed to Rouen. On the 9th August Maurilius, the Archbishop of Rouen, died. The cathedral clergy and the people of the city unanimously desired to elect the Abbot of Caen, and sent an urgent invitation to him. He declined the burden and responsibility of so great an office, 'humbly desiring rather to be ruled than to rule.'[2] The Duke deferred to his wishes, though probably with Canterbury in view for him. John, Bishop of Avranches, was promoted to Rouen. But Lanfranc only purchased his immunity at the cost of a third journey to Rome. It was necessary to obtain the papal consent to the election. He speedily performed the journey, and returned with the papal licence and the pallium for John, to the exceeding satisfaction of all Normandy.[3] While at Rome Alexander urged him to spend three or four months with him in the following year,[4] but it is doubtful whether the Papacy ever seriously contemplated removing him from Normandy.[5] He was too valuable a servant to the Church in that country. If the papal interests were to be adequately fostered, it was necessary that a strong-minded and able diplomatist should be close at hand to watch the active grasping character of William, especially in view of the reforming policy which the curia was beginning to develop.

After Lanfranc's return from Rome in 1067, less than three years were passed at Caen before he left Normandy for England. We are told nothing of his doings during that period, though we learn from one of his letters that the government of a monastery turned out to be an irksome

[1] Milo, 14; Ord. iv. 6 (ii, p. 211). [2] Milo, 14.

[3] Milo, 14, and Migne, cl (col. 87). [4] Lanfranc, Epis. III.

[5] Cf. Epis. of Nicholas, II (Migne, cxliii; Epis. XXX), in which the Pope says that he tolerates Lanfranc's absence unwillingly. He would like to have Lanfranc's counsel at the Roman synods. Milo, 5; Ord. iv. 6 (ii, p. 212), who allege that the curia sent letters in which they attempted, both by persuasion and threats, to secure his transference to Rome.

task for him.[1] He hastened forward the completion of the new buildings towards the day of consecration and the opening ceremony. He laid down the principles for the future organization of the community and made purchases of land.[2] Unless he returned from Rome before the King went back to England (6th December 1067), Lanfranc did not see William again until he came over to Canterbury. But the frank understanding between the two men, which characterized all their relationships in England, was by this time firmly established. What Lanfranc's feelings were towards William we are not told, but William of Poitiers writes in picturesque language that William 'respected Lanfranc as a father, venerated him as a teacher, loved him as a brother or a son, and confided to him the oversight of ecclesiastical affairs throughout Normandy.'[3]

Thus amid much work for Bec, for Caen and for Normandy generally, were the thirty or thirty-five years of Lanfranc's life in the duchy brought to a close. If not the most fruitful, they were no less active than the later and more famous days spent in England. Three journeys to Rome and one to Tours; the foundation and conduct of two if not three schools of letters; the organization and supervision of a new monastic foundation, together with all the domestic and public business, both for Church and State,

[1] Lanfranc, Epis. III.

[2] Cf. Charter of Henry, Bishop of Bayeux, in favour of Caen (Migne, cl, cols. 75-7).

[3] This passage probably refers to William's first departure for England, at the end of September 1066, when the civil administration of Normandy was left to his duchess, Matilda, and to his eldest son, Robert. To them also would be confided the nominal control of ecclesiastical affairs, but some practical arrangement must have been made, such as Poitiers suggests, whereby Lanfranc was entrusted with the care of the Church. William returned to Normandy in March 1067, and remained until the 6th December in the same year, and Lanfranc left for Rome some time after the end of August (Maurilius of Rome died on the 9th August), so that the period of his oversight of Church matters came after his return from Rome at the end of 1067, or beginning of 1068, with the exception of the six months during William's absence on the Hastings campaign.

which these matters involved, are no mean record for the best years of a man's life; and if he had ended his days as Abbot of Caen, we should still have owed him a debt of respect and veneration for the sound work done in quickening the religious life of Normandy, and especially for the part taken by him in the reform of the monasteries. These were the formative years of his life. They were late indeed, and came at a period when most men are already fixed in ideas and rigid in habits. Lanfranc's career proved that the later years of middle life may provide opportunity for an entirely new orientation both of habit and enterprise in a man of sufficient resolution and adaptability. He was not less than sixty-five when he arrived in England, but he achieved a success and reputation which are denied to most men in the prime of life. His training in Italy counted for much, but those years in Normandy counted for more, as a preparation for the work of mastering and reforming the Church in England, even as the King conquered and reformed the politics and social life of the country.

Election to Canterbury

By the year 1070 the Saxon resistance had been almost entirely quelled. Only one last effort was to be made at Ely in the following year. William's hands were free to deal with the English bishoprics. At the Conquest there were thirteen sees in the province of Canterbury and two in the province of York. Three sees were already occupied by foreigners,[1] two others became vacant in 1070,[2] and it was found possible to create four more vacancies by deposing their occupants without unduly exciting Saxon feeling.[3]

The King proceeded by diplomatic as well as by constitutional methods. The support of the Papacy was secured by the presence of three legates—Ermenfrid, Bishop of Sion, and John and Peter, two cardinal canons.[4] The business

[1] Gisa of Wells, Walter of Hereford, Remi of Dorchester.

[2] York and Winchester.

[3] Canterbury, Durham, Elmham and Selsey.

[4] Florence (Thorpe, ii, p. 5).

was undertaken at the Easter and Whitsuntide meetings of the Council, and not at any specially convened assembly. At the Easter meeting held at Winchester, Stigand of Canterbury was deposed on grounds to which no exception can be taken. Similar treatment was meted out to his brother Ethelmar of Elmham, but the nature of his offence is not known.[1]

The business was then adjourned to the Whitsuntide council at Windsor. At this meeting, Thomas, the Treasurer of Bayeux, was nominated to the see of York. Walkelin, a royal chaplain, was promoted to Winchester. Ethelric of Selsey was deposed, on a charge which has not been reported. Elmham was given to Herfast, Lanfranc's former adversary, and Stigand, another foreigner, was promoted to Selsey. By virtue of an understanding between William and Alexander II, Lanfranc was nominated to Canterbury.[2] The baronage concurred,[3] although they may have been surprised that Odo of Bayeux, the Conqueror's half-brother, was not chosen. The election is said to have been canonical,[4] but although the monks were not consulted, the new Archbishop was welcomed on his arrival at Christ Church.[5]

The legates were dispatched to Normandy to acquaint Lanfranc with the nomination, and much pomp was gathered in order to make the election impressive. A council of Norman bishops, abbots and barons was convened,[6] and the appointment was publicly announced. Lanfranc's attitude was foreseen by Ermenfrid, and the Legate was careful to announce that the election was the special desire both of the King and the Holy Roman Church, as well as of himself and the other legates.[7] This precaution was justified. Lanfranc was so disturbed by 'holy ire and sadness', pleading his own incapacity, and his ignorance of the

[1] Florence (Thorpe), ii, p. 5. Freeman says that at one time he was married. *Norman Conquest*, iv. p. 335, quoting Domesday, ii. 195.

[2] Gilbert, p. 99; Milo, 12; Lanfranc, Epis. III.

[3] Gilbert, p. 99; Milo, 12.

[4] Or. iv. 6 (ii, p. 213).

[5] Milo, 15.

[6] Lanfranc, Epis. III.

[7] Milo, 15. Hubert had joined them; cf. Lanfranc, Epis. III.

language and people,[1] that the legates thought that he intended to refuse altogether when he asked for time to consider his answer.[2]

Lanfranc's hesitation was quite natural. He had reached the time of life when ambition no longer sheds a lustre on promotion. As Abbot of Caen and adviser of William he had reached a pinnacle lofty enough for a man of scholarly habits with a desire for seclusion from active life. He saw clearly that he could not combine the business of an archbishop with the leisure of a monk.[3] But in the Middle Ages a man was the servant of the community. The theory of both the Hildebrandine Church and the feudal state made obedience imperative. Life in both Church and State was influenced by the obligations and tone of military service. To the persuasion of the legates was added the united influence of Matilda and Robert and of Herluin and the Norman baronage. Matilda's attitude as the wife of the Conqueror was certain, and no woman would forget the service he had done her at Rome on the question of her marriage.[4] The separation of Robert and Lanfranc was the most regrettable feature in the whole affair. Robert was now between fourteen and sixteen years of age. His future might have been very different if the rest of his youth had been passed in close proximity to Lanfranc in Normandy.

Herluin was at first unwilling that Lanfranc should leave Normandy. Shortly before the event took place he dreamed that he saw in his orchard an apple-tree with far-spreading branches and abundance of fruit. The form and flavour of the apples were of surpassing loveliness. The King demanded the tree for one of his own orchards, and with reluctance Herluin was compelled to yield. But when it was removed, the roots could not be torn up. New shoots sprang up above the soil, and were shown by the rejoicing Abbot to the King, who came to tell him of the wonderful fruits which the tree was bearing in its new environment.[5] The

[1] Lanfranc, Epis. III.

[2] Milo, 15.

[3] Ord. iv. 6 (ii, p. 212).

[4] He had doubtless assisted with the plans for her foundation at Holy Trinity, Caen.

[5] Gilbert, p. 100.

interpretation of the dream reported by Milo is obvious. Whether authentic or not, the tale reflects the reluctance with which the Norman monks at first regarded the transference of Lanfranc from their midst. But by this time the reform movement in the Norman monasteries was so well advanced that Herluin could bring no cogent objection against the departure of the Abbot of Caen. Indeed, Orderic says that he used his influence to persuade Lanfranc to comply.[1]

Sadly he crossed the sea in the early days of August, hoping to persuade William to allow him to decline the honour and to return to Caen. The King was fully sympathetic. Kindly he talked to his despondent counsellor, but emphasized the needs of the decayed English Church and the Abbot's fitness for the work of restoration. 'With grace and dignity' the King overcame his reluctance,[2] and the formal induction took place on the 15th August.[3] It was the feast of the Assumption, and the unwilling stranger must have been comforted by remembering the troubles which had filled the life of the Virgin before she was elevated to queenly rank in heaven, as the tradition of the Church said. The monks of Christ Church, though coming together at the King's order, received him 'happily and festively',[4] and they were joined by the brothers from the other house of S. Augustine's at Canterbury.[5]

The consecration followed a fortnight later, on Sunday,[6] the day of the Decollation of S. John the Baptist (29th August).[7]

[1] Ord. iv. 6 (ii, p. 212). A letter of congratulation was sent by Anselm (Migne, clviii, Lib. I, Epis. I).

[2] Milo, 15.

[3] Florence (Thorpe), ii, p. 7, Roger de Hoveden (Rolls), i, p. 124, and Ralph de Diceto (Rolls), i, p. 202 ; Malmes., *G. P.*, p.39, says the induction took place a few days after he landed.

[4] Milo, 15.

[5] Sax. Chron., *Lat. Acta*.

[6] Florence, ii, pp. 7–8.

[7] Sax. Chron. E., Orderic, Milo, Malmesbury, Eadmer. But Florence, Diceto, Matthew Paris, and *Flores Hist.* are wrong as to the year. They give 1071. Moreover, Florence gives 24th June, and Paris and *Flores Hist.* give the 24th April as the date of the consecration. Mr. Luard (Matthew Paris, Rolls Series) suggests that Paris was misled by Diceto, who gives S. John Baptist's Day as the date of the consecration, i. e. octo kal. Julii, and that Paris carelessly

Whatever consolation Lanfranc gained from the associations of the day of Assumption must have been dispelled by the recollection of the end of John's ministry. Moreover, the charred ruins of the cathedral, burned down on the 6th December 1067, were typical not only of the decay of the Church but of the fiery blast which had swept over the people of the land. Only a temporary shelter was available for the scene of what should have been a ceremony of surpassing splendour within the old walls of Christ Church, but an attempt was made to give dignity and impressiveness to the occasion. Nine bishops were present.[1] The rest sent letters, and some sent presents, with their apologies.[2] Other influential ecclesiastics and barons,[3] together with the monks of Christ Church and S. Augustine, and the townspeople of Canterbury, assembled.

Lanfranc's own feelings on this occasion, and in the months which followed, are expressed in his letter to Alexander II.[4]

> I have not any one to whom I can explain my trouble with more propriety than to you, Father, who of these calamities are the cause. When the Duke of Normandy forced me from the monastery of Bec, and appointed me to preside over that of Caen, I found myself quite unequal to sustain the government of a few monks, and therefore it appears to me a mysterious decree of Providence that I should be appointed and compelled by you to undertake the supervision of an innumerable multitude. When the Duke became King of England he laboured in vain to effect this object, until your legates Ermenfrid, Bishop of Sion, and Hubert,[5] a cardinal of the Holy Roman Church, coming into

wrote octo kal. Maii. But Diceto does not actually mention octo kal. Julii, although by S. John Baptist's Day, like Florence, he apparently means the Nativity of the Baptist (24th June) and not the Decollation (29th Aug.). As Lanfranc did not land in England till Aug. 1070, they were thus compelled to place the consecration in the following year.

[1] Sax. Chron. A., Milo, 30. The Bishops of London, Winchester, Dorchester, Rochester, Elmham, Selsey, Sherborne and Wells. The name of Walter of Hereford is added by Florence.

[2] Sax. Chron., *Lat. Acta*; Malmes., *G. P.*, p. 39. The first letter in Anselm's collection is one of congratulation to Lanfranc on this occasion.

[3] Ord. iv. 6 (ii, p. 213).

[4] Lanfranc, Epis. III.

[5] Hubert was not present at the English council which had nominated Lanfranc.

Normandy, and convening the bishops, abbots, and nobles, enjoined me on the authority of the Holy Roman Church to accept the see of Canterbury. In vain did I plead my own incapacity, my ignorance of the language, and of the barbarous people. They would not admit my plea, and why should I say more? I gave my consent, I came, I took the burden upon me, and such are the unmitigated cares and troubles to which I am daily subjected, such the perturbation of mind caused by parties pulling in the opposite direction, the harrowing incidents, the losses, the harshness, the avarice, the meanness, the evil conduct I see around me, such the danger to which I see the Holy Church exposed, that I am weary of my life, and lament that it has been preserved to witness such times. But bad as is the present state of things, when I look around me I feel the future will be still worse. That I may not detain your Highness, whose time must be fully occupied by much business, longer than is necessary, I entreat you for God's sake and for the Lord's sake, since it was by your authority that I was involved in these difficulties, by the same authority to extricate me from them and permit me once more to return to the monastic life, which above all things I delight in. Let not my petition, I entreat you, be rejected or despised, for I only ask what is right in itself, and, so far as I myself am concerned, what is necessary to my highest interests.

I beg you to remember what you ought never to forget, how ready I always was to entertain in my monastery, not only your relatives, but all who brought introductions from Rome. I instructed them in sacred as well as secular learning, and I might mention other things in which, whenever an opportunity occurred, I endeavoured to render good offices to you and your predecessors. Do not imagine that I am saying this by way of boasting in regard to myself, or with a view of reproaching others. My conscience acquits me of any such intention, my only object is to adduce some reason why this favour should be granted me for Christ's sake. If you place your refusal to accede to my request on public grounds, instead of furthering the cause of the Lord, you will probably impede it, which God forbid, for as regards the salvation of souls, I have neither directly nor indirectly met with success, or if any, it has been so slight as not to be weighed for a moment against my discomforts. But enough of this.

When I had the pleasure of seeing you and conversing with you at Rome, you invited me to visit you at your palace the following year at Christmas and spend three or four months with you. But I call God and the holy angels to witness that I could not do it without personal inconvenience and the neglect of my affairs. I need not enter further upon these matters, but if my life be preserved, and if circumstances permit, my desire is to visit you and the Holy Apostles and the Holy Roman Church. To this end I ask your prayers that long life may be granted to my Lord the King of England, and peace from all his enemies.

May his heart and mind be love to God, and His holy Church. For while he lives we enjoy safety, such as it is, but after his death, neither peace nor any manner of good is likely to befall us.

There is no reply of Alexander II extant, but the Pope, like William, could not be moved, even by a strong personal appeal from his old master and friend. In a letter to the King, Alexander II admitted that it was not without sorrow that he allowed the Archbishop to remain absent from his side, but he found consolation in the fruits which Lanfranc was reaping for the Church in England.[1]

During the first year or two of his archbishopric, Lanfranc referred repeatedly to Alexander for guidance on points of detail. He was a 'novus Anglus', and being ignorant of English customs, sought the Pope's advice about the ritual to be employed at consecrations.[2] Herman, Bishop of Sherborne, had sought permission to retire to a monastery in the time of Leo IX. He had done good work, but was now too enfeebled by age to carry on further. Lanfranc asked what action should be taken; the matter ought not to be delayed lest damage might be done to the souls under Herman's charge.[3]

Alexander placed the fullest confidence in his judgement and capacity. The King was urged to be guided by him in matters ecclesiastical.[4] A matrimonial case, which came within the jurisdiction of Stigand of Selsey, was referred by the Pope to Lanfranc for settlement.[5] The case of Ailric of Chichester was to be retried by him, although the legates had previously deposed the bishop.[6] Thus the friendship of the Pope and King made less difficult the opening years of his pontificate, and this, coupled with his industry and practical common sense, enabled Lanfranc rapidly to overhaul the load of work awaiting him who undertook the reorganization of the English Church.

[1] Alex. II, Epis. IX (Migne, cxlvi). Cf. Epis. LXX.

[2] Lanfranc, Epis. IV.

[3] Ibid. Herman was allowed to retain his see until his death in 1078, when Osmund was made bishop.

[4] Alex. II, Epis. LXXXIII (Migne, cxlvi).

Lanfranc, Epis. XXXI.

[6] Alex. II, Epis. LXXXIII.

VI

THE YORK CONTROVERSY

THE forebodings of coming trouble, expressed by Lanfranc in his letter to Alexander II, soon began to be fulfilled, even if the letter was not inspired by difficulties already incurred. Shortly after his consecration a dispute began which was to hinder the harmony of ecclesiastical relationships in England for fifty years. It was occasioned by a small point of precedence, but the cause centred in one of the fundamental principles upon which the new Norman rule was being based. The question whether Canterbury was senior to York or merely co-equal was not of serious importance. But the necessity for organizing the national Church from one centre was a matter of supreme urgency for the political solidarity of the new government.

There can be little doubt that the argument presented by Lanfranc to William expressed not only what he knew would be acceptable to the King, but what any prudent statesman of the day, who perceived the political tendency of the north of England, would surely admit. At the same time the ecclesiastical motive was also present. If it was sound policy to centre the political organization of the country in London, it was equally desirable that during the period of reform about to be inaugurated, ecclesiastical affairs should be controlled from one centre, and that centre could only be Canterbury. Thus in the interest of ecclesiastical no less than political unity, Lanfranc began a quarrel, which on any less solid foundations must have revealed in him a meanness of spirit and excess of ambition almost inexplicable in a man who possessed his experience and reputation. To make this preliminary statement is by no means to prejudice the case between Lanfranc and Thomas. The actual points in dispute were much smaller matters, but unless the general bearing of the bigger questions upon them is kept in view, they assume a proportion larger than their due, and become *ipso facto* prejudged against Lanfranc.

The controversy was concerned not only with questions of

personal precedence, ecclesiastical policy, or even political expediency. Nor was it a mere question of the authenticity and interpretation of documents. It was a historical question ranging back to the earliest days of the archbishops of Canterbury. What were the historical facts behind the contentions upheld by Lanfranc at the Councils of 1070–2? Upon the answer to this question must depend our judgement upon Lanfranc's claims.

Four years after the arrival of Augustine in Kent, Pope Gregory sent over to England a constitution for the ecclesiastical organization of the new mission. Under that scheme two archbishoprics, each containing twelve sees, were to be founded at London and York respectively. During the lifetime of Augustine an actual primacy over the whole of England was to be the privilege of the Archbishop of Canterbury. On the death of Augustine, the archbishop who was senior according to consecration should possess precedence. Thus the story of the relationships between Canterbury and York began with a clearly-defined primacy for Canterbury.

But the scheme of Gregory was not destined to materialize within the period of our survey. Not until the time of Theodore, nearly a hundred years after the coming of Augustine, were even half the number of bishoprics planned by Gregory consecrated, and the full number of twelve sees has been created in the northern province only during our own times. Not until 734, with the exception of the short sojourn of Paulinus at York (627–33), was an archbishop of the northern province established. Hence, for a hundred and thirty-seven years the metropolitan supremacy of the archbishops of Canterbury over the whole of England was almost unchallenged.

With the coming of Theodore (668) the pre-eminence of Canterbury reached its second stage. Theodore reorganized the English Church, and centred it more definitely around the archbishopric of Canterbury than even the constitution of Gregory had permitted to Augustine. He was the first archbishop to whom the whole English Church submitted.[1] The Northumbrian bishops and clergy, who had formerly

[1] Bede, iv. 2.

looked to Iona as their Mother Church, now turned their eyes southward to the Mother Church of Roman Christianity in these islands. The Council of Hertford (673) recognized Theodore as the Metropolitan of the whole of Britain.[1]

The history of this period is of enhanced significance because of the long dispute waged between Theodore and Wilfred, who struggled to maintain his rights as Bishop of York. But although Wilfred had a large following he was never recognized as Archbishop of York, nor did he once challenge Theodore's unquestionably high-handed action on the ground that the Bishop of York was independent of the jurisdiction of the Archbishop of Canterbury, a fact hardly to be explained save on the ground that the Archbishop's actual primacy was willingly recognized by Wilfred and his supporters. Wilfred must have known of the constitution of Gregory. But probably he regarded Theodore as a second Augustine, sent to England by the Papacy with special powers, and therefore worthy of special pre-eminence. Even Eddius, Wilfred's supporter and biographer, did not raise the question. In England the *de facto* hegemony of Theodore was at this time undisputed, although the Bishop of York and a powerful following were in open revolt against him on matters involved with all the delicate points centring in personal and ecclesiastical precedence.

The course taken by the dispute at Rome was equally significant. Wilfred's case was tried by Pope Agathon in 679. Theodore was throughout the proceedings referred to as Archbishop. Wilfred was merely styled Bishop. Wilfred made no claim even to metropolitan dignity, and did not allude to the constitution of Gregory, an appeal which would have strengthened vastly his own case, if he had been desirous of challenging the primacy of Theodore. Agathon decided in favour of Wilfred, but the primacy of Theodore was carefully preserved. Wilfred was to be restored to his see, with authority to select suffragan bishops, but these were to be sent to Theodore for consecration.[2]

[1] Bede, iv. 5.

[2] Eddius, *Vita Wilf.* xxix–xxxi; Haddan and Stubbs, *Councils*, iii, pp. 136–40; Bede, v. 19.

Wilfred's case was again heard at Rome by Pope John VI in 704, and, except in the formal charge read by the ambassadors of Bertwald, Wilfred was referred to throughout the proceedings as Bishop of York, while Bertwald received the title Archbishop. But although in his formal charge Bertwald alluded to both Wilfred and himself as Bishops, the Canterbury claim to the primacy was also asserted. Wilfred was charged with showing contempt for the judgement of Bertwald, the 'Bishop' of the Church of Canterbury and of all Britain.[1] Yet Wilfred lodged no complaint against this claim to primacy, nor did Eddius, in his long report of the proceedings. John VI acquitted Wilfred, and confirmed the decisions of Agathon, Benedict II, and Sergius I in his favour. The whole case was then referred back again to an English synod. But the one point which would have finally settled the dispute in Wilfred's favour, the claim for independence, on the basis of Gregory's original grant to Augustine, was never raised, nor was any counter-charge lodged against the encroachment upon this privilege by Theodore, even by those most interested in asserting Wilfred's rights.

Further evidence for the papal attitude to the hegemony of Theodore is to be found in the report of another council held at Rome in 679 (October), a council to be distinguished from that which decided upon Wilfred's business.[2] This meeting appears to have been held before Wilfred arrived, and before his case came up for discussion. It may have arisen out of some forgotten appeal to Rome, concerning Theodore's division of the English provinces. This council decreed that England was to be divided up into twelve bishoprics under the Archbishopric of Canterbury. This was clearly a different arrangement from that contemplated by Gregory, but it was much more in harmony with the conditions of the time. It had not been found practicable, so far, to introduce the northern arrangements of Gregory's scheme. Theodore's plans agree much more closely with the decree of this council than with the constitution of Gregory I.

[1] Eddius, xlviii (Haddan and Stubbs, iii, p. 259).
[2] Haddan and Stubbs, iii, pp. 131–5; cf. *supra*, p. 72.

He divided England up into fourteen sees under his own primacy.[1]

A third stage in the development of the pre-eminence of Canterbury was the creation of an archbishopric at Lichfield (787). With the sanction of the papal authority Lichfield ceased to be an archbishopric in 803. During the Lichfield controversy York played a minor part. It was not, of course, concerned with the affairs of Lichfield, but from scattered references it appears that popular opinion still regarded Canterbury as the pre-eminent metropolitan centre. In 793 Alcuin addressed Ethelhard of Canterbury in a letter as 'the light of all Britain'.[2] In 801 he addressed Ethelhard as 'Archbishop', but alluded to Eanbald of York as 'Bishop'.[3] In the same year he referred to Ethelhard, in a letter to Charles the Great, as Metropolitan of Canterbury, and Bishop of the chief see in Britain.[4] In some verses at the foot of a letter sent to Ethelhard (793–804) Alcuin addressed him as 'pontificalis apex'.[5] These admissions on the part of

[1] Haddan and Stubbs, iii, pp. 131–5. Haddan and Stubbs regard the report of this council as doubtful, on the ground that it does not appear in Eddius, Bede, or William of Malmesbury, and first appears in a manuscript copied by Spelman, and because of its bearing upon the York controversy in the eleventh and twelfth centuries. On the other hand, they admit that the long list of bishops, which it contains, is authentic, and that these bishops were in Rome in 680, a fact which is proved by the signatures of the letters addressed by the Council of Rome to that of Constantinople in 680, with the exception of George of Catania, whose name does not appear among the signatories; and especially by reason of the mention of Deodatus of Toul, who was not an Italian bishop, but who did accompany Wilfred to Rome. They admit that an error of two years in the date 'post consulatum eius anno x°', which should read 'XII°', need not affect the authenticity of the record.

But the acts of this Council were not quoted, so far as we know, at any point in the York dispute. It is therefore difficult to see for what purpose they can have been forged. The suggestion that they are to be regarded as questionable on the ground of their bearing upon this controversy is hardly feasible, unless it can be shown that they were used with this object in view.

[2] Haddan and Stubbs, iii, p. 476: 'lux totius Britanniae'.

[3] Ibid., p. 532.

[4] Ibid., pp. 533–4: 'primae sedis in Britannia pontificus'.

[5] Ibid., p. 553.

Alcuin are remarkable, because Eanbald of York was his pupil and personal friend,[1] and because Alcuin lost no opportunity of emphasizing the dignity of York. For example, in the letter to Ethelhard of 801 he speaks of Ethelhard and Eanbald as ' you two, the two eyes of the body, which are to shine through the breadth of the whole of Britain '; but in addition to giving Ethelhard alone the title of Archbishop, he seems to allow, even in this passage, some precedence to him, if ' the subtraction of the right eye ' refers to the damage done to the prestige of Canterbury by the Lichfield question. Again, in a letter to Eanbald in the same year (801) he speaks of Ethelhard as the co-episcopus of Eanbald,[2] and in a letter to Ethelhard in the following year, in which he congratulates the Archbishop on reviving the dignity of the see, apparently in relation to Lichfield, Alcuin refers to Canterbury and York as the two chief bishops of Britain, and two metropolitan cities,[3] but only once (796) does Alcuin appear to have addressed Eanbald as Archbishop.[4]

A fourth epoch in the story of the pre-eminence of Canterbury was the period of Dunstan. The Church had become disorganized by the first Danish invasions. A revival in the south had been accomplished in the time of Archbishop Plegmund (891–914) under the influence of Alfred. But Northumbria, which was part of the Danelaw, remained almost completely cut off from the Church in the south of England. It now possessed its own Archbishop of York, who was assisted by only one suffragan. Church life was far less flourishing than in the days when Theodore had openly controlled ecclesiastical affairs in the north. With the consecration of Dunstan (959) Canterbury once more

[1] He usually addressed him as ' filio Simeoni '. Haddan and Stubbs, iii, pp. 505, 507, 534.

[2] Haddan and Stubbs, iii, p. 534.

[3] Ibid., p. 540. But had there been any conflict of prestige between Canterbury and York ? In the letter of 801 to Ethelhard, Alcuin congratulates him on the result of a conference with Eanbald. If the letter of 802 refers to the Lichfield business, the papal decision was already known, although the Archbishopric of Lichfield was not suppressed until the next year.

[4] Ibid. iii, p. 501.

regained its prestige. Dunstan's pre-eminence was based upon sheer personal merit. He called no councils, and passed no canons, but the great revival of church-life in the latter half of the tenth century emanated from his efforts at Canterbury.

In 988 the second Danish invasion began. Ecclesiastical affairs again became disorganized, though less so, perhaps, than the civil administration of the country. Order was never restored by the Saxon rulers, until the time of Godwin, and in Godwin's time no great churchmen, like Theodore or Dunstan, arose to restore the influence of the Church. Canterbury reached the lowest depth of its degradation, indeed the only depth of degradation to which it ever declined, when Robert of Jumièges and his successor Stigand ruled the southern province. During the pontificate of Stigand, Aldred of York performed the great civil functions which by use and wont had long been attached to the see of Canterbury. He crowned both Harold and William the Conqueror, and although this was on account of the irregular nature of Stigand's appointment, the pontificate of Aldred of York formed the only real historical precedent to which Thomas might have made any claim against the demands of Lanfranc. But the claim was never made, probably because Thomas realized the peculiarly temporary nature of the relationship between the two provinces at that date.

In the year 1070, soon after Lanfranc's consecration, Thomas of Bayeux, an old pupil of Lanfranc, who had been elected to York before the latter was nominated to Canterbury, came to him to be consecrated, according to a custom which derived its authority from Gregory's letter to Augustine (601).[1] Before proceeding to the consecration Lanfranc demanded that a written profession of obedience, together with an oath, should be made to him, in accordance with 'the practice of his predecessors'. Thomas declined to comply unless he was presented with written authority for the submission, supported by witnesses, who would swear to its antiquity, and unless, in addition, he was given cogent reasons why he ought to do it, reasons which would not

[1] Although nominated after Thomas, Lanfranc was consecrated first.

involve the dignity of his Church. In the presence of those who had come together for the consecration, Lanfranc gave his reasons for the demand, but without convincing Thomas. Lanfranc then ordered the assembled bishops and monks to disrobe, and Thomas departed without being consecrated.[1]

One report says that Thomas was a new man, unacquainted with the customs of England, and was influenced by flatterers to raise the objection.[2] But when Lanfranc based his claim to a written profession of obedience, accompanied by an oath, upon custom, he showed himself equally ignorant of English traditions, for, as the York historian says, this was the first occasion upon which such a demand had been made upon York,[3] although there are in existence numerous examples of the written professions of obedience made to Canterbury by the suffragan sees.[4] At the same time, if Lanfranc was at this date unacquainted with the documents, he had accurately appreciated the traditional relationship between Canterbury and York, while he also realized the necessity for getting the authority of Canterbury recognized speedily, if the reforms contemplated by him were to be successfully introduced. But he blundered in the method selected. Thomas, perhaps already aware of the traditional primacy awarded to Canterbury by public feeling, as well as by the tacit consent of his predecessors, was none the less sensitive upon a point where rather an implicit understanding than a clearly prescribed arrangement seemed to touch the honour of the northern province. He was therefore alert for the slightest suggestion that a primacy already well understood should be given a legal form. So when Lanfranc's demand for a written profession of obedience was made he refused to comply.

[1] Malmes., *G. P.*, p. 39; Sax. Chron., *Lat. Acta; Hist. of York*, ii. p. 360; Milo, 33. Malmes., *G. P.*, p. 39, which is a quotation and appears to be an account of the controversy drawn up by Lanfranc (cf. Boehmer, *Die Fälschungen Erzbischof Lanfranks*, p. 165, for the best text).

[2] Malmes., *G. P.*, p. 39. Boehmer assigns Malmes, §§ 25–9 to Lanfranc under the title *Scriptum Lanfranci* (*Die Fals.* pp. 141–3, 165–73).

[3] *Historians of York*, ii, p. 357.

[4] Haddan and Stubbs, cf. *infra*, p. 86, n. 2.

Thomas appealed to the King, who at first admitted the justice of his refusal. William held that Lanfranc's attitude was created rather by an academic cast of mind than by common sense and the merits of the case. But a few days later Lanfranc quickly convinced William that something much more solid than a mere academic quibble lay behind his request. He pointed out the political significance of his case. The political unity of England might be endangered by the existence at York of an archbishop who was quite independent of the control of the southern primate. The contingency might arise during the Conqueror's reign, or in that of one of his successors, in which the Archbishop of York would crown another king, selected from the Danes or Norsemen or Scots. It is noteworthy that the northern historian supplies this detail, a detail which would not have been invented by him. He continues by admitting that the King and the Normans were convinced by Lanfranc's arguments,[1] but makes the absurd statement that William was influenced by bribes and promises.[2] The southern writer tells us that the Englishmen present gave their testimony in support of Lanfranc's claims.[3]

A royal order was issued, with the consent of those present, commanding Thomas to return to the mother Church of the whole kingdom at Canterbury, to write a profession of obedience, and after reading what he had written, to hand it to Lanfranc, in order that the document might be examined in the presence of the bishops. In his written submission Thomas was to promise that he would obey, without reservation, all the demands of Lanfranc in everything pertaining to the Christian religion. But his successors were not to be bound to repeat the submission unless it should be first proved by competent testimony, either publicly or in a council of bishops, that his predecessors had rendered, or clearly ought to render, such homage to the primate of the Church of Canterbury.[4]

[1] *Historians of York*, ii. pp. 100, 357. Some years later the Danes did effect a landing in Northumbria and marched as far as York.

[2] Ibid., p. 100.

[3] Malmes., *G. P.*, p. 40 (*Scriptum Lanfranci*).

[4] Ibid.

Thomas still remained obdurate. William thereupon tried to persuade him by entreaties, blandishments and promises, emphasizing the point that his submission was necessary for the unity and peace of the kingdom. Thomas answered that he was not under any obligation to the King to comply, that such a submission would not be canonical, and that it would not be right or useful to the King if he did submit. William then threatened to expel him from England and his relations from Normandy. Thomas gave way, though it was reported that he said on a later occasion that he would not have submitted if there had been an opportunity for him to escape from England.[1] However, Thomas did what was commanded, and Lanfranc performed the rite of consecration.[2]

Hugh the Chanter elaborates the story. Before consecrating him Lanfranc submitted him to an examination, in which he said, 'Are you willing to be subject to the holy Church of Canterbury, both to me and to my successors?' Thomas, overcome by emotion, weeping, gasping and scarcely attending, replied, 'I will be subject to you so long as you live, but not to your successors, except with the consent of the supreme pontiff.' He was then ordered to read a confession of obedience, written by the Canterbury monks, and to deliver it to Lanfranc. He declined to comply with either of these two demands. Refusing to be defeated, the Canterbury monks thereupon stole the royal seal, and signed a document which stated that the council had admitted Lanfranc's right to demand the profession of obedience, but that Lanfranc 'for love of the King' had remitted the oath.

But there is confusion in this account. It is a combined report of the original meeting before the King (1070) and of the Council of 1072 which finally settled the dispute. At this stage of the controversy the written profession was the chief point in dispute. The oath was remitted at the Council of 1072. The statement of Malmesbury appears to be more probable. No oath was taken at the Council of

[1] *Historians of York*, ii, p. 101.

[2] Malmes., *G. P.*, p. 40 (*Scriptum Lanfranci*).

1070, but Thomas promised, under the royal compulsion, to offer a written submission on the day of his consecration.[1] It is hardly probable that, having convinced the King of the political expediency of securing the submission of York to Canterbury, as Hugh admits, Lanfranc would modify his demand at the same council, unless William showed signs of wavering, and for this there is no evidence.

Again, on the day of Thomas's consecration Lanfranc would scarcely risk the success of his case by repeating his original demand for an oath of submission not only to himself but to his successors. His case was progressing well. At the Council (1070) he had secured the royal consent to Thomas's written submission. The larger question of the liability of Thomas's successors had been remitted to a future council of bishops, when the historical evidence for Lanfranc's case would be produced. Nothing was to be gained by forcing the pace at this juncture. Moreover, if Thomas had refused to comply with the royal judgement by declining to give a written statement of submission, Lanfranc would have appealed immediately to the King, and the northern Archbishop would not have been consecrated. But on the fact of his consecration at this point all the writers agree.

The statement that no bishop took an oath of obedience to his metropolitan [2] showed a complete ignorance of the customs of the province of Canterbury. For centuries a written confession of obedience had been handed to the metropolitan, and several of these documents existed.[3] The dispute arose when Lanfranc, without documentary precedent, but with sound political and ecclesiastical insight, and supported by a traditional primacy, demanded the same from Thomas. His statement that such an oath had been taken by Thomas's predecessors was also made in ignorance of the facts.

Having consecrated Thomas [4] under this provisional arrangement, a few days later Lanfranc sought and received

[1] Malmes., *G. P.*, p. 40 (*Scriptum Lanfranci*).

[2] *Historians of York*, ii, p. 102.

[3] Haddan and Stubbs, *passim*; cf. p. 86, foot-notes 1 and 2.

[4] Sax. Chron. A. says that the consecration took place after the return from Rome. This, of course, is wrong.

professions of obedience from the English bishops.[1] Most of the suffragans had been consecrated by other metropolitans: some, during the time of Stigand, by Aldred, and some by the Pope. No opposition occurred. Lanfranc was on absolutely safe ground in making this demand. But Thomas probably raised an objection against the professions made by the Bishops of Lincoln, Worcester and Lichfield, for his claim to metropolitan rights over these bishoprics constituted one of the later points in dispute with Canterbury.

In the following year both Archbishops went to Rome to receive the pallium,[2] accompanied by Lanfranc's kinsman Paul.[3] Lanfranc was received with more than usual honour by Alexander. The Pope rose at his approach, saying, 'I have not risen because he is the Archbishop of Canterbury, but because I was at his school at Bec, and with others I then sat as a listener at his feet.'[4] Lanfranc prostrated himself and kissed the Pope's feet, saying, 'And I by duty bound, reverence and honour thee, who art humble, even as Ananias reverenced Paul, and Sixtus reverenced Laurentius.'[5] The Archbishop then rose to receive the Pope's kiss.[6]

Lanfranc received two palls, one taken in the usual manner from the high altar of S. Peter's, the other from Alexander's own hands as a mark of the Pope's personal regard for him, the latter to be used during the celebration of Mass.[7] The rest of the day was devoted to the exchange of friendly reminiscences.[8]

[1] Malmes., *G. P.*, p. 40 (*Scriptum Lanfranci*), says that 'all' the English bishops made their submission.

[2] Ibid. Lanfranc had, apparently, written to Rome, asking the pall to be sent. Hildebrand replied regretting that it could not be given without troubling Lanfranc with the long journey. If it had been possible, the pall would certainly have been sent to a dignitary of Lanfranc's eminence (Giles, *Op. Lan.*, Epis. VIII).

[3] Walsingham, *Gesta Abb. Mon. S. Alb.*, i, p. 46.

[4] Milo, 31; Eadmer, *Hist. Nov.*, p. 11.

[5] Walsingham, *Gesta Abb. Mon. S. Alb.*, i, p. 46; *Ypodigma Neustriae* (Rolls), p. 71.

[6] Eadmer, *Hist. Nov.*, p. 11.

[7] Malmes., *G. P.*, p. 40 (*Scriptum Lanfranci*); Milo, 33. The editors of Migne (*ad loc.*) state that this honour was done to Hincmar of Rheims in the ninth century and to Bruno of Cologne in the tenth century.

[8] Eadmer, *Hist. Nov.*, p. 11.

It was not possible that the visit should conclude without reference to the York controversy. The matter was doubtless privately discussed between Lanfranc and the Pope, but as the case was *sub judice* in England, it is improbable that Lanfranc would have raised it formally at this stage, especially since he had not yet had time to get up his documentary evidence. But Thomas did not allow the opportunity of appealing to Alexander to pass by. On the next day he opened his case by raising the question of the allegiance of the Bishops of Lincoln, Lichfield and Worcester, claiming that Canterbury had no jurisdiction over them and that they had been subject to York in former times.[1] He then passed on to the disputed question of the relationship between the two Archbishops, and maintained that the honour of priority should be shared in turns, but that neither should be in any way subject to the other, according to the original arrangement of Gregory. He who consecrated should have priority and precedence over him who was consecrated.

The reply to Thomas took the form of a charge against him and Remi of illegally holding their sees.[2] The charge is not stated as coming from Lanfranc, though it can hardly have come from any one else, and it bears all the appearance of his lawyer-like diplomacy. Lanfranc was annoyed.[3] He was not anxious to have the matter discussed at Rome at this point. No appeal to the papal court could be usefully made until after the English bishops had met. He therefore pressed home the counter-charge. Thomas was the son of a priest. Remi had been promoted to Lincoln in return for services rendered to William at the Conquest.[4] He had supplied a ship with twenty knights for the expedition to England,[5] and appears to have joined in the fighting.[6]

[1] Eadmer, *Hist. Nov.*, p. 11; Malmes., *G. P.*, p. 40 (*Scriptum Lanfranci*); Milo, 33.

[2] Eadmer, *Hist. Nov.*, p. 11.

[3] Malmes., *G. P.*, p. 41 (*Scriptum Lanfranci*).

[4] Eadmer, *Hist. Nov.*, p. 11; Malmes., *G. P.*, pp. 66 and 312.

[5] Freeman, *N. C.* iii, p. 380.

[6] Malmes., *G. P.*, p. 66: 'divinum munus bellicori laboribus mundinatus', but the words need not mean that Remi actually

Moreover, Remi had been consecrated by Stigand.[1] Thomas was taken off his guard. It was not the only occasion when he was silenced by Lanfranc's quicker intelligence. If we may accept the testimony of Eadmer, Thomas and Remi having no excuse to offer, surrendered their staves and rings to the Pope and sought mercy. The report suits the hesitating and emotional nature revealed by Thomas on other occasions.

Lanfranc's anger then passed away. If he was unscrupulous, as he has been alleged to have been, he would have pressed his advantage right home and secured the deposition of Thomas. The two bishops asked him to intercede for them. He at once complied, and drew attention to their knowledge of public business which was useful to the King at a time when the kingdom was being reorganized. He also referred to their capacity as preachers and speakers. Alexander pointed to the two staves, and ordered Lanfranc to dispose of them in a manner most suitable to the interests of Christianity in England.[2] The Pope declined to take any responsibility in the matter upon himself, and left it to Lanfranc's discretion. He might reinvest them if he desired, or if not, he might do what he felt to be best in the circumstances of the case.[3] The Pope's non-committal attitude in this matter, as on the York question, was unmistakable. Did he fear William? Or had Lanfranc convinced him that the English bishops could settle the matter? Anyhow, Lanfranc reinvested the two bishops with the symbols of their authority.

After this damaging beginning Thomas's appeal on the larger question had become hopeless. Lanfranc pointed out that Thomas's contention was not valid because Gregory issued his constitution not for the churches of Canterbury and York, but for those of London and York. Gregory had

fought, and it was stretching the point to allege that his contribution amounted to simony.

[1] Giraldus Cambrensis (Rolls), vii, p. 151.

[2] Eadmer, *Hist. Nov.*, p. 11; Malmes., *G. P.*, pp. 66 and 312; Girald. Cambren. vii, p. 152. A dispute between Thomas and Remi was referred to Lanfranc for settlement, cf. Alex. II, Epis. LXXXIII (Migne, cxlvi):

[3] Malmes., *G. P.*, p. 66.

made arrangements for a condition of affairs very different from the actual relations existing between Canterbury and York. The appeal to Gregory's scheme was inadmissible because it had never been possible to put Gregory's scheme into operation. A considerable discussion upon this point and upon the question of the allegiance of the three bishops followed. Details have not been reported. Alexander finally decreed that the case should be tried in England, and settled by the testimony and opinion of the bishops and abbots of the kingdom.[1] Malmesbury says that Lanfranc regarded the dispute as settled, so far as he personally was concerned, by the submission already made by Thomas, but that he determined to carry it on, in the interests of his successors, so that all cause of future disturbance might be removed.[2]

The case was reopened at the royal council of 1072 held at Easter at Winchester.[3] The King exhorted the bishops, abbots and nobles who attended the Council, by virtue of the loyalty and oaths by which they were bound to him, to follow the evidence carefully, and to bring the dispute to a definite and just conclusion, without favour to either side. The Council promised to obey the royal wishes.

Lanfranc produced the documentary evidence for his claim. The history of Bede was brought into court and examined there. To the satisfaction of all,[4] it was shown that from the time of Augustine down to the time of Bede, a period of nearly a hundred and forty years, the predecessors of Lanfranc had possessed the primacy over the Church of

[1] Malmes., *G. P.*, p. 41 (*Scriptum Lanfranci*); Milo, 31.

[2] Malmes., *G. P.*, p. 41 (*Scriptum Lanfranci*).

[3] Malmes., *G. P.*, §§ 27, 29, and Lanfranc, Epis. V. Malmesbury omits the beginning of Lanfranc's letter. The date in the margin (p. 44) should be 1072. A doubtful passage in Eadmer (*H. N.*, p. 253) and Ralph de Diceto, i, p. 206, reports that the case was not finally settled until the Whitsun council at Windsor. Upon this same doubtful passage Boehmer builds up his case against Lanfranc (cf. *Die Falschungen*, pp. 29 and 169). According to Boehmer, Malmes., *G. P.*, § 27 (Milo, 33) is a report of the Council of Windsor, minus the reference to Windsor (cf. *Die Falschungen*, pp. 167–9); cf. *infra*, p. 285, n. 4.

[4] *Pace omnium.*

York and the whole island of Britain and Ireland. They had exercised the pastoral cure not only in the city of York itself, but in the neighbouring districts, wherever they happened to be.[1] In those places they had conducted ordinations and held councils. The archbishops of York had been summoned to these councils, and when necessary had been compelled to explain their conduct at them.[2] Moreover, the bishops, whom Thomas claimed as his suffragans, had, during that hundred and forty years, been consecrated by the archbishops of Canterbury. They had likewise been called to the councils, and some of them, when convicted of crimes, had been deposed with the authority delegated by the Roman see. The reports of numerous councils were produced.[3] These councils had been held at various places, in connexion with different disputes, and although they did not agree upon the form in which the primacy was instituted, yet they all agreed upon the fact of the primacy and the subjection of the bishops. Reports were read of both elections and consecrations to the same three bishoprics effected by the archbishops of Canterbury, together with the written professions of obedience which they had left behind. Evidence was produced which claimed that when a certain King of Northumbria committed simony by selling the bishopric of York, he was summoned to appear before the Archbishop of Canterbury, and when he did not appear, he was excommunicated. The whole Church of Northumbria thereupon abstained from communication with him, until he appeared personally at the council.[4]

As a statement of precedent Lanfranc's conclusions from the History of Bede may, with some qualification, be allowed to pass. Lanfranc's contention that the practical supremacy of Canterbury over York was established by the record of Bede is incontrovertible. For nearly half the period covered by Bede there was no Bishop of York, except

[1] Malmes., *G. P.*, p. 44. 'Ubi eis visum fuit.'

[2] The case of Wilfred.

[3] The acts of the synods of Clovesho (747, 803, 825), Brentford (781), Chelsea (787–9), at least were available.

[4] Not reported by any early English authority.

during the short sojourn of Paulinus in Northumbria (625–33). Wilfred was consecrated Bishop of York in Gaul (665) and Chad was consecrated to the same see in the following year. Chad was deposed by Theodore and sent to Lichfield (669), and Wilfred was expelled by Theodore (678). The claim that the bishoprics of the three sees in dispute had formerly given written professions of obedience to the Archbishop of Canterbury is fully established by records independently of Bede,[1] and there are examples of similar professions made by other sees.[2]

In support of the evidence drawn from purely English sources, Lanfranc produced in court privileges and letters sent by Popes Gregory, Boniface, Honorius, Vitalian, Sergius and Leo,[3] to Canterbury, or to English bishops and kings, at different times, and concerning different disputes. He stated that the relics of other documents, both originals and copies, were consumed in the destruction of Christ Church, which had occurred four years previously.[4] The defects in the legal aspect of the Canterbury case were made good by these documents. Although of uncertain cogency in some cases, the documents contained one or two privileges which proved that the primacy of Canterbury throughout England had been recognized by some of the Popes.[5]

The Council was impressed by Lanfranc's evidence, especially as Thomas could produce no documents to controvert Lanfranc's charters. There had, indeed, been a fire at York, when William sacked the city, and the charters and privileges of S. Peter's Church had been burned,[6] but it is improbable that any charter which

[1] Worcester (798, 822), Lichfield (814–16, 828–30, 832–6, 841–4), Lincoln and Worcester (814–16, 839–44); cf. Haddan and Stubbs, iii, *passim*.

[2] Haddan and Stubbs, iii, pp. 511, 528, 529, 568, 569, 578, 591, 592, 608, 621, 622, 633, 650, 655, 658.

[3] I have followed the list given in Lanfranc's letter to Alexander II. This does not agree with the list of Popes contained in the accounts of Malmesbury and Eadmer. Cf. *infra*, p. 271.

[4] Epis. V and Malmes., *G. P.*, p. 46. Cf. *infra*, pp. 271–9.

[5] But cf. Appendix i.

[6] Hugh the Chanter (*Historians of York*, ii, p. 98).

definitely granted an equal status to York would have been altogether forgotten. Thomas was an emotional man,[1] and therefore liable to succumb to a sudden attack, and he seems to have obtained little support from his own supporters, who were not small in numbers.[2] His case was badly handled. While Lanfranc's position was strong on the general and practical aspect of the question, yet his evidence was not altogether relevant to a dispute which centred round the demand for an oath and a written promise of obedience. As a statement of law upon that specific point, it was imperfect. Lanfranc stated at this council, as in 1070, that he possessed historical authority for this demand, but he did not attempt to produce evidence.[3] Although the fact of the primacy was established, that did not carry with it an implication that the oath was lawful. It could only create a presumption in favour of Lanfranc's claim, which really attempted to establish a new custom. One piece of evidence was available. Wulfstan I (931–54), Oswald (972–95), Ealdwulf (995–1003), Aldred (1061–70), all held the see of Worcester together with that of York. They may have sworn obedience by letter or viva voce, or both, to Canterbury, as bishops of Worcester. We have no trace of such oaths taken by these particular bishops of Worcester, but if they existed in Lanfranc's time, they would have provided some basis for his first hurried claim as to the evidence for the oath. But it is to be observed that Lanfranc did not make use of this point in conducting his case.

Thomas was able to do no more than to reiterate his original point. He did not even quote the letter of Honorius I transcribed by Bede.[4] He contended that the primacy over the bishops consecrated by the Archbishop of York, and indeed over all the priests of Britain, had been granted to Augustine alone. After his death precedence was to be shared by the Bishops of London and York, priority going to him who was consecrated first. Gregory desired Augustine to fix his bishop's chair at London, but, influenced by love for King Ethelbert, Augustine had fixed it at Canterbury.

[1] Ibid.
[2] Lanfranc, Epis. V; Malmes., *G. P.*, p. 62.
[3] Ibid.
[4] Bede, ii. 17.

It would have been quite easy for Gregory, if he had thought it desirable, to have settled any uncertainty by adding some such words as 'To thee Augustine, and to thy successors, I concede. . . .' But really, it was only waste of time, said he to revert to this argument.[1]

It is strange that Thomas made no attempt to question Lanfranc's documents. It may well have been that they took him by surprise, and by sheer mass and weight appeared to render any doubt impossible. Even the York historian, Hugh the Chanter, does not suggest that Thomas expressed any doubt as to the documents, either at the Council or later. Nor does he charge Lanfranc with forgery.

Thomas's reply added nothing to his case. But Lanfranc gave an elaborate answer to this renewed appeal to the constitution of Gregory. He said that the argument upon which Thomas relied was far from sound. If the subjection of all the bishops of Britain, and of those consecrated by the bishops of York, had been confined by Gregory to Augustine, the Pope would have bestowed a very lean and restricted office upon his friend, for during Augustine's life the Archbishop of York consecrated no bishop who could be subject to Augustine, for the simple reason that there was no Archbishop of York. Paulinus was the first bishop to be sent to York, not in the time of Augustine, but in the time of Justus, the fourth Archbishop of Canterbury. Those who knew the history of the English would agree with what he said, and it was upon the basis of these facts that the bishops of the apostolic see had confirmed the subjection of the bishops of England to the successors of Augustine, as the privileges which had been read testified, nay they adorned the Gregorian constitution, as it was called, with amplifications, developing it with munificent liberality—judges in the same chair, upholders of the same decision. In the same manner they maintained that all the churches of England should derive their discipline of life from that place from whose fuel they had seized the torch of belief. Who, indeed, did not know that faith in Christ had flowed from Canterbury to York, and to the other English churches?

[1] Malmes., *G. P.*, p. 62.

Thomas's statement was altogether true to the effect that the blessed Gregory might have confirmed, by a word, to the successors of Augustine, that which he had conceded to Augustine, and he did not deny it. But what prejudice, he asked, did this offer to the see of Canterbury? He quoted as an illustration a similar case. When our Lord and Saviour Jesus Christ said to the blessed Peter, 'Thou art Peter, and upon this rock will I build my Church, and I will give to thee the keys of the Kingdom of Heaven,' He could have added, if He had wished, 'and the same authority I grant to thy successors'. But the omission of these words diminished in no way the reverence due to the successors of Peter. Could Thomas say anything to the contrary? Indeed it was rooted in the consciences of all Christians that they trembled before the successors of Peter, and the threats of them, as before S. Peter himself, and gladly acclaimed the serene kindness of his successors, when they were indulgent. The arrangement, then, of all Christian matters was fixed if the jurisdiction of the successors of the blessed Peter was settled. What did that mean if not that the virtue of the divine concession was dispensed through the Lord Jesus, by the blessed Peter, to his representatives? If Thomas knew anything of logic, he would be able to deduce a similar judgement from this illustration.

Moreover, what was true of the whole was true of a part. What was true of the greater was true of the less. The Roman Church was, as it were, the whole of all the churches. The other churches were parts of it. So indeed, in a certain sense, a man was the type of his species, and in each individual there was present the whole constitution of all mankind. So, from one point of view the Roman see was the type and whole of all the churches, and in every church the whole content of the Christian faith was present. The Roman see was the greater part of all the churches, and what applied to it ought to apply to the less, so that the authority of the chief of each metropolitan church devolved upon his successors, unless any one was personally and by name exempted. Wherefore as Christ said to all the bishops of Rome what he said to Peter, so Gregory said to all the successors of

Augustine that which he said to Augustine. Hence it was concluded that as Canterbury was subject to Rome, since it received its faith from her, so York was subject to Canterbury, which sent missionaries to it.

Thomas's statement also, that Gregory wished Augustine to reside at London, clearly fell to the ground. Could any one assert that he would have opposed the will of his master by ignoring his decrees? But he (Lanfranc) declined to detract from the trustworthiness of a tradition supported by the assent of many. Even if Augustine did migrate at another time, what was it to him who was not Bishop of London? It was no business of his—except that the practice of antiquity did not sanction it—if he shared the honour of primate with the Bishop of London. If Thomas wanted to discuss that business before Lanfranc's jurisdiction, when the present cause had been peaceably settled, he would not be wanting in a right judgement.

The cogency of Lanfranc's final speech was somewhat uncertain. The suggestion that if Gregory had confined his plan to Augustine personally it would have been a lean privilege to award to a friend, and that Gregory must have given some later sanction for the removal of the archbishopric from London to Canterbury was mere trifling, and must have been impossible save in the case of a pleader, led away by his love of debate. It shows the immense influence of tradition in those days, since even Lanfranc was not able to break entirely away from the traditional significance of Gregory's grant, and was ready to resort to a feeble argument to circumvent it. But his contention that Gregory's plan fell to the ground because there was no bishop of York at the time was sound enough, and the analogy drawn from the grant of Christ to Peter, together with the argument based upon the supremacy of the Roman see over the parts of the Church of which it was the whole, reveal Lanfranc's forensic ability in its best form.

Thomas said nothing more. He was not so completely convinced as Malmesbury suggests.[1] In later years, after the death of Lanfranc, he raised the question again.[2] But

[1] Malmes., *G. P.*, p. 65.

[2] Cf. *infra*, p. 280.

as the court appeared to be convinced by Lanfranc's reasoning and evidence, the only course open was to surrender, especially in view of the royal attitude. The King asked Thomas how it was that he had dared to oppose such arguments supported by so little authority on his own side. He replied that he did not know beforehand that Canterbury possessed so much proof in support of its claim.[1] At the close of Lanfranc's final speech the court was in a state of suppressed excitement, and Lanfranc himself was labouring under intense emotion, for when Thomas declared his surrender, he leapt to his feet, and gave an order for the proceedings to be committed to writing for the benefit of posterity.[2] This document was sealed with the royal seal, and distributed to the leading churches and monasteries of England.[3]

After Thomas's submission the court proceeded to define the terms of settlement. These were drawn up in three sections.

The river Humber was adopted as the boundary line between the two provinces. All the region on the northern bank, including the whole of Scotland, was placed under the jurisdiction of Thomas.[4] Thus the three disputed bishoprics of Worcester, Lincoln and Lichfield were left to the jurisdiction of Canterbury, which retained its sway everywhere south of the Humber, including Wales. The only see remaining under the jurisdiction of York was Durham.[5]

The Archbishop of York and his suffragans were to attend

[1] Lanfranc, Epis. V. Boehmer, *Die Fälschungen*, p. 28, says that Thomas must have come to the Council fully prepared. What then became of his defence?

[2] Malmes., *G. P.*, p. 65.

[3] Eadmer, *Hist. Nov.*, p. 16; Gervase, ii, p. 366. But Gervase says that the King gave the order for drawing up this document. Mr. Shepherd, *Litt. Cant.* (Rolls), i, p. xli; iii, Append. i, says that the original exists in the muniment room at Canterbury. It is the report quoted by Milo, 33, and Malmes., § 27.

[4] Malmes., *G. P.*, § 27. The final terms may have been submitted at an adjourned meeting at Windsor. Cf. *infra*, p. 285, n. 4.

[5] Gervase, ii, p. 366. The Scottish bishops were never brought under the control of the northern archbishop.

any council summoned by the Archbishop of Canterbury, wherever it happened to be held, and they were to be bound by any decisions therein canonically made. On the death of an archbishop of Canterbury, the Archbishop of York was to come to Canterbury, and there to consecrate as primate him who had been elected, assisted by the suffragans of the province of Canterbury. On the death of an archbishop of York, his successor, after being invested by the King, was to come to Canterbury or to any other place named by the primate, for consecration.[1]

A written submission was received from Thomas, but the verbal oath was remitted. The King intervened to bring about this compromise. Thomas asked William to intercede for him with Lanfranc, in order to bring about the restoration of friendly relationships between them.[2] Lanfranc then remitted the oath for 'love of the King', though without binding his successors to this qualification.[3] Thomas made an unconditional surrender in his written submission.

> I Thomas, already consecrated metropolitan Bishop of the Church of York, having heard and recognised the evidence, make an absolute profession of obedience to thee Lanfranc, Archbishop of Canterbury, and to thy successors, and whatever by thee or by them is lawfully and canonically ordered, I promise to obey. But concerning this matter, at the time when I was consecrated by thee, I was doubtful, so I promised to obey thee without conditions, but thy successors conditionally.[4]

Hugh the Chanter supplies a sequel to the story. On a later occasion when the King was embarking from the

[1] Malmes., *G. P.*, § 27 (*Scriptum Lanfranci*).

[2] Lanfranc, Epis. V.

[3] Malmes., *G. P.*, § 27 (*Scriptum Lanfranci*).

[4] Malmes., *G. P.*, p. 42; Milo, 32. In the *Gesta Regum*, ii, pp. 351–2, Malmesbury gives the names of the signatories to the settlement. These include the King, the Queen, Hubert the legate, Lanfranc, Thomas, William of London, Herman of Sherborne, Wulfstan, Walter of Hereford, Gisa, Remi, Walkelin, Herfast, Stigand of Chichester, Siward of Rochester, Osbern, Odo of Bayeux, Geoffrey of Coutances, Scolland, Abbot of S. Augustine's, Elfwin of Ramsay, Elnoth of Glastonbury, Thurstan, Ulnoth of Chertsey, Elfwin of Evesham, Frederick of S. Albans, Geoffrey of Westminster, Baldwin of S. Edmunds, Turold of Peterborough, Adelinus of Abingdon, and Rualdin, Abbot of Winchester.

Isle of Wight for Normandy, both archbishops were present. It was reported to William that a forged charter of submission was in existence, sealed with the royal seal. The King repudiated the charter, and said that if Thomas had done anything from personal love or fear of him it should not prejudice the dignity of the Church of York, and that on his return, justice should be done.[1] Several witnesses were present, among them Ralph, who at the time Hugh wrote was Bishop of Durham, and at the time of the incident was chaplain and keeper of the royal seal; and also Gilbert Crispin, afterwards Abbot of Westminster, the author of the life of Herluin, both of whom were prepared to swear to this incident. But Ralph was the notorious Ralph Flambard, who would swear to anything; moreover, the report does not say that Ralph alleged that the Canterbury monks had stolen the seal from him, a point which would not have been missed. Again, the story is weakened by the fact that William is not reported to have taken exception to the charter, but to its contents. Of more importance still is the fact that we do not read in either of the northern historians that William took up the case on his return, a step he most certainly would have taken if a forgery had been brought before his notice, and a step which would, with equal certainty, have been reported by the northern writers. Some such incident probably took place, but it took the form, not of a charge of forgery by Thomas, but of some general restatement of his original complaint. This was smoothed over by William with an equally general promise of amendment. The story represents an attempt on the part of the York writer to discredit the sealed account of the proceedings of 1072, sent by Lanfranc to the churches of England.

A report of the proceedings of the Council of 1072 was sent by Lanfranc to Alexander II.[2] In a covering letter Lanfranc asked for an authoritative confirmation of his right to the primacy, and supported his claim by a letter to Hildebrand.[3] His actual supremacy had already been recognized, when he

[1] *Historians of York*, ii, p. 102.
[2] Lanfranc, Epis. V.
[3] Epis. VII. Hildebrand was at that time Archdeacon of Rome and head of the papal chancellery.

was in Rome (1071), by his appointment as apostolic vicar in England, and by the Pope's order that Lanfranc should re-invest Thomas and Remi with their pastoral staves. But the papacy was not prepared to issue a decree formally recognizing a permanent primacy at Canterbury. Hildebrand went so far as to write that if Lanfranc appeared personally at Rome, his claim would receive attention.[1] But it did not suit the political policy of the papacy to run the risk of creating a rival to its own hegemony in the west, especially as the character of both William and Lanfranc was known to be very independent. From the papal point of view Hildebrand's guarded action in 1072 became fully justified as time went on, for William and Lanfranc tended to withdraw more and more from a wholehearted support of Hildebrand's policy after the latter became Pope, and at the close of Gregory's pontificate a rupture occurred in the relations between him and both William and Lanfranc.[2] But Lanfranc's failure to secure from Rome a written confirmation of the settlement of 1072 left the way open for Thomas and Urban II to reopen the case after Lanfranc's death, and it was not finally settled till fifty years later.[3]

[1] Giles, *Op. Lan.*, Epis. VIII.

[2] Cf. *infra*, pp. 220–31.

[3] Cf. Appendix I (*b*). For an account of the alleged forgery of the documents produced by Lanfranc in 1072, cf. Appendix I (*a*).

VII

THE REVIVAL OF THE COUNCILS

A PROMINENT feature in the Norman reformation was the revival of conciliar action. After the time of Theodore, the national assemblies of the Church fell into disuse. Two causes chiefly contributed to this result. Under the stress of the Danish invasions political unity and national cohesion were indefinitely postponed, and the organization of the Church became disintegrated. The successors of Theodore were weak men who allowed the predominance of Canterbury, established by him, to be diminished. Even the great Dunstan, who restored Canterbury to much of its former dignity, took no steps to re-establish the conciliar activity of the Church. The result was fatal for the dioceses. The suffragan bishops became more and more isolated and local. Laxity of discipline, secularization of spiritual life and decay of learning became prevalent.

Having settled the question of the primacy, Lanfranc began the great Norman reformation of the English Church. It is true that this was based upon the assumption of the primacy of Canterbury, and that an even earlier step had been taken by the appointment of Norman clergy to the vacant bishoprics in the spring of 1070. Without the establishment of a centralized ecclesiastical authority, and without the appointment of capable agents, it would have been impossible to make the decrees of the Councils effective for the whole Church. There was, indeed, a reciprocal action between the primacy and the Councils. If conciliar action owed much to the successful issue of the York contest, the most effective means of exerting the primacy was by the exercise of primatial authority in the general ecclesiastical assemblies. So intimately connected were the primacy and the Councils, that in earlier times, when the Councils were regularly held, the supremacy of Canterbury was widely recognized, and when conciliar activity ceased, the influence of Canterbury declined. It need not be contended that Lanfranc revived the primacy and the Councils with the ostensible object of restoring the two most effective factors of old Saxon church life. But the sureness of his appreciation of the needs of the situation is revealed by the fact that he perceived that those conditions demanded a strong central ecclesiastical executive operating through general councils.

A second factor in the conciliar movement was the influence of the Hildebrandine policy. The great reforming councils held at Rome from the days of Leo IX onwards set up a *modus operandi* for the western Church, and the reform programme was published to the dioceses through the metropolitan synods modelled on the Roman Councils. At the Easter and Whitsuntide gatherings in 1070, when Ermenfrid and the other legates dealt with the deposition and appointment of the English bishops under the eye of William, the necessity for some separation between the functions of the royal gemot and the episcopal synod and for the revival of the ecclesiastical councils must have been perceived by Ermenfrid, and urged by him then or later upon William.[1]

[1] Sax. Chron., *Lat. Acta,* 'multoque de Christianae religionis cultu servanda instituit.' The date given is 1071, but the reference to the settlement of the York dispute enables it to be corrected to 1072. Milo, 29, writing of the year 1070, says a council was held 'ad renovanda decreta et instituta sanctorum Patrum de synodis celebrandis, de consuetudinibus ecclesiasticis'.

The acts of two early undated councils have been preserved (Spelman, ii, p. 12; Wilkins i, p. 360; Mansi, xx, cols. 459–60). These editors assigned them to a Winchester Council of 1076. But the acts do not agree with the acts of the Winchester Council of that year (cf. *infra*, p. 103 ff.). The first list contains thirteen canons; the second, sixteen. Johnson, *Canons* (1720), dates them 1071, on the ground that they are bound up in two old volumes with a Penitentiary (cf. *infra*, p. 111, n. 1) which appears to have been drawn up by the legate Ermenfrid in 1070, and left to be confirmed by a later council. Confirmation for a council held in 1070, which dealt with ecclesiastical customs, is found in Henry of Knighton (Rolls), i, pp. 70 ff. (a late writer); but the acts, which are given in detail, do not agree with the lists of the Council reported by Spelman, Wilkins, and Mansi. Mansi (xx, col. 6) also assigns a council held in London to 1070, but the acts are concerned with the change of sees and the attack on Wulfstan.

Lanfranc was not slow to adopt this feature in the Hildebrandine programme. He called the bishops and abbots together at frequent intervals. The first council of which we have any certain record was the Winchester Council of 1072, when the question of the primacy was settled. Ulric, the Abbot of New Minster, was deposed by Lanfranc, and many details concerning public worship were arranged. A few days later, at London, the Archbishop consecrated Osborn, Bishop of Exeter, and Scolland, Abbot of St. Augustine's, Canterbury. At Gloucester, in the same year, at Christmas, he consecrated Peter to the see of Lichfield.[1]

By 1075 the conciliar revival was well established. It had secured the approval of the King.[2] The great London Council of that year was held in S. Paul's.[3] A report of the proceedings, which has been preserved in the Canterbury registers, was drawn up by Lanfranc, or by his order, at the request of many who were present.[4] All the bishops of England were present, with the exception of the Bishops of Rochester and Durham. At that date the see of Rochester was unoccupied.[5] The Bishop of Durham had been excused by Lanfranc. The list of bishops present is headed by Thomas of York. Then follow the names of William of London, Walkelin of Winchester, Geoffrey of Coutances—who although not an Englishman held two hundred and eighty English manors—Herman of Sherborne, Wulfstan of Worcester, Walter of Hereford, Gisa of Wells, Remi of Dorchester, Herfast of Elmham, Stigand of Selsey, Osbern of Exeter and Peter of Lichfield. The presence of Thomas of

If we can rely upon Milo, 29, the second list and the Penitentiary may be the acts of the legatine Council held in April 1070. The first almost certainly belongs to 1072 and contains the acts of the Council mentioned by the Sax. Chron., *Lat. Acta.* I find that Boehmer, *Kirche und Staat*, pp. 62–4, n. 3, agrees.

[1] Sax. Chron., *Lat. Acta.*

[2] Malmes., *G. P.*, p. 66.

[3] Gervase, ii, p. 367.

[4] Sax. Chron., *Lat. Acta*; Spelman, ii, p. 8; Wilkins, i, p. 363; Mansi, xx, col. 450; Malmes., *G. P.*, § 42; Milo, 35–42.

[5] The Englishman Siward was dead, and Ernest had not yet been appointed.

York[1] and the Bishops of Worcester and Dorchester shows that the settlement of the primacy dispute had been entirely favourable to Lanfranc. In addition to the signatures of the bishops, the names of twenty-one abbots and one archdeacon appear. It was the first great council over which Lanfranc presided as the undisputed primate of all England, and steps were taken to make it as impressive and imposing as possible.

The agenda had been carefully prepared. Authority for the proposed reforms had been amassed from the records of previous Councils of the Western Church, and from the papal decrees. The report of the proceedings states that these steps were necessary because for many years no Council had been held in England. This refers, of course, to specifically ecclesiastical Councils, assembled for the confirmation of ancient canons or the creation of new ones. The legal and methodical mind of Lanfranc appears to be behind the acts of this assembly. Everything enacted was based upon canonical authority, for which exact quotations were given. In the York dispute Lanfranc had learned the value of documentary evidence, as well as its weakness, and he was determined that the reorganization of the English Church should be conducted by unimpeachable methods, based upon unimpeachable authority.

The question of the precedence of the bishops was decided first, for having settled his own status, Lanfranc was anxious that the dignity and status of his suffragans should receive adequate recognition. The canons of the second Council of Milevis (416),[2] the second Council of Braga (563),[3] and the fourth Council of Toledo (633)[4] were quoted, in which it was decreed that at such assemblies the bishops should take precedence according to the date of their consecration,

[1] Thomas was present at all Lanfranc's councils, and also at the consecration of Ernest of Rochester at Westminster, and Maurice of London at Winchester. Spelman, ii, p. 15; Wilkins, *Concilia*, i, p. 369.

[2] Milevis in Numidia. Canons 13 and 14 seem to have been quoted (Mansi, iv, cols. 330–1).

[3] Braga in Spain, Canon 6 (Mansi, ix, col. 778).

[4] Canon 4 (Mansi, x, col. 617).

except where preference was due to individuals on account of ancient customs or special privileges held by their churches. A whole day was taken up with this question. As at the assembly on Penenden Heath, the opinions of the older men were taken, and they were asked to report on what they could recollect of early traditions. The Council then either adjourned or passed on to other business. On the next day the senior members made their report. It was the privilege of the Archbishop of York to sit on the right-hand side of the Archbishop of Canterbury, with the Bishop of London on the left.[1] The Bishop of Winchester sat next to the Archbishop of York. If the northern metropolitan was absent, the Bishop of London sat on the primate's right hand, and the Bishop of Winchester on the left. This was an arrangement which the historical importance of those sees made quite obvious, but Lanfranc's diplomacy was quite sound in allowing it to appear as if the Council were making the arrangement.

The status of the monastic clergy was then settled. On the authority of S. Benedict, and the customs of regular monastic houses, it was agreed that monks should have their due rank without possessing property.[2] If any monk died in the possession of property which he had not confessed, he should not be buried in the cemetery. Feudal and monastic organization threatened to come into conflict. The status of the bishops was based upon their possession of real property, and, consequently, their ecclesiastical status depended upon their status as territorial lords. The abbots were the heads of monasteries owning large properties, and therefore they possessed the status of property owners, without being theoretically the owners of the property attached to the house. That they were legally feoffees in the eyes of the King is proved by the fact that they did homage, and had to provide knight service, but the ecclesiastical authorities were prevented

[1] In 1075 Lanfranc consecrated Hugh to the see of London (Stubbs, *Reg. Sac. Ang.*, p. 22, quoting the Canterbury Profession Rolls).

[2] Malmes., *G. P.*, p. 67. Ut monachi proprium ordinem habeant, et proprietate careant.

from recognizing them as property owners because of the monastic vow of poverty. In Milo's report the point appears to be confined to the varying status of monks within the monastery. They were to hold the rank due to them,[1] and the boys and younger men, especially, were to be subject to the masters set over them. They might carry lights at night on special occasions, but generally they were to be without such indulgences. If any one was found, after death, to have held property without permission, no bell could be tolled for him, no mass could be sung for his soul, nor could he be buried in the cemetery. It is not certain whether the rule of Benedict[2] bearing upon these points was quoted at the Council in the form reported by Milo. But whether it was quoted or not, it is clear that, together with the reorganization of the episcopate, Lanfranc began the reform of the monasteries at an early date.

The work of the episcopate was hampered by the survival of the Saxon practice of fixing diocesan centres in country villages. Until the eleventh century there were few towns of sufficient size to form obvious centres for the diocesan organization. The people lived in scattered hamlets. Even in the eastern counties, where Danish influences prevailed, the villages were no more than a few huts collected together in one village street. In days when communications were not easy, the bishop was thus isolated, and if he remained for any length of time at his cathedral centre he was kept separated from the main course of national affairs. Much of the provincial rusticity and indifferent learning of the old Saxon bishops was due to this cause.

The organization of the English Church had been arranged on a scheme very different from that of the rest of the Western Church. Continental Christianity had fitted itself into the town life which formed the characteristic feature in the organization of society of all countries comprised within the area of Roman administration. The Romans were townsmen, and they organized conquered territories around the towns. But the village life of old England, which had

[1] Milo, 37: 'monachi ordinem debitam teneant'.

[2] Milo refers to a rule of Gregory, but no such rule is known.

been its strength as well as its weakness, was rapidly losing its importance in the civil administration of the country. As town life developed, the political centres of gravity moved away from the villages, and although the Council of 1075 quoted from the canons of the Council of Laodicea (320),[1] the Council of Sardica (343),[2] and a decree of Leo I,[3] Lanfranc's reform was only a natural adaptation of the older ecclesiastical organization to the new conditions which he found existing in England, but it permanently raised the tone and character of the English episcopate.

The Council decreed that no episcopal see should for the future be set up in a village centre. The royal sanction was obtained for the removal of certain sees from the villages to the towns. The process had begun so early as 1050, when Leofric, Bishop of Devonshire and Cornwall, removed his cathedral centre to Exeter. Since then Remi of Dorchester had removed to Lincoln (1072–3). The see of Sherborne was now transferred to Salisbury, that of Selsey to Chichester, and that of Lichfield to Chester. Apparently the King's consent to these alterations had been obtained beforehand, for Milo tells us that certain other cases were deferred for his attention, because he was at that time oversea. William can have raised no difficulty, because the process of removing the episcopal centres went on. The Bishop of Chester made a second move to Coventry (after 1086). Herfast of Elmham moved to Thetford (1078), and Herbert Losinga from Thetford to Norwich (1091). Gisa moved from Wells to Bath (1085).[4]

While the bishops were brought into closer touch with the central life of the Church and nation, the parochial clergy were placed under more adequate episcopal supervision. A weakness of parochial organization has always been shown in the tendency of the parish priests to wander. We need

[1] Canon 57 (Mansi, ii, col. 590).

[2] Canon 6 (Mansi, iii, col. 14). Mansi dates this council 347. This has been corrected by Gwatkin to 343 in *Studies of Arianism* (1900), p. 124.

[3] The 49th decree of Leo. The decrees of Damasus I mentioned by Milo (38) were forgeries ; cf. Johnson, *Canons*, ad loc.

[4] There is also a report of the movement of these sees at a Council held in 1078. Spelman, Wilkins, Mansi. Cf. *infra*, p. 109, n. 3.

not attribute this tendency to the influence of Celtic monks, who certainly wandered far and wide, from kingdom to kingdom, and later from diocese to diocese. Originally it was their function to wander as itinerant missionaries, though S. Paul's method and the Roman method of working from definite urban centres produced better results. The tendency was not inherited from the Celtic clergy, but was due on the one hand to the ' wander lust ' which every Teuton, whether priest or soldier, felt as insistently as the Celts ; and, on the other hand, to the slackness of episcopal supervision, which had always been a characteristic feature of the Saxon bishops in contrast with the bishops of the Continent. The Council of London now (1075) decreed, on the authority of Roman pontiffs and synodical statutes, that no clerk was to be allowed to settle in a diocese, or to seek ordination in any diocese but his own, without letters demissory from the bishop of the diocese from which he came.

One of the three special abuses aimed at by the Hildebrandine reformers was the prevalence of simony. To what extent this had been common in England in earlier days it is difficult to say,[1] and certainly William's administration was almost entirely free from it, although Remi of Dorchester was accused at Rome of having bribed the King to secure the see of Dorchester. The Council of London passed a decree against simony, forbidding the purchase of holy orders and offices and benefices where a cure of souls was attached, on the ground that this was the sin of Simon Magus, condemned by S. Peter, and afterwards placed under the ban of excommunication by the fathers.[2]

Another statute aimed a blow at the cruel jurisdiction of the times which far too readily condemned a man to death or mutilation. On the authority of the eleventh Council of Toledo (675),[3] the clergy were forbidden to take part in such

[1] Cf. *infra*, p. 111. [2] Malmesbury omits this canon.

[3] Canon 6 (Mansi, xi, col. 141). The Spanish Council of Elvira (305) is also quoted, but this matter is not mentioned in the canons of Elvira (cf. Mansi, ii, cols. 6–20). Spelman, ii, p. 8, and Wilkins, i, p. 363, refer to canon 19 of Elvira, but this regulation deals with sexual offences.

sentences, or to give any sanction to those who passed them. The case of Abbot Thurston at Glastonbury shows that the prohibition was needed to check the arrogant tendencies of some of the new Norman clergy.

Another decree restricted free speech in the councils. It was agreed that no one save bishops and abbots might speak without the primate's permission.[1] Freedom of debate was, of course, for long a thing unknown in England, though it had originally formed one of the special features of a Saxon gemot. But this decree seems to be coloured by Lanfranc's distrust of the Saxon clergy and by his contempt for their ignorance and simplicity—a contempt which does not appear to have saved even the saintly Wulfstan of Worcester from attack.[2]

At the Council of the following year (1076), held at Winchester, a full dress discussion took place on clerical marriage. So early as 1049 Leo IX had issued a prohibition in the synod at Rome against this practice. Nicholas II repeated the prohibition at the synod of Melfi ten years later. His successor, Alexander II, passed a similar decree at Rome in 1063. But the prohibition did not become a matter of acute importance, except in northern Italy, until Gregory VII issued his famous decrees at the synod of Rome in 1075. Letters were dispatched by him ordering the metropolitans to make similar demands at their provincial councils, and to take steps to see that the order was carried into effect.[3] In England, France, Germany, and Northern Italy, the parochial clergy were often married men. The practice was

[1] Cf. Epis. XXX. Priests holding cures in the diocese of Chichester, under Lanfranc's patronage, were not allowed to speak at the diocesan synod.

[2] Two other decrees are more general in character. One of them dealt with superstitious practices, cf. *infra*, p. 111. The other applied to the laity only. The decrees of Gregory the Great and Gregory II were quoted against marriages within the seventh degree, either among a man's own kin or those of his deceased wife. Milo, 40. But Gregory allowed marriages above the fourth degree; cf. Johnson, *Canons*, ad loc.

[3] Jaffé, *Mon. Greg.* i. 30; ii. 10, 25, 30, 45, 55; iii. 3, 4; iv. 11; v. 18; vi. 5b; *Epis. Coll.* 3, 4, 5, 28.

certainly uncanonical, but while public feeling condoned the marriage of the parochial and even capitular clergy, there was considerable feeling against the marriage of bishops. In Western Europe the clergy, outside the monasteries, did not disapprove of clerical marriage. The decrees of Lanfranc's council in 1076 prove that many of the English parochial clergy were married. Orderic states that the practice was common in France,[1] and attributes it to the influence of the Danish settlements in Normandy. In Lombardy, and especially in Milan, the marriage of the clergy was a recognized custom, for which they claimed the sanction of S. Ambrose. Strong opposition to the Cluniac reform was led by Guido of Velate, the successor of Heribert, as Archbishop of Milan, and the conservatives succeeded in making headway against the powerful advocacy of Peter Damiani, who was sent by the papal court to preach against clerical marriage.[2] But the most violent, if not the most successful outburst against the marriage prohibition broke out in Germany, when Gregory's decree of 1075 was made known there.[3] The German clergy protested against the decree as that of a heretic whose teaching was mere raving, and who attempted to compel men to live according to the habits of angels. The only result would be, said they, to give rein to the bridle of fornication and uncleanness. They quoted the Gospel which said that not all could accept this saying, but only he who was able, and they quoted S. Paul, who said that a man who could not contain himself should marry, for it was better to marry than to burn. Finally they declared that they would rather give up their priesthood than their wives.

It is thus misleading to state that the general feeling of the age was opposed to clerical marriage. At the most, public opinion condemned outright the marriage of bishops, and was not even able to insist upon absolute compliance in their case. The parochial clergy were often in favour of the institution. Among the monastic clergy the prohibition

[1] Ord. v. 12 (ii, p. 297).
[2] Gregorovius IV, Pt. I, p. 127 ff.
[3] Lambert of Hersfeld, Annals 1074 (Holder-Egger, p. 199). The date is, of course, wrong.

was of course in force, and as most of the writers belonged to their ranks, the authorities are all coloured by their view. Doubtless also, the Cluniac ideal was exerting influence, but its observance had not yet become widespread.

There was much to be said for the Hildebrandine discipline. In days when family influence was supreme, largely through the feudal organization of society, the marriage of the clergy tended to lock up ecclesiastical emoluments in the hands of particular families. The clergy were naturally influenced by the local jealousies and feuds of their own families and those of their wives. The control of the Church over the private lives of the clergy was hindered. The cares of family life hindered them, as now, from the complete performance of duty. Moreover the scandalous behaviour of the Popes of the house of Tusculum, who for so long degraded the dignity of the apostolic see, made the rigorous attitude of the reforming pontiffs almost a necessity. If the reputation of the Roman bishops was to be re-established, only drastic action could effect the change, and the Popes from Leo IX to Gregory VII were influenced by the domestic affairs of the papacy as much as by the Cluniac ideals.

The decrees of Lanfranc's council at Winchester (1076) [1] dealt considerately with the parochial clergy. While cathedral clergy were forbidden to have wives, and while it was decreed that, in future, no priest or deacon was to be ordained, until he had sworn to observe the rule of celibacy, the parochial clergy, in both town and country, were allowed to retain the wives to whom they were already married. This was in direct contradiction to the decree of Gregory, which had ordered the separation of the clergy from their wives, under pain of degradation from their orders. We read of no other council where a similar modification of the papal demand was made. At Rouen (1072) [2] and Lillebonne (1080),[3] decrees were passed without qualification. The Winchester decrees point not only to the prevalence of clerical marriage in England at that date, but reveal the

[1] Spelman, ii, p. 13; Wilkins, i, p. 367; Mansi, xx, col. 462; Sax. Chron., *Lat. Acta*.

[2] Ord. iv. 9 (ii, pp. 240–1).

[3] Ibid. v. 5 (ii, p. 317).

moderating wisdom of Lanfranc's statesmanship. It was not the only occasion upon which he undertook to soften the rigour of Gregory's demands, and even to go contrary to the advice of his friends.[1] Moreover, his action does not appear to have been taken with the object of pleasing the King, but with the humane desire of disturbing as little as possible the settled customs of the Saxon clergy. This lenient legislation should be remembered when the appointment of Norman ecclesiastics to English benefices is quoted as evidence of the ruthless treatment of the English Church. If English bishops were not appointed it was because no suitable candidates were to be found, and the treatment of the married clergy shows that Lanfranc was quite ready to recognize the claims of the Saxon clergy, whenever it was possible.[2]

On the other hand, within the limits of sanity and reasonableness Lanfranc energetically carried out the policy of the reformers. So early as 1070 he had concurred in the deposition of Leofwin, Bishop of Lichfield, on the ground of his being a married man.[3] A deacon, who had been ordained, though married, and whose case was referred to Lanfranc by Herfast, was degraded from the diaconate, but was allowed to be eligible for promotion to minor orders.[4] Whether the prohibition against future clerical marriage was obeyed at once or not, at least the Saxon clergy were made to understand that they were now under the control of a new discipline, and that the monastic ideals of the Continent were to

[1] Epis. XX. John of Rouen challenged him upon this point.

[2] It must also be recollected that Lanfranc was a Lombard, and may have been influenced by the views of the Milanese clergy, in spite of his long sojourn as a monk in Normandy. Moreover, if he was in early life a married man, he possessed another reason for showing sympathy to the married clergy in England.

The action of Lanfranc at this council proves that the references of the monastic writers to clerical concubinage were the exaggerated expressions of monastic prejudice. In whatever manner the marriages of the clergy were contracted, the tie was loyally observed by them, otherwise the Council of Winchester would not have set its imprimatur upon their unions.

[3] Epis. IV.

[4] Epis. XXIV.

be adopted as the standards for the parochial clergy of Saxon England.

The same kindly consideration for the interests of the Saxon clergy was shown in the decree which protected the clergy from rendering greater service to their lords, in return for the tenure of the benefices, than was rendered in the days of Edward the Confessor. By this enactment the Norman bishops took a step in the defence of the whole clerical order. It was no more to the interest of a Norman ecclesiastic than to that of a Saxon to remain inactive while new feudal or allodial burdens were placed upon his order. These burdens were payments in kind or money, paid in lieu of personal services, and demanded by a lord from the villein tenants. At this point in the development of feudal tenure the ecclesiastical benefice was regarded like any other feudal holding. Service or payment of some kind had to be rendered for it. The parochial benefices were upon a footing similar to that of bishoprics or abbeys, which had to supply knight-service to the King as tenants-in-capite. The case of the King, and of any feudal lord in the investiture contest, was based upon this economic factor in the ecclesiastical organization of the day. However definitely, in point of fact, the royal claims throughout Western Europe were substantiated in that contest, yet the struggle issued in a moral victory for the clergy, and this achievement had some influence in quickening the general tendency, which became in course of time the main current of English constitutional development, to restrict the rights of the King over individual tenures. The beginnings of that process of development are to be found in this decree of the Council of 1076, which was but a re-echo of the larger claims in the matter of lay-control of ecclesiastical benefices that were being made by Gregory VII against Henry IV.

The attack upon the security of the Church, which consisted in the attempt to create new burdens, was accompanied by an attempt to forfeit endowments which were not covered by charters.[1] A decree of 1076 interdicted this practice Very few of the churches, apart from monastic houses, were

[1] 'Supplantatio'; cf. Johnson, *Canons*, ad loc.

in possession of such charters. If the decree was also intended as a protection against temporary but violent encroachment, such as pillage of Church ornaments, on the part of civil or ecclesiastical superiors, it constituted yet another effort to guard the Saxon clergy against the interference of Norman occupiers. During the period of resettlement, much violence of this kind undoubtedly took place in local areas, and the necessity for such a decree indicates the prevalence of the abuse. William and Lanfranc were both determined to do at least justice to the old occupiers of lay and ecclesiastical holdings, where submission to the new régime had been made.

In 1076 the regulation of the previous year, against the movement of clerks and monks, without letters of recommendation from their bishops, was confirmed, with the additional provision, that in any case monks were not to be allowed to serve in the parish churches. This provision was part of Lanfranc's general revival of ecclesiastical discipline.[1] The same distinction between seculars and regulars was maintained in the decree on the marriage question. An attempt was being made to reserve capitular preferment for monastics, while, as this decree shows, the parochial cures were to be reserved for the secular clergy. Possibly the fact that many married clergy were to be left in charge of their cures influenced the Council to draw up this decree. Constant communication between the monks and married clergy might have weakened the discipline of the monastic houses.

Two decrees were concerned with laymen. One dealt with the jurisdiction of the new spiritual courts. If a man who was accused of a crime which came within the cognizance of the bishops' court refused to appear, after being summoned three times, excommunication was to be pronounced against him. But if, after excommunication, he wished to submit, then he must pay a fine to the bishop for each summons which had been neglected. But side by side with this regulation, the royal injunction against the excommunication of the great barons must be recollected.

[1] Cf. Epis. XXVII.

The other decree regulated the procedure of marriage. No man should be permitted to give away in marriage his daughter, or a woman related to him, without the priest's blessing. Otherwise, the marriage would be deemed unlawful.[1]

Three other councils are recorded, but no reliable details of the business transacted have been preserved.[2] At the Council of 1078,[3] held in London, Ailnod, Abbot of Glastonbury, was deposed. He was succeeded by the infamous Thurstan. Possibly at this council Osmund was consecrated by Lanfranc to the see of Salisbury. Two years later (1079) Robert of Losinga was consecrated to Hereford.[4] At the Gloucester Council of 1081, Thomas of York, under a royal mandate, and with the consent of Lanfranc, consecrated William of S. Carilef to the see of Durham. Thomas had been unable to secure the attendance of the Scottish bishops at the consecration.[5] Four bishops of the southern province—Wulfstan, Osbern, Gisa and Robert were deputed by Lanfranc to assist at the rite. The last council of which we possess a record was also held at Gloucester (1085–6), where Ulfcetel, Abbot of Croyland, was deposed, and three royal chaplains, Maurice, William and Robert, were elected

[1] At the same Council the case of Ailric, Bishop of Chichester, was brought to a conclusion. But the facts relating to his offence are unknown.

[2] A complete list of these councils, with dates, is to be found in the Latin life of Lanfranc, attached to the Canterbury Chronicle. Gervase, ii, p. 367, followed this list. But cf. p. 116, foot-note, on the dating in the Chronicle. Cf. Spelman, ii, p. 15, Wilkins, i, p. 369, who report that Lanfranc held five general Councils, at Winchester (twice), London and Gloucester (twice). This list agrees fairly well with the sequence given above in the text, but not with their own lists of the acts of the Councils.

[3] Sax. Chron., *Lat. Acta*. Cf. Spelman, ii, p. 14, Wilkins, i, p. 367, and Mansi, xx, col. 606, who report a council held at Westminster in 1077, without details. They also report a London council in 1078, which Mansi, in addition, reports again in 1070 (xx, col. 6), all dealing with the removal of the sees and the case of Wulfstan. The repeated reference to these two matters in their series renders their reports useless for fixing dates.

[4] Florence, ii, p. 13; Gervase, ii, p. 367.

[5] Sax. Chron., *Lat. Acta*.

to the sees of London, Thetford and Chester.[1] Later in the year, Robert and William were consecrated by Lanfranc at Canterbury, and Maurice was consecrated by him at Winchester. A few days after his consecration Maurice came with presents to the mother Church at Canterbury.[2]

The intense conciliar activity of Lanfranc's pontificate has an intrinsic importance apart from the work performed by the Councils. The transference of the sees from rural to town centres and the introduction of marriage regulations were matters of far-reaching consequence for the life of the Church, but their success depended largely upon the method by which they were introduced. The series of great Councils maintained throughout Lanfranc's time supplied the reform movement with an organization, and made possible a constant supervision of the reform policy. The haphazard methods of Saxon days had ended. The English Church was again moving along the orderly lines introduced by Theodore. The most striking contrast between the period of the Norman and the later Saxon Church is created by the reappearance of the Councils through Lanfranc's agency, and it is a contrast which has never been sufficiently emphasized by Church historians.

[1] The election of the bishops is mentioned in the Sax. Chron., *Lat. Acta,* which gives 1085 as the date of the Council. For the discrepancy cf. p. 116, foot-note 1. Wilkins, i, p. 368, Mansi, xx col. 603, also give 1085. Spelman does not record this council.

[2] Sax. Chron., *Lat. Acta.*

VIII

REVIVAL OF DIOCESAN LIFE

WHEN Lanfranc came to England the secular administration had broken down under the ravages of William's campaigns. Murder and robbery were common offences. It was inevitable that human life should be regarded lightly by men who had witnessed the great slaughter of William's battlefields, who lived under constant terror of attack by the local Norman lords, or who were moved by the impulse of revenge for injuries received. The difficulty of securing food, which sent them roaming over the country, and the desire to secure the rewards offered to mercenary fighters and hired assassins, created additional motives for homicide.[1] Moral offences were rife, both those which are common to men of all ages, and those which belong to more violent conditions of life.[2] The marriage rules were broken.[3] The robbery of churches was frequent.[4] Tithes were not paid,[5] and small respect was shown to clergy and monks.[6] The decay of religion and the prevalence of unruly conduct were accompanied by widespread superstition. The bones of dead animals were hung up as charms against disease contracted by animals. Sorcery, divination and soothsaying were common.[7]

A similar decay was seen in the lives of the clergy. Bishops, parochial clergy and monks bore arms, and had taken part in the fighting. Bishops moved about from diocese to diocese and plotted against the King. Simony was prevalent. Bishoprics, abbeys and even holy orders were secured by the payment of money. Clerks were often unchaste.

[1] Cf. the Penitentiary of 1070 (Spelman, ii, p. 12; Wilkins, i, p. 365; Mansi, xx, col. 460).

[2] Ibid., § 12.

[3] Winch. Council, 1076.

[4] Winch. 1072, § 11 (i.e. the first undated council, cf. *supra*, p. 96, n. 1).

[5] Winch. 1070, § 14 (i. e. the second undated council); Winch. 1072, § 10.

[6] Winch. 1072, § 13.

[7] Winch. 1076

Apostate clergy roamed over the country, and monks associated too freely with the parochial clergy. Mass was celebrated by clerks who had not been regularly ordained. Water only was sometimes used in the Sacrament, and the chalices were sometimes made of wax or wood.[1]

The decline of clerical life and discipline contributed as much to the decay of religion and morals as the campaigns of William. No help was forthcoming from the diocesan organization, and the failure of the old Saxon system was the chief factor in the widespread evils of the times. The straggling rural sees lacked the cohesion of the continental bishoprics, which were organized from populous cathedral centres. The diocesan boundaries were badly defined ; there were few archdeaconries ; parochial life was decadent and the services in the churches were badly conducted. The jurisdiction of the bishops, even in spiritual cases, was confused with that of the ealderman and other secular officers, who sat in the same courts and dealt with civil and ecclesiastical business alike. There had been no attempt to codify ecclesiastical law.[2]

Before the decrees of the Councils could be applied to the work of reform, it was necessary to separate the ecclesiastical from the civil jurisdiction ; otherwise conciliar activity must have come to an end. It would have been useless for the Churchmen to pass regulations which the shire gemot had power to modify or rescind.

The royal charter, giving effect to this new arrangement, is undated. But it was probably issued before the great reforming Council of 1075, and must have been in contemplation earlier.[3] The charter is addressed to the three sheriffs and the liegemen of Essex, Hertfordshire, and Middlesex. It claims to have been drawn up at the advice of the archbishops, bishops, abbots and chief men of the realm. It states that ecclesiastical laws have not been kept according to the decrees of the sacred canons. No bishop or archdeacon

[1] Cf. the acts of Winch. Councils, 1070 and 1072, and the Penitentiary of 1070. [2] Boehmer, *Kirche und Staat*, pp. 43–8.

[3] Cf. Curtis H. Walker, *Eng. Hist. Rev.*, July 1924, who dates the Charter 1072–6.

was henceforth to hold a plea touching upon ecclesiastical law in the Hundred courts, or to bring a matter concerning the government of souls before a secular tribunal. Any ecclesiastical cause must be tried before the bishop at such place as he should arrange, and according to canon and episcopal law.[1]

The Conqueror found it necessary to place some restraint upon English institutions. The superior clergy were now nearly all new men of foreign birth. The Hundred courts were, and continued to be, the strongholds of Saxon feeling. The solidity of the Conquest, and more especially of the new ecclesiastical organization, ran the risk of being impaired if the episcopal jurisdiction remained at the mercy of the twelve good men of the old Saxon courts. So, also, affairs which belonged to high ecclesiastical policy were placed unreservedly under the control of the Norman prelates, subject only to the secular prerogative of the royal supremacy.

We may with confidence perceive the hand of Lanfranc behind this measure, but even more confidently can we trace signs of his influence in the widespread revival of diocesan life, which took place during the reign of the first Norman king. Before the decrees of the great Councils of 1075–6 were passed, some attempt had been made to deal with clerical abuses during the years 1070–2. Every diocesan was ordered to hold one or even two councils a year.[2] Confession for crimes was to be heard by the bishop only, and both bishops and clergy were to urge confession upon the laity. The bishops were ordered to visit the parishes, and facilities were to be provided for them by clergy and laity alike. Ordination was to take place at fixed times, and only in the cathedral churches. Baptism was to be administered, as a rule, only at Easter and Whitsun, unless death seemed imminent. The altars were to be made of stone. Burials were not to be permitted within the churches. Church building and endowment were encouraged.[3]

[1] Stubbs, *Select Charters* (1895), p. 85; Gee and Hardy, *Documents* (1896), pp. 57–8.

[2] Cf. Mansi, xx, col. 754, for the acts of a Council held by Wulfstan.

[3] Cf. the acts of the Winchester Councils, 1070, 1072, and the

The case of Wulfstan of Worcester indicates Lanfranc's zeal for a well-educated and well-trained episcopate, and also his recognition of spiritual qualifications. At the Easter council at Winchester (1070), when the legates deposed several English bishops, Wulfstan claimed from the see of York certain lands which had been alienated from Worcester by Aldred of York. The see of York was at that time vacant, and the case was deferred until a new candidate had been consecrated.[1] At one of the early councils Lanfranc charged Wulfstan with illiteracy, and attempted to secure his deposition. Wulfstan was invited to surrender his see. He left the council room to take the advice of his monks before replying, but he remembered that the hour of Nones had not been sung. The monks said that it would be wiser first to conclude the business for which they were assembled, when there would be ample time for Nones, for if the King and nobles heard of the suggestion that Nones should first be sung, they would laugh at the idea. But the Bishop insisted that they should first render the service due to God, and then go on with the business of men. Nones were accordingly sung, but the monks then tried to dissuade Wulfstan from re-entering the council chamber because his reply was not prepared. But he assured them that he had that day seen the blessed Archbishops Dunstan and Oswald, and that these good men would answer his prayers against lying tongues. He returned to the council and obtained straightway a favourable judgement.[2] Thomas thereupon invited Wulfstan to assist

Penitentiary. Henry of Knighton (Rolls), i, pp. 78 ff., reports a Council held in 1070, which passed regulations for the revival of patronal festivals and provided protection for those passing to and from the festivals. This is doubtful, at least at the beginning of the period, in view of the Norman attitude to Saxon saints. Some of the other regulations in his report are more probable. They secured the property of the clergy, the safety of those seeking absolution, precedence of ecclesiastical over secular cases in a royal court, protection for church tenants, rights of sanctuary, payment of tithes and Romescot, &c.

[1] Florence (Thorpe), ii, p. 6.

[2] Malmes., *G. P.*, § 143. This incident has been worked up by

him with the administration of the York diocese, on account, says Malmesbury, of his own fear of the Saxon people, or because of ignorance of their language.[1] Wulfstan, as a Saxon, could meet both these difficulties.

At the trial on Penenden Heath (1072), when Lanfranc regained from Odo the Canterbury lands, he secured the

Ailred of Rievaulx (Twysden, *Decem Scriptores*, 406) into a monkish legend. When challenged by Lanfranc to surrender his pastoral staff, the Bishop replied that he would only surrender it to him who had handed it to him, and advancing to the tomb of the Confessor, offered the staff to the dead King. The tomb opened and closed round it, and the repeated efforts of those who stood by were not able to remove it. Lanfranc sent a message requesting the King to come to see the marvel, and when the King had arrived, Lanfranc also failed to withdraw the staff from the tomb. Whereupon Lanfranc said: 'Truly God is just and loves righteousness, and His face looks upon probity. Truly He walks with the simple and His speech is with the humble. Thy righteous simplicity was derided by us, brother! Involved in woeful darkness we call evil good and good evil. Our judgment has erred, it has erred! But God raised His Spirit in the Holy King Edward to make empty our opinion and to reveal thy happy simplicity before all. Therefore by the authority which we enjoy, yea, by the divine indication by which we are convinced, we hand back and place with thee again the cure which inadvisedly we took from thee, knowing from experience that a little with righteousness is better than the great riches of sinners. Clearly a little scholarship, together with faith which labours in simplicity with love, is better than the riches of secular wisdom and knowledge, which many abuse for the vanity of human praise, or the base pursuit of avarice. Approach therefore, my brother, approach thy Lord, yea and ours, for we believe that the holy hand which denied the staff to us, will easily relax and resign it to you.' Wulfstan complied and the staff was released. Lanfranc and the King fell at his feet and asked for the Bishop's blessing.

The tale also appears in Paris, *Hist. Ang.* i, p. 53, *Flores Hist.* ii. p. 7, and Richard of Cirencester, ii, pp. 300–4, and Bromton (*Decem Scriptores*, 976). The reference to the tomb of the Confessor suggests a London council, and the allusion to Bishop Gundulf, who did not become bishop until 1077, suggests the London Council of 1077–8. But 1078 is far too late, so also Ailred's date (1075); cf. *supra*, p. 109, n. 3.

[1] Malmes., *G. P.*, § 143; but the sequence of events is uncertain. The story may represent an attempt of Thomas to strengthen his claim upon the Worcester lands.

consent of Thomas to the restoration of the Worcester lands, alienated by Aldred.[1] At this meeting Lanfranc appointed Wulfstan as his commissioner in the diocese of Chester,[2] and at a later date assisted him to repress the slave trade at Bristol.[3] Complete harmony was created between Lanfranc and the Saxon bishop, and we shall find him co-operating with Lanfranc in repressing the Norman rebellion of 1075.

In Lanfranc's correspondence there is proof of the constant reference of all kinds of business to the Archbishop, which in normal circumstances would have been dealt with by the

[1] Florence, ii. 8. The date and sequence of events are quite obscure. Florence fixes the settlement of the dispute between Wulfstan and Thomas in the same year as the Legate's Council (1070), but he runs the events of 1070–2 together. He records the death of Ailwin, Bishop of Durham, in 1070; makes him appear in the rebellion of Edwin and Morcar (1071); and again records his death on the 15th October 1072. Under 1070 he mentions the accession of Ernest and Gundulf to Rochester. But Ernest was not consecrated till 1075, nor Gundulf till 1077. Another difficulty is his statement that the King presided at Penenden, but this is not borne out by our authorities for that meeting (cf. *infra*, p. 126). Malmesbury (*G. P.*, § 143) also runs the events together, but without giving dates. Ailred dates the attempt to displace Wulfstan at the London Council of 1075, but Lanfranc must have made up his mind about Wulfstan before that time. The dates in the Saxon Chron. (*Latin Acta*) are misleading, owing to the alternative system of beginning the year from Christmas or Easter. Both methods are employed. (Cf. Plummer, vol. ii, pp. cxxxix–cxli.) Further confusion is caused in the Saxon Chron. by the dating from the Indiction in some years: this also has the effect of throwing events, in some parts of the record, a year forward (cf. Armitage Robinson, *The Times of Saint Dunstan*, p. 27; cf. p. 21 ff., where a similar effect was produced by the carelessness of the scribe who allowed the year 930 to slip from his record). Spelman, Wilkins and Mansi are almost valueless for Wulfstan's case. They report it under 1074 and 1078. Mansi also places it under 1070. The only fixed dates are the opening of Wulfstan's case before the Legate (1070) and the settlement at Penenden (1072). The attempt to dislodge Wulfstan, made by Lanfranc, must have fallen between these two dates. Lanfranc's attitude may have been connected with the York dispute and with Thomas's claim to the allegiance of Worcester. When Wulfstan refused to consent to the cession of the Worcester lands to York, Lanfranc changed his attitude and befriended him.

[2] Wharton, *Ang. Sac.* ii, p. 256.

[3] Malmes., *G. R.* ii, p. 329.

diocesans independently. Although details are often lacking, it is clear that a thorough revival of diocesan life was being undertaken by the vigilant care of the new primate. Perhaps the most impressive feature in the correspondence is this close connexion maintained by Lanfranc with the bishops, on matters of purely local interest, at least in normal times. Abbot Baldwin of S. Edmund's was concerned in a dispute with a man named Richard, who apparently lived in the diocese of Exeter. Lanfranc wrote to Osbern, the Bishop of Exeter, saying that for the present he was detaining Baldwin, who, at the King's order, was taking care of the Archbishop during a time of sickness. A settlement of the quarrel was deferred until Lanfranc and Osbern could meet and examine the details of the case.[1] The Archbishop's letter makes it clear that the episcopal rights of Exeter were not allowed to be overridden by the Abbot of S. Edmund's.

Shortly before Maurice was consecrated Bishop of London (1086) he referred to Lanfranc's judgement the case of a man who was found dead in the hands of his captors. Lanfranc refused to give a verdict until he had heard details of the incidents which had preceded the murder. The rest of the letter is concerned with other matters. The Archbishop said that he had not yet had an opportunity of consulting the King concerning Maurice's lands, but he would do so when an opportunity occurred. A clerk named Godfrey, who had been guilty of apostasy, was not to be allowed to leave the diocese, at least not without the formal letters of commendation demanded by the canons. A date was appointed on which Maurice was to go to Chichester to be ordained to the priesthood.[2]

Walcher, Bishop of Durham, referred to Lanfranc the case of

[1] Epis. XXI. The letter was sent from the manor of Freckenham in Suffolk, which Lanfranc referred to as ' villam nostram '. It must therefore have been written before the manor was restored to Rochester. Cf. p. 131.

[2] Epis. XXVII. The letter was addressed to Maurice as ' Londiniensis ecclesiae electo antistiti ', and must therefore be dated 1086. Maurice was consecrated at Easter 1086 (Sax. Chron., *Lat. Acta*); Stubbs, *Registrum Sacrum Anglicanum*, quoting the Canterbury Profession Roll.

a priest who had been found in a monastery without having been formally admitted to the religious life. Lanfranc apologized for the delay in his reply. He had been absent from Canterbury, and Walcher's messenger had only reached him on the octave of S. Martin. He declined to give an opinion on the case. The canons certainly made it clear that the priest should not be prohibited from returning to secular life, but if Walcher chose to act differently he might do so on the authority of S. Luke xiv. 23, which said 'Compel them to come in '.[1] It is remarkable that Walcher did not refer this case to his own metropolitan at York.

A letter sent to Stigand of Chichester reveals a somewhat extreme use of the Archbishop's metropolitan authority. Certain clergy in the diocese of Chichester, who held livings in the gift of Canterbury, had been fined by Stigand's archdeacons. Lanfranc reminded the Bishop that contrary to previous custom he had sanctioned the appearance of these priests at Stigand's synods, where they might listen to discourses on the Christian faith, on condition that they took no part in the discussions, and that if any fault were proved against them, they should be handed over to the Archbishop's authority. Stigand was ordered to take steps for the refund of the money paid by them in fines, and he was warned that for the future the clerks on the Archbishop's manors were not to attend the synods of Chichester, or any other synods; nor were they to be summoned to them. Lanfranc would deal with their misdeeds when he came to visit the manors. The only thing they might accept from Stigand was the chrism.[2]

The letter affords an indication of the extent to which the organization of the Church had become feudalized. Although resident within the authority of the Bishop of Chichester, the clerks appointed by Lanfranc were regarded as feoffees of Canterbury, and the spiritual jurisdiction of the Bishop of Chichester was thereby almost completely nullified in their case. On most occasions Lanfranc loyally upheld the rights of the diocesan bishops, especially against the abbots, but personal interest, when supported by feudal sanctions,

[1] Epis. XXIX. [2] Epis. XXX.

was sometimes too strong, even for so clear-headed a man. Moreover, across the diocesan, and across the metropolitan authority another tribunal tended increasingly to assert itself. Lanfranc once communicated with Stigand, concerning a matrimonial dispute or some such issue, which Stigand had referred to the Papacy. Lanfranc said that the Roman court had transferred the case to him, and gave orders that until he could come to try it before a council of bishops, the woman in question was to remain quietly with her husband.[1]

This interaction of the royal and archiepiscopal authority on the one hand and the papal and metropolitan authority on the other is revealed by four letters addressed to Herfast, Bishop of Elmham, which exhibit the same general features that characterized the relations between Lanfranc and the other bishops. Moreover, in one letter, Lanfranc appealed, with quotations from tradition, to his primatial authority, in a manner reported nowhere else in the correspondence.

The affairs of the Abbey of Ely were of particular interest to the King.[2] Although Herfast, the Bishop, was an ex-royal chaplain, William supported the Abbot of Ely, who had taken exception to certain actions of the Bishop, which were regarded as encroachments upon the liberties of the house. They may also have been regarded as encroachments upon the royal rights. The dispute came to a head during a quarrel between some clerks of Abbot Baldwin's household and the Bishop. William, who appears to have been at Ely at the time, ordered Herfast to let the matter rest until either he himself could inquire into it or until a convenient opportunity should present itself to Lanfranc for the settlement of the dispute. In his letter Lanfranc reminded Herfast of these points, and wrote saying that as the King had now gone abroad, he would himself shortly come to Ely to adjudicate upon the dispute,[3] but in the meantime the clerks were to be absolved from excommunication.[4]

In this matter Lanfranc was acting rather as the royal vicegerent than as the primate of England, though the two

[1] Epis. XXXI.

[2] Cf. p. 217, n.

[3] He had been authorized by the King. *Memorials of S. Edmund's* (Rolls), i, p. 65.

[4] Epis. XXII.

functions reacted upon each other.[1] Whether he fulfilled his promise and went to Ely on this occasion is not clear, but certainly harmony between the Bishop and the Abbot was not established. Details of the dispute were reported to Gregory VII, who wrote to Lanfranc ordering him to rebuke the Bishop and to take steps to prevent any encroachment upon the liberties of the monastery of Ely.[2] Thus the matter was swept into the main current of the Hildebrandine reform. The freedom of the monastic houses from episcopal control was a prominent feature in that programme. But it was one of the points to which Lanfranc unwillingly gave his support. While, as primate of England, he maintained constant supervision over the bishops, he generally reserved to them some supervision over the monasteries within their jurisdiction.[3] However, the papal order was carried out, the more easily because Herfast had personally made himself obnoxious to the Archbishop, partly by treating disrespectfully his previous letters, and partly through his coarse and secular mode of life. But Lanfranc's letter, which has not survived, produced no effect, and he wrote again in terms which are of special interest for their graphic details and for the Archbishop's insistence upon his metropolitan rights.[4]

Berard, a clerk, and one of the household of Abbot Baldwin, delivered to you our letter relating to his affairs, which, as he afterwards informed me, you impudently ridiculed, and, in the hearing of many, spoke very vilely, and said much that was discreditable to me, declaring most positively that for me you would do nothing in that matter. For this, at another time and place, account shall be rendered. I now charge you, however, not to grasp at anything belonging to S. Edmund, unless you can shew, by authentic documents, that it has been sought by your predecessors. Dismiss the said Berard in peace and uninjured until the matter shall come to our hearing, and shall receive a decision agreeable to canonical authority and our judgment.

[1] Cf. p. 208 f.

[2] Jaffé, *Mon. Greg.* i. 31. 1073, which roughly fixes the date of this correspondence.

[3] Cf. p. 152.

[4] Epis. XXVI, addressed to Herebert, but Herbert of Losinga was not made bishop until 1091. The letter must have been sent to Herfast, especially as its contents refer to the dispute with Baldwin.

Give over dice playing, not to speak of graver misconduct in which you are said to waste the whole day. Study theology and the decrees of the Roman pontiffs, and give special attention to the sacred canons . . . you will discover how vain is your expectation of escaping ecclesiastical discipline. In the decrees it runs thus: 'In every province let him attend to the regulations of his bishop in all things.' At the Council of Nicaea: 'The confirmation of everything done in each province is to be left to the metropolitan by the bishop.' At that of Antioch: 'In every province it is fitting that the bishops acknowledge the metropolitan bishop as having charge of the whole province, for since all who have any business resort from all parts to the metropolis, it is right that he has the precedence.' At the Council of Toledo: 'It is proper that each should receive rules of discipline from the place where he received the honour of consecration, that in accordance with the decrees of the fathers, the see which is the mother of each one's priestly dignity should be the mistress of his ecclesiastical rule.' And a little after: 'If any one violate these decrees, let him for six months be debarred from the communion, and undergo penitential correction as the metropolitan may direct.' There are many other passages on the precedence and power of primates and archbishops, both in the aforesaid writings and in other authentic books of orthodox fathers, which, if you had read more studiously, and when read had remembered, you would not think disrespectfully of your mother Church, nor have said what you are reported to have said. Nor would any one in his senses have considered this to be a rash presumption in another's diocese, when through God's mercy, this one island, which they call Britain is evidently the diocese of our single church.

Remove entirely from your company and from your household Herman the monk of whose life so many scandalous reports are circulated, for I desire that he live regularly in a monastery, subject to rule, or if he refuse, depart from this realm of England.[1]

Lanfranc was careful to conserve the traditional rights of the bishop, even against the orders of the supreme pontiff. But no extant writing of his contains a more complete statement of his metropolitan right to watch over the personal and official conduct of the bishops. At the same time, the closing passage reveals his characteristic watchfulness over the manners of the inmates of the monastic houses.

Two other letters, addressed to Herfast with a fraternal salutation, have been preserved.[2] They seem to have been

[1] Epis. XXVI.

[2] Epis. XXIV and XXV

written some time before the quarrel with Baldwin broke out, for they are replies, couched in friendly terms, to a communication received from Herfast concerning the case of a married deacon, and of a clerk who had performed priestly functions without being ordained to them. Lanfranc ascertained that the deacon was unwilling to be separated from his wife. He was not, however, to be completely degraded. Lanfranc ordered that he should cease to act as a deacon, but on a convenient occasion should be promoted to minor orders, unless he altered his mind and put away his wife, when he was to be restored to the diaconate, without reordination. The other offender was to be placed under discipline, but, again, if he showed penitence, and remained chaste, the Bishop should deal mercifully with him, and, as the letter seems to suggest, have him regularly ordained to the priesthood.

In the correspondence with Stigand the reference to the archdeacons of the diocese of Chichester is of more than passing interest. When Lanfranc came to England few archdeaconries were in existence.[1] We are almost entirely without information about the steps taken to revive or to introduce this feature of diocesan organization, which was so highly developed in Normandy. But we know that by the beginning of the twelfth century five archdeacons had been appointed in the York diocese, seven in Lincoln, four in Salisbury,[2] one in Wells,[3] and an unknown number in the Chichester diocese.[4] In the sees of London and Canterbury similar reforms appear to have been introduced, but the details are obscure. Florence refers to an archdeacon at Canterbury under the year 1011, and an ecclesiastic named Hamo appears as Archdeacon of Canterbury in the time of the Confessor. Lanfranc appointed an archdeacon of Canterbury,

[1] Boehmer, *Kirche und Staat*, p. 44.

[2] Ibid., p. 91. Cf. Council of Winch. (1072), c. 5, which restricted the ordination of archdeacons to the cathedral churches.

[3] Armitage Robinson, *Somerset Historical Essays* (1921), p. 74. By 1120 there were three at Wells. Cf. Frere, *Visitation Articles and Injunctions* (1910), i, pp. 35–53.

[4] Lanfranc, Epis. XXX; Boehmer, *Kirche und Staat*, p. 91. By 1116 there were three in Wells; by 1125–7 three in Norwich.

and we find his nominee signing before all the abbots at the Council of London in 1075.[1] But there is some obscurity surrounding this appointment. A suffragan bishop who had existed at Canterbury from the time of Theodore, performing episcopal functions, and resident at the monastery of S. Martin, was suppressed by Lanfranc. A clerk named Valerius was appointed to take his place, holding the functions of an archdeacon. But no jurisdiction over the churches in the archbishop's patronage was allowed to him, nor was he permitted to supervise matrimonial causes.[2] When we read that the new dignitary resided in a dwelling outside the north gate of Canterbury, near the monastery of S. Martin, it appears that Lanfranc's official was appointed to fill a special vacancy created by the suppression of the suffragan bishopric.

There are indications that the Archbishop used his influence to secure a revival of popular preaching, even to the extent of supplying the preachers with useful illustrations. Two of these illustrations have been preserved by the monk Osbern, who records a story of the Bishop of Bayeux who had thrown a man into bonds because he had hunted a stag with dogs in his woods, and had killed it with arrows. The chains did not prevent him from coming to church at Canterbury, at all hours of the day and night, when he lamented his misdeeds. The sound of the clanking fetters had a great effect upon the people. One day, two years later, while he prostrated himself before the altar of the Cross, his bonds were broken in the sight of all present, though he himself was not at once aware of the fact. But on rising up, he picked up the chains and carried them through the choir to the altar, where he placed them as an offering to God, and thus gave as a reward what had been to him a burden, at the same time praising the Almighty Christ.[3]

A few days later, Lanfranc was relating this story to a certain important man, who told him a similar tale. Three

[1] Wharton, *Ang. Sac.* i. p. 798. There is evidence for an archdeacon at Canterbury in 803, 830, and 859. During 863–70 there were four of them. Cf. Frere, *Visitation Articles*, i, pp. 41–3.

[2] Ibid., i. p. 150.

[3] Osbern, *Mem. of S. Dun.* (Rolls), p. 154.

days before, seven pirate ships were driven on shore by a gale. The pirates were either drowned or captured by the royal officers.[1] The chief, who desired to be called Barabbas because he had always been so cruel, and had killed a large number of men with his own hands, was captured and bound by the feet. But he escaped, and took the road which led to Canterbury, hoping to reach Christ Church, where he knew he would find sanctuary. When he drew near to the city, he saw above the church golden cherubim which prevented him from coming any farther. He pressed manfully against the empty air, but always felt something opposing him, as it were a wall of iron. After repeated efforts he gave up the attempt, and turned back to find that he could then run as fast as he wished. But if he changed his mind and turned again towards Canterbury, he was always met by the same opposition so soon as he came in sight of the church. So he despaired of his safety and the mercy of God, and said, 'It is clear that I have my lot with the damned, for whom it is not lawful to see the church. What does it profit to call upon a cruel Christ, from whom it is not possible to ask mercy. As fortune decrees, so be it. I will not take flight, but return whence I came, to meet death.' He retraced his steps at a rapid pace and related what had happened to many thousands of men, and afterwards paid the just penalty for his deeds.

Osbern adds that he received these two stories from Lanfranc, who ordered him to preach them to the people. He was to point the moral that one man had been repulsed because he had approached the church with a false heart, but the other was wonderfully delivered in the church, because he came in a devout spirit.[2]

The organization of the diocese was still simple. The archidiaconate was only gradually introduced, and we read of no rural deaneries, such as existed in the York diocese,[3] but the policy of reform, laid down at the great councils, was consistently applied in the correspondence which Lanfranc maintained with the bishops. The Archbishop's

[1] *Exactoribus.*

[2] Osbern, *Mem. of S. Dun.*, p. 155.

[3] Boehmer, *Kirche und Staat*, p. 91.

personal relationship with the diocesans produced energetic effects upon the progress of reform. The regulations of the great Councils were not allowed to be relegated to the cathedral muniment rooms. In diocese and parish the practice of the bishop-like and priestly life was regarded by him as the necessary outcome of the deliberations of the great reforming Councils of the reign, and as the justification of his general programme of reform.

IX

RESTORATION OF CANTERBURY, ROCHESTER AND S. ALBANS

WHEN Lanfranc came to Canterbury he found not only a ruined church, but a patrimony reduced by the carelessness of his predecessors,[1] and by the inroads of Odo, Bishop of Bayeux and Earl of Kent.[2] Odo was the Conqueror's half-brother. He had fought at Hastings, and until the coming of Lanfranc, was left in charge of the kingdom whenever William left England. He was a man of considerable ability and munificent habits, but while vividly impressing the imagination of contemporaries, he was an unpopular administrator. He had seized certain lands [3] belonging to Christ Church, and had handed them over to Herbert Fitz Ivo, Turold of Rochester, Ralph Curbespine, and other feoffees of his own earldom of Kent, together with all the local rights and customs belonging to them. Several other claims were outstanding against Odo and his vassals; for example, Lanfranc appealed for certain rights over Hugh de Montfort, another of Odo's men, and for the payment of sixty shillings from Ralph Curbespine, for the use of pastures in the island of Ingrean.

Lanfranc appealed to the King, who ordered the case to be tried by Geoffrey, Bishop of Coutances. The trial took place on Penenden Heath, near Maidstone, in the autumn of 1072.[4]

[1] Malmes., *G. P.*, p. 69. [2] Ibid.; Milo, 27.

[3] Ernulf of Rochester (Wharton, *Ang. Sac.* i. p. 334) speaks of 'many holdings'.

[4] A full account of the trial and its antecedents appears in Wharton, *Ang. Sac.* i, p. 334; Wilkins, *Concilia*, i, pp. 323–4; W. Levison, *Eng. Hist. Rev.*, Oct. 1912 (taken from a Canterbury document older than those quoted by Wharton and Wilkins); Hook, *Archbishops*, ii, pp. 127–9. The date of the trial in Sax. Chron., *Lat. Acta*, appears to be 1073, but cf. p. 117, foot-note. Florence places it under 1070 (but cf. *supra*, p. 116, n. 1). Boehmer, misled by Florence, also gives 1070—*Kirche und Staat*, p. 88. The date (1072) is fixed by Levison's charter.

The magnates, both Norman and Saxon, from different parts of the kingdom, were present, and among them Richard of Tunbridge, Hugh de Montfort, William Dacres and Haimo the sheriff. Special emphasis was laid upon the testimony of the Saxon representatives to the ancient laws and customs of the land. The aged Ailric, lately deposed from the bishopric of Chichester, who was unusually learned in Saxon customs, was by the King's command conveyed to the trial in a wagon drawn by four horses.[1]

No details of Lanfranc's presentation of the case nor of the defence are reported, but he pleaded with his usual ability and success.[2] All the lands and customs claimed by him were regained, and he made use of the opportunity to secure the confirmation of the archiepiscopal rights over the rest of the Canterbury lands, and also to secure a definition of the royal rights within the same area, and of his own rights in the rest of the kingdom. All customs relating to lands, fields and meadows, woods and pathways, streams and ponds, and all local rights in the townships and villages on the property were confirmed. He proved that the King possessed no rights over the lands of Canterbury apart from control over the highways. Three points were established. Firstly, the Archbishops' tenants could not dig up the highway between one town and another. Secondly, they were forbidden to cut timber so that it fell across the roads. In each of these cases offenders were liable to a penalty in a royal court, whether they had paid on being convicted or not. Thirdly, if murder or bloodshed or any crime was committed on the highway the offender fell under the King's jurisdiction if he was taken in the act, but the royal court could not impose any penalty if the offender had been allowed to depart from his first examination without bail. The Archbishop's tenants were thus protected against malicious informers. At the same time considerable freedom

[1] The *Text. Roffensis*, from which the copies of Wharton and Wilkins are taken, mentions Ernest, Bishop of Rochester. But Ernest did not become bishop until 1075. Levison (*Eng. Hist. Rev.*, Oct. 1912) points out that this text has been much altered in process of copying.

[2] Eadmer, *Hist. Nov.*, p. 17; Sax. Chron., *Latin Acta*.

was left for crimes like highway robbery, unless the Archbishop's court dealt with the culprits. The royal courts could only take action if the offender was caught in the act.

Several customs of the Archbishop on the royal property and on the lands of the Earl of Kent were defined. These included the right to try all cases of bloodshed committed between the first day of Lent and the octave of Easter. During Lent the whole of the fine[1] for illegitimate parentage fell to the Archbishop. At other times of the year he sometimes received only half the fine. All cases of a general spiritual character, within the royal demesne and the earldom of Kent, fell within Lanfranc's jurisdiction.

The decisions of the court were approved by William, with the consent of the lay magnates, and were declared by the King to be inviolate for all time. The King's action in this case illustrates his general practice of resorting to legal methods for the settlement of disputes, when no act of insubordination prejudiced a plea. The adjudication of the dispute by a court where Saxon custom and Saxon witnesses instructed the president may have been suggested by the difficulty of the royal position in a matter where the litigants were his half-brother on the one hand and a favourite prelate on the other, but William was always ready to preserve Saxon customs when they did not conflict with his administration. The unhesitating confirmation of Geoffrey's finding points to the fact that William was already losing confidence in Odo.

There is a doubtful report that the Bishop of Bayeux was not satisfied with the judgement given at Penenden. He perceived that the decision had turned on the evidence of local custom produced by the Saxon representatives at the inquiry. With the consent of the King he obtained a rehearing of the case, and produced witnesses for his cause, equally learned in the laws and customs of England. Lanfranc did not think it necessary to appear at the opening session of this meeting. But while he was in the midst of theological study, the course of the proceedings was reported to him. He replied that the action of his adversaries was not

[1] 'Cildwite', cf. Freeman, *N. C.*, iv, p. 814.

in order, and secured an adjournment of the meeting until next day. During the night he dreamed that S. Dunstan visited him and promised him a favourable conclusion of the discussion on the morrow. When the meeting reassembled Lanfranc appeared, and completely demolished the arguments of his opponents.[1]

Milo tells us that Lanfranc recovered twenty-five manors by ecclesiastical process.[2] This must refer to the result of the Penenden trial. A Canterbury writer of the next century gives a long list of the property recovered from the King.[3] Most of these manors were situated in Kent, so that Gervase probably refers to that meeting. But some of them were new grants to the church of Canterbury, for Gervase says that in addition to restoring property which had been alienated, William 'increased the rights' of Canterbury. This property was divided by Lanfranc between the archbishopric, the cathedral chapter of Christ Church, and that of Rochester, in accordance with an ancient custom which came down from the time of Theodore.

The traditional tie between Canterbury and Rochester was strengthened by the personal relationships existing between Lanfranc and the bishops of Rochester. On the death of the Saxon bishop, Siward, in 1075,[4] Lanfranc

[1] Eadmer, *Hist. Nov.*, pp. 17–18. The whole story is doubtful. It follows directly upon Eadmer's account of the gathering at Penenden, and may well describe the proceedings of the court on the second and third days. But according to Eadmer, Lanfranc was not present on the first day of this second trial, because he did not attend legal cases unless necessity required his presence, but Eadmer says that Lanfranc was present at Penenden, and it is not conceivable that he would have left the opening stages of this important case to his agents. Moreover, there was no opportunity at Penenden for Odo to have gathered during the night following the first day's discussion, people learned in Saxon law and custom who could counter the evidence of those already assembled, unless Odo found them already at Penenden. If Eadmer's account is to be accepted it must refer to a late rmeeting. Was it the court which dealt with the Rochester lands ? Cf. *infra*, pp. 129–30.

[2] Milo, 25.

[3] Gervase, ii, p. 64 ; cf. Malmes., *G. P.*, p. 70.

[4] Wharton, *Ang. Sac.* i, p. 342. Siward had not been displaced during the episcopal changes of 1070–2.

secured the appointment of Ernest, one of his old pupils at Caen. At the consecration the Archbishop noticed that Ernest was ailing in health and prophesied that he would not live long.[1] The infirmities of the monks of Bec and Caen are a constant feature of comment in the correspondence of the day,[2] and if Ernest was suffering from a malignant malady the prophecy may well have been made. At any rate in the next year he died, and Lanfranc recalled to mind another old pupil, Gundulf, who had been with him at Bec and Caen. He determined to appoint him on account of the holiness of his life, but before doing so consulted his friends, and then sent him to William in Normandy for approval. The King had already heard of Gundulf's sanctity, and readily gave his consent. The clergy of Rochester were then assembled, and Lanfranc made known to them the wishes of the King and of himself. They agreed to the appointment, but we are naïvely told that no one could withstand the authority of King and Archbishop.[3] Gundulf was consecrated on 21st March 1077.

As at Canterbury so at Rochester the revival of church life was accompanied by lawsuits in which Odo of Bayeux again appeared, though not always as a defendant. We certainly read that Lanfranc obtained from him the manor of Stoke in Kent,[4] and of Falkenham in Suffolk, the latter by despatching a royal chaplain to the King in Normandy, together with a promise to pay sixty pounds, a payment which was reduced by the King to thirty pounds.[5] But in the protracted dispute over Freckenham in Suffolk,[6] Odo appears

[1] According to the story this was the interpretation placed by Lanfranc on the passage ' bring forth the best robe ' which came in the Gospel at the Consecration. Milo, 46.

[2] Cf. *infra*, pp. 178–80.

[3] Wharton, *Ang. Sac.* ii, pp. 280. Ernest and Gundulf were nominated by Lanfranc in the chapter house at Canterbury before their consecration. Cf. Sax. Chron., *Lat. Acta.*

[4] Domesday (5 b) quoted by Freeman, *N. C.*, iv, p. 367, n. 4. Cf. Wharton, *Ang. Sac.*, i, p. 336.

[5] Wharton, *Ang. Sac.* i, p. 337. Another manor, named Denitunam, was recovered from Odo, but no details are given. Ibid. p. 336.

[6] Ibid. p. 339.

in a more favourable light than was usually accorded to him by the ecclesiastical writers of the day. So far from being the defendant, as Ernulf the Rochester writer suggests,[1] he appears as the friend of the Rochester chapter, while Gundulf and the Sheriff Picot are plaintiff and defendant. Picot claimed the lands of Freckenham on behalf of the King. Odo awarded the property to the Bishop. We hear nothing of Lanfranc during the proceedings of this case, but the plea appears to have been instituted by him,[2] and a royal writ formally handed over the property to him.[3] All fields, meadows, woods and villages, with the customs relating to them, were to be held as in the time of Harold. While retaining nominal rights over the manor, Lanfranc restored it to Rochester for the use of the monks, but being situated in Suffolk in the diocese of Elmham or Norwich,[4] it was too far distant from Rochester to be of practical value to the monastic community, so, with the consent of Lanfranc, Gundulf secured the exchange of Freckenham for another manor situated nearer to Rochester,[5] and retained Freckenham for the use of the bishops of Rochester, preferring to ride there annually to consume the harvest of the manor, than to allow the monks or villagers to expend labour in transporting the harvest to Rochester.[6]

The right of nominal possession over the manor of Freckenham,[7] granted by the King to Lanfranc, suggests that the see of Rochester was to some extent dependent upon Canterbury. This is confirmed by the fact that similar rights over the lands of S. Albans were preserved by Canterbury, by virtue of an ancient tradition.[8] Rochester was, of course, originally a suffragan see to Canterbury, in the modern sense of the term, and an indication of its dependence is afforded by the fact that the Archbishop was able to arrange that the

[1] Wharton, *Ang. Sac.* i, p. 336. [2] Ibid. [3] Ibid.

[4] Freckenham was at that time part of the parish of Isleham, Cambs., bordering on Suffolk (cf. Wharton, *Ang. Sac.* i, p. 339).

[5] Uldeham (*Ang. Sac.* i, p. 337) possibly Aldham in Essex, although another parish of this name lies in Suffolk.

[6] Wharton, *Ang. Sac.* i, p. 337.

[7] Cf. Domesday (190 b), quoted by Freeman, *N. C.*, iv, p. 816.

[8] Gervase, ii, p. 373.

property which had been withheld from the predecessors of Gundulf, and after his arrival restored to Rochester by Lanfranc's influence, should be held on condition that Gundulf revived a monastic community at that church.[1]

REBUILDING

The work of restoring the cathedral and monastic buildings was already in process at Canterbury when the trial at Penenden took place. The fire of 1067 (6th Dec.) had completely gutted the church. Parts of the walls and the roof were lying about in heaps of rubbish.[2] But Canterbury now possessed in her chief shepherd one of the most experienced builders in an age of great builders. The Abbey of Bec had been rebuilt by Lanfranc. For many years he had supervised the rising fabric of the splendid new house of S. Stephen at Caen, and doubtless watched over the construction of Matilda's new church of Holy Trinity in the same city. S. Stephen's, Caen, became the model for Christ Church, which in turn influenced the majestic conceptions of Norman Romanesque to be erected later at Durham, Ely, Winchester, Norwich, Rochester and Hereford. Romanesque had already been introduced to the Saxon churches by the influence of Wilfred and Benedict Biscop, but in the revival of the greatest Italian architectural creation of the Dark and Middle Ages we must see chiefly the influence of the Lombard archbishop. The Norman builders were not content to patch up the old Saxon schemes by merely adding Lombard details, as when the Italians, in later times, reshaped Milan Cathedral on Gothic lines. They took the broad spaciousness of the Lombard design, and developed it by giving it strength and massiveness, and when the age of decoration came, a Gothic transformation of arch and lancet was introduced, together with a remodelling of pillar, capital and corbel, whereas the Italians were content to add mere details to the western façade and to the apse. Indeed, at Canterbury the ground had been cleared for the

[1] *Vita Gundulfi* (Migne, clix, col. 820).

[2] Malmes., *G. P.*, p. 69.

introduction of an entirely new style of cathedral architecture. Not only the cathedral but the monastic houses and the archbishop's residence were in ruins.[1] Although at first in despair, through the magnitude of the task before him, Lanfranc commenced the rebuilding from the foundations, and completely restored the church and monastery within seven years.[2] This was half the time spent by King Edward in building the Abbey, and long before his death Lanfranc was able to gaze upon his magnificent achievement shining in the sunshine,[3] its Caen stone and ornate pinnacles flashing like ivory surmounted with gold.[4] Although it could not compare in size with the vast structures about to be erected in other cathedral cities, Lanfranc's cathedral at Canterbury worthily took its place among the splendid triumphs of Norman architecture.

The eastern tower stood between the choir and the nave, in the middle of the church, and was flanked on each side by the transepts. It was supported by a circle of huge pillars, arranged like the circumference around a central point. A gilded figure of an angel was erected on the pinnacle of the tower. To the west stretched the nave, supported on each side by eight pillars, and completed at the western end by two lofty towers, surmounted by golden pinnacles. In the middle of the nave was a gilded corona or lantern. The interior of the cathedral was richly furnished and decorated. Vestments ornamented with gold, copes, chasubles, tunics, also palls and vessels of gold were wrought by the finest workmanship, with no saving of expense. Magnificent pictures attracted the eye to the ceilings, which were made splendid by richness

[1] Eadmer, *Hist. Nov.*, p. 13.

[2] Ibid.

[3] Cf. *supra*, p. 124.

[4] A detailed description of his work has been left by Gervase, the Christ Church monk, who was born about 1140. At the time when Gervase wrote, the whole of Lanfranc's work was standing, with the exception of the east end of the choir, which had been pulled down twenty-five years after its construction, and rebuilt by Prior Ernulf under Anselm's supervision. Gervase was not able to recover any description of Lanfranc's choir. (Gervase, i, pp. 9–16; cf. Willis, *Architectural History of Canterbury Cathedral*, 1845, pp. 37–41.)

of colour as well as beauty of mural design, so far as it was known to the artists of that time.[1]

While the foundations of the new church were being laid, and before a palace was built for himself, the Archbishop began the restoration of the monastery.[2] A large part of the buildings had been destroyed by the fire, and those which remained were old and unsuited to the growing community at Christ Church. The ruined buildings were pulled down, and the remains of the fire were cleared away. The foundations were dug out anew, and before the church was completed, new monastic quarters, on a larger and more magnificent scale than the old monastery possessed, were erected.[3] The church and monastery were then surrounded with a high wall. Stone for all these works was brought from Caen in sailing ships.[4]

Meanwhile Lanfranc was assisting the restoration at Rochester, where his friend Gundulf, a greater builder than himself, was rebuilding S. Andrew's. In later years Gundulf designed the Tower of London and the castles at Malling and Rochester. On his arrival at Rochester he found the cathedral almost a ruin through neglect and the attacks of time. A new church, together with habitations for the monks, was built, commencing from the foundations and so far as the confined space of the site would allow.[5] Lanfranc assisted the work with large grants of money, and with rich gifts. One day he sent twenty-five copes made of fine silk, embroidered with gold fringes; two large silver-gilt candlesticks; two crosses of gold; a dalmatic made of white diaper, with gold embroidery; two chasubles, one crimson and one purple; a silver table to stand before the high altar; and a silver thurible. He also caused the body of Paulinus to be raised and placed in a silver casket bought with the proceeds of a successful plea against Gilbert de Glanville.[6]

[1] Malmes., *G. P.*, p. 69; Eadmer, *Hist. Nov.*, pp. 12–13; Milo, 25.

[2] Eadmer, *Hist. Nov.*, p. 13.

[3] Ibid., and Malmes., *G. P.*, p. 69.

[4] Milo, 25.

[5] Gervase, ii, p. 368; Wharton, *Ang. Sac.* ii, p. 280.

[6] *Flores Hist.* ii, pp. 20–1. I suggest twenty-five 'copes', but a word is missing in the text.

A third work of church-building in which Lanfranc took part was the restoration of the Abbey at S. Albans. The new abbot, Paul (1077), who came over with him from Caen, was a nephew of the Archbishop. Paul found the walls of the Abbey tumbling down, and the interior so dilapidated as to be beyond repair.[1] He first rebuilt the church, bake-house, and other necessary offices,[2] leaving the monks' houses and other parts of the monastery to be completed eleven years later.[3] Stone in abundance was found amid the ruins of ancient Verulam, which had long been used as a quarry. The timber, collected by Paul's predecessors for the work of restoration, was lying ready to hand.[4] The woods of the old Abbey had been cut down by the King after the death of Abbot Frederick.[5] Lanfranc contributed the sum of one thousand marks to the building fund,[6] and secured the return of the property of Redbourn, on condition that it was used for the monks.[7] Paul also obtained the restoration of some of the property of the Abbey alienated either before or during the Conquest,[8] and then enriched it with a gift of twenty-eight books—a most liberal donation at that time—as well as relics, phylacteries, palls, copes, albs and other ornaments.[9] By the order of the King, S. Albans was to be held perpetually by the Church of Canterbury 'in alodio'.[10]

[1] Eadmer, *Hist. Nov.*, p. 15.
[2] Walsingham, *Ges. Abbat. S. Alb.* i, p. 52.
[3] Ibid. pp. 52 and 54. [4] Ibid. p. 52. [5] Ibid.
[6] Ibid. i, p. 54; cf. Eadmer, *Hist. Nov.*, p. 15; Gervase, ii, p. 368.
[7] Walsingham, *Gest. Abbat. S. Alb.* i, p. 54. Redbourn, Herts.
[8] Ibid. i, p. 53. [9] Ibid. i, p. 58.
[10] This privilege had come down from earlier times. The precise significance of a tenure 'in alodio', and its distinction from a holding 'in feudo', is doubtful. It has been suggested that the distinction lay with the person who originally formed the connexion between the two churches. In the case of a tenure 'in feudo', the holding was first created by the overlord. In the case of the tenure 'in alodio', the relationship was created by the tenant who offered the holding to an overlord. The alod was heritable, while the feud was held only for life. But it is not clear that any such distinction was made by the Norman lawyers. Maitland, *Domesday Book and Beyond* (1907), p. 153.

It is probable that the relationship between S. Albans and Canter-

The building of great cathedrals and abbeys and the restoration of alienated church properties were characteristic activities of the munificent and enterprising churchmen of the Norman period. Lanfranc was the representative of a whole class, rather than the original source from which the work of building was inspired. Before his arrival in England, Thomas had commenced the cathedral at York (1070). Before the close of his life, eight other cathedrals in addition to Canterbury and Rochester had been commenced—Salisbury (1075); Winchester and Hereford (1079); Ely (1083); Worcester (1084); Lincoln (1085); London (1086); and Bath (1088).[1] At York, Winchester, and Lincoln, new monastic houses and bishops' palaces were built. The survival of Norman churches in the parishes all over England testifies to the enthusiasm of the Norman builders and founders. But if Lanfranc shared this enthusiasm with other ecclesiastics and with generous laymen of the day, and if many building schemes sprang into existence quite independently of his example at Canterbury, yet his works at Bec and Caen, from which a large number of the Norman bishops and abbots of the Conquest were drawn, supplied the original inspiration for the rebuilding of the great cathedrals of England.

bury was less precise than in the case of a lay holding 'in alodio'. But the use of this term implies a closer connexion than that which existed between Rochester and Canterbury, unless the term 'sub Archiepiscopo Lanfranco' describes a similar relationship. Moreover, according to Maitland's definition, the tenure 'in feudo' probably more accurately describes the connexion between both churches and Canterbury. In the case of both S. Albans and Rochester, it is more probable that these churches originally received grants of land from Canterbury, than that they voluntarily commended themselves to Canterbury.

[1] Before the close of the Norman period, this list was increased by Chichester (1091), Durham (1093), Norwich (1101), Exeter (1107).

X

REVIVAL OF MONASTICISM

WHEN Lanfranc joined the community at Bec the monastic revival in Normandy was well established. But the English monasteries at the time of the Conquest were in a state of serious disorganization, following on the sudden revival under Dunstan, Ethelwold and Oswald. Beyond the Humber no house existed save at Durham.[1] In the south, reforms had been introduced during the time of the Confessor by William of London, Gisa of Wells, Walter of Hereford and Herman of Sherborne, all foreign bishops. Three English bishops, Leofric of Exeter, Aldred of York, and Wulfstan of Worcester, had also been influenced by the reforming spirit of the Continent.[2] The only new foundations were Edward's house of S. Peter at Westminster, and Harold's secular foundation at Waltham. The houses at Wells and Exeter were organized according to the rule of Chrodegang of Metz, which was neither so lax as the secular communities nor so strict as the reformed rule of Cluny.

In 1066 not only were the buildings of most of the English monasteries dilapidated, their lands diverted to other uses, and their rule of life disorganized by secular habits, but in some cases the community had been almost entirely scattered, and the few brethren who remained existed in a condition of extreme indigence. At Rochester Siward found only four or five inmates,[3] clothed like laymen, enervated by lack of nourishment, barely able to secure daily bread, which they had to beg or buy when they could.[4] At Gloucester, Serlo, who was appointed by the King,[5] found only two old monks and eight boys.[6] At Christ Church, Canterbury, the trouble was of a different nature. The monks had so far abandoned the regular discipline that their lives could scarcely be distinguished from those of laymen. They hunted,

[1] Boehmer, *Kirche und Staat*, p. 73.
[2] Ibid., p. 68.
[3] Malmes., *G. P.*, p. 136; Eadmer, *Hist. Nov.*, p. 15.
[4] Malmes., *G. P.*, p. 136.
[5] Ibid., p. 292.
[6] *Hist. and Chartul. Mon. Glouc.* (Rolls), i, p. 10; Malmesbury says he found only three monks.

hawked, rode on horseback, and played with dice. They indulged in fine cloaks and delicate food, and were waited upon by so many servants, that, to quote the words of Malmesbury, they 'lived like Lords'.[1] A secular mode of life, not poverty, had relaxed the monastic rule at Christ Church.

The material condition of most of the English houses was made worse by the confiscations ordered by William soon after the first victories of the Conquest. By the advice of his friends, the King ordered the removal of the treasures from all the monasteries in the country.[2] This was unusual conduct for William, but the ruinous condition of the English houses may well have disposed him to think that the treasure was lying idle. Moreover, he was anxious to send oversea presents to the churches and abbeys of Normandy, as a worthy thank-offering for victory. The new houses of S. Stephen and Holy Trinity at Caen doubtless received a large share of the spoils of the English abbeys.

The first step in the reform of the ruined houses was to secure abbots who had been trained in the great monasteries of the Continent. The King and Archbishop worked in conjunction, and although there are traces of some independent action by William, Lanfranc sometimes secured the appointment of his own nominee, and always secured his nominee in houses like Rochester and S. Albans, which were closely allied with Canterbury. The Archbishop generally promoted monks trained at Caen or Bec. We have seen that Ernest and Gundulf, who were Bishops of Rochester, were brought over from Caen, and also Paul, who was made Abbot of S. Albans. On the death of the Saxon Abbot of Evesham, Lanfranc sent Walter, his Norman chaplain, who was trained at Cerisy, to succeed him. In the same year he concurred in the royal appointment of Vital of Fécamp, the Abbot of Bernay, to Westminster. All these appointments were made in 1077, with the exception of that of Ernest, who was

[1] Malmes., *G. P.*, p. 70.

[2] *Annales Monastici* (Rolls), ii. p. 29; iv. p. 372. Florence (1070) says that William Fitz-Osbern made the suggestion. Cf. Matt. Paris, *Hist. Maj.* ii, p. 6.

promoted in 1075. In 1085 Vital died, and was succeeded at Westminster by Gilbert Crispin, who had come to England some years before.[1] Gilbert wrote to Lanfranc concerning some lands belonging to Westminster. In his reply Lanfranc disclaimed any authority over the property, but suggested that it should be used for the benefit of the monks and the monastic life.[2] In the last year of his life Lanfranc created a Benedictine community at Bermondsey,[3] and we have a charter issued by him granting property to S. Mary of Southwark.[4]

According to the new reformed theory, the appointment of an abbot was vested in the hands of the community. The Constitutions of Cluny[5] and the rules drawn up by Lanfranc for Christ Church, Canterbury,[6] clearly insist upon the rights of the members at the appointment of their abbot. A similar right appears to have been admitted at the appointment of a prior. A certain 'father William' wrote to Lanfranc concerning the appointment of a prior to one of the Norman houses. Lanfranc replied that he had consulted the brothers who were with him, and their advice was that Ernest should receive the preferment, but if he was unwilling, or if the Abbot declined to accept him, then a candidate selected by the community should be appointed.[7]

However, in spite of these regulations, the communities

[1] Cf. Armitage-Robinson, *Gilbert Crispin*, p. 19, n. 1, for the date of Gilbert's appointment.

[2] Epis. LX. Like Epis. LI and LII this letter is addressed to the 'Beloved G. . . .', and opens with an almost identical ascription. Then it refers to the friendship existing between Lanfranc and 'G.' 'a primordio' (cf. *infra*, p. 178, n. 1). Thus it suits Gilbert better than Gundulf. But the reference to the property would agree well with the uncertainty surrounding some of the Rochester lands. Another epistle (LXVIII) addressed to Abbot G. . . . may also refer to Gilbert. It is addressed in more formal terms, but the opening paragraph refers in characteristic manner to the friendship existing between Lanfranc and the recipient.

[3] *Flores Hist.* ii, p. 21 (cf. Matt. Paris, *Hist. Maj.* ii, p. 29). For a list of the English houses cf. Boehmer, *Kirche und Staat*, p. 73, n. 2.

[4] Lanfranc, Epis. LXVII.

[5] *Constitutions of Cluny*, Lib. III. 1; Migne, cxlix.

[6] *Decreta pro Ord. S. Ben.* ii.

[7] Lanfranc, Epis. LIV.

were allowed little more than a consultative voice in the appointment of the abbots, and this is confirmed by the history of the elections at S. Evroult.[1] The English appointments during Lanfranc's régime may have been necessarily confined to the nominees of the King and Archbishop, on account of the decayed state of those houses. But if the right of appointment decreed by the Constitutions of Cluny and Christ Church had been actually put into operation, the investiture contest between Anselm and Henry I would have been avoided. On the other hand, the feudal organization of England made the concession of this right on the part of the King impossible without a struggle. The abbots were great landholders, and it was essential that their appointment should be controlled by the King. Moreover, it was not in accordance with Lanfranc's bias in favour of episcopal prestige that the monasteries should be allowed untrammelled rights in the appointment of the abbots. While willing to limit the royal power by sanctioning a theoretical right to the monks, the English bishops were not in practice prepared to hand over so much power to the monasteries. In England the abbeys never gained more than the shadowy rights conferred upon them by the *congé d'élire*.

We read of only two attempts on the part of the monks to contest the appointment of an abbot who was not selected by them. But both at Glastonbury and S. Augustine's the opposition was influenced by national feeling expressed by Saxon monks against a Norman abbot, and while the S. Augustine's monks claimed a constitutional right to appoint their abbot, this claim was not put forward at Glastonbury. The mutiny at Glastonbury was caused by the harsh behaviour of Thurstan towards his new charges. Although Lanfranc had preserved the right of election to the monks of Christ Church in the constitutions of that house, he made no allowance for the rights of the community at S. Augustine's and Glastonbury. The monks of S. Augustine's were coerced into accepting Guido,[2] and Thurstan received a very mild rebuke.[3]

[1] Ord. iii. 5 (ii, pp. 68–92).

[2] Cf. *infra*, pp. 245–7.

[3] *Infra*, p. 145.

The most important feature of the restoration was the revival of the Benedictine rule. Every appointment in which Lanfranc was concerned appears to have been made on the stipulation that regulars and not canons should be restored to the revived foundations. Where secular canons had been installed, the regulars were reinstated; and where the regular rule, though not abandoned, had yet become slack, it was revived.

At Christ Church, Canterbury, Lanfranc introduced his reforms slowly, and seized opportunities as they arose, with due regard for the confirmed habits of the inmates.[1] The constitution of the house was amended, and the Prior and convent were invested with the administration of their own property.[2] The community gradually increased until it numbered one hundred and fifty brothers.[3]

While the reform of Christ Church was Lanfranc's special care, he gave his attention to the affairs of the rival house of S. Augustine. The Abbot was his friend Scolland, who had been trained at Mont S. Michael, and was appointed to S. Augustine's in 1070.[4] The oath of obedience to Lanfranc was taken by Scolland wherever and whenever the Archbishop demanded it, and the relations between them were so intimate that the Archbishop loved Scolland 'as a father loves a son'.[5] This is merely the formula of the writers of the day for describing any close friendship, but in view of the unhappy relations between the monastery of S. Augustine and Lanfranc in later years, it seems clear

[1] Malmes., *G. P.*, p. 71.

[2] Gervase says that hitherto the lands of Canterbury had been so divided that the Archbishop retained control over the barons and knights, while the supervision of the agriculturists was left to the convent, although according to the same writer some said that Lanfranc himself introduced this system. The position is not clear, but this division of proprietary rights may indicate the formal introduction of knight-service upon the Canterbury lands. Possibly the process of sub-infeudation was confined to the property which remained in the Archbishop's hands. Gervase, i. p. 43.

[3] Gervase, ii, p. 368.

[4] Thorn (Twysden, *Decem Scriptores*), but Sax. Chron., *Latin Acta*, says 1072.

[5] Gervase, i. p. 70.

that during the earlier period, when harmony was absolutely essential for reform, Lanfranc and the Abbot of S. Augustine's worked cordially together, although not without murmuring on the part of the S. Augustine's monks.[1]

At Rochester the old canons, of whom only four or five remained, were liberally pensioned off by the Archbishop.[2] The alienated property was restored to S. Andrew's on the express condition that monks should be reinstalled. The regular clergy were introduced, and the community grew to the number of fifty or sixty monks. We are told that Lanfranc watched the revival of the monastic life with joy. Gundulf was frequently called into his presence to talk over the affairs of the house. He was seldom allowed to depart without a present for the adornment of S. Andrew's. If he omitted to give a present to Gundulf after one of these visits, he ordered something to be sent after him, lest the Bishop should be offended, and with a request that prayers might be made for him to S. Andrew. With the Archbishop's approval, Gundulf reorganized the administration of the property of the community on the model of the reforms at Christ Church. It was divided between the Bishop and the monks, and the larger share fell to the monastery. The manor of Haddenham in Buckinghamshire, purchased by Lanfranc, was handed over to Rochester.[3] The living is still in the gift of the Dean and Chapter.

The details of the new régime at S. Albans have been described at some length.[4] Paul took with him Lanfranc's Benedictine statutes,[5] and introduced new rules for both monks and nuns.[6] He followed Lanfranc's example at Canterbury, and introduced his reforms slowly, but in a few years the monastery and its school became famous throughout England.[7] S. Albans became a centre not only of the

[1] Cf. *infra*, pp. 245–8. [2] Eadmer, *Hist. Nov.*, p. 15.

[3] *Vita Gundulfi* (Migne, clix, col. 820 ff.), Malmes., *G. P.*, pp. 136–7. At York, Salisbury and Lincoln the prebendal system was instituted, i. e. each prebend managed his own share of the property. (Cf. Boehmer, *Kirche und Staat*, pp. 98–9.)

[4] *Gesta Abbat. S. Alb.* i. pp. 53–60.

Ibid. i. pp. 52, 58, 61.

[6] Ibid. i. pp. 58–60. [7] *Gesta Abbat.* i. p. 52.

Benedictine reform of the English monasteries, but of a great school of historical writers. The works of Matthew Paris and of Walsingham, together with the different recensions of Paris, are among the richest of our historical treasures of the Middle Ages The work at S. Albans was completed by the grant of a new charter by the King.[1]

Lanfranc was instrumental in securing the continuance and reform of the regular clergy at Winchester and Durham.[2] At Worcester the Benedictine rule was introduced by Bishop Wulfstan, who probably influenced reforms at six abbeys allied with Worcester.[3]

Although the introduction of the Cluniac reforms into the cathedral foundations was only partial, the reforming movement became general in the abbeys, and improved the discipline of those cathedral chapters which retained the secular Rule. Thirteen of the twenty-one abbots who signed the decrees of the Council of 1075 were Englishmen, but by the time of Rufus only three of the thirty abbeys which then existed were ruled over by Englishmen.[4] The English abbeys were gradually filled with abbots trained not only at Bec and Caen, but at all the principal Norman houses, including Jumièges, S. Michael, Fécamp, S. Wandrille, Cerisy, Bernay, and Lire, which were the chief centres of the Benedictine reform.[5]

The Archbishop's letters contain numerous indications of his watchfulness over the affairs of the monasteries. We have seen that he repeatedly rebuked Herfast, Bishop of Elmham, for interfering with the property of S. Edmund's.[6] A worse case of episcopal encroachment upon the liberties of a monastery was that of Robert, Bishop of Chester. Not only had Robert confiscated lands and goods from the house at Coventry, he had also violently broken into the dormitory and the stables, and had carried off all the horses and other movable property. Even the buildings were dismantled, and the materials were carried away to Robert's own

[1] Matt. Paris, *Hist. Maj.* vi, p. 33.
[2] Cf. *infra*, pp. 227–8.
[3] Freeman, *N. C.*, iv, pp. 387–91.
[4] Boehmer, *Kirche und Staat*, p. 107.
[5] Ibid., pp. 106–9.
[6] Epis. XXVI; cf. *supra*, pp. 120–22.

manors. To this pilfering was added a sojourn of eight days, when the Bishop and his train consumed the supplies of the monastery. Lanfranc ordered him to make full restitution, and reminded him that he had no warrant for such conduct, and that he should set a worthy example, by his words and actions, of good behaviour and holy life.[1]

The bishops did not always look kindly upon the Archbishop's supervision. Herfast publicly ridiculed a letter of Lanfranc in the presence of Berard, the bearer, and abused the Archbishop.[2] Robert hardly deigned to read the letters, and with open contempt hurled them behind a chair.[3] But in spite of some restlessness on the part of the bishops and abbots, Lanfranc's firm grasp upon the affairs of the Church was maintained. We read of only one instance when, either through favour or too marked a readiness to overlook a fault, a guilty abbot escaped his censure. After the scene of slaughter before the high-altar at Glastonbury, where the Saxon monks were shot down by Thurstan's Norman archers, the Abbot appears to have come into a better frame of mind, not untempered perhaps by fear of the consequences, when the matter came to the ears of William. He wrote asking for Lanfranc's short and candid advice.[4] Whether the Archbishop had already rebuked him in the severe terms which his crime demanded is not clear from this letter. In any case the Abbot should have been removed from his charge, but Lanfranc wrote :

> You have asked me to indicate briefly my advice to you, and I have taken care to do it in a few words. Pray God that He may remember you and have mercy upon you, and do this instantly, both for yourself and your friends. Do satisfaction to our Lord the King through friends and faithful intermediaries. If he spurns you, do not be very sad or anxious about it. God will visit His people when He decrees to hasten. May mercy be with thee.[5]

Lanfranc appears to have been thinking rather of his own

[1] Lanfranc, Epis. XXXII.

[2] Epis. XXVI ; cf. *supra*, p. 120.

[3] Epis. XXXII.

[4] Lanfranc, Epis. LIX.

[5] Epis. LIX (1082–3, after Thurstan's appointment to Glastonbury).

misfortune and that of his friends who had advised William to send Thurstan to Glastonbury. Or had he begun to lose a due sense of proportion owing to advancing age? The rebuke issued to Herfast and Robert was much stronger, although their misdeeds had been far less serious. But whereas Thurstan made his submission, Herfast and Robert spurned the Archbishop's reproofs and were therefore treated as contumelious.

Another monastic dispute, connected with a delicate question of precedence, which came up before Lanfranc for settlement, occurred at Barking. Maurice, Bishop of London, was ordered to go to Barking, if it was convenient, and to settle a quarrel between the Abbess and Prioress if possible.[1] When he had heard the accounts of both sides, he was to order the 'Abbess to be Abbess' and the 'Prioress to be Prioress'; each should retain befitting rank, and as the rule of S. Benedict said, the superior should give orders, and the inferior should obey them. Provided that the Abbess commanded things which were reasonable, and not contradictory to canonical rules, whether in spiritual or secular matters, and due respect being observed towards the dignities of their respective ranks, harmony should exist between them. The nuns, clergy and laity, both within and without the monastery, must obey them both. If any one ventured to question the Archbishop's ruling, Maurice should repress his presumption; but if the quarrel had passed beyond possibility of reconciliation, the Bishop was ordered to notify the Archbishop, who would deal out severe discipline to the offender.

We are not told whether Lanfranc intervened in this dispute as the result of an appeal by the parties concerned. But he was always ready to listen to individuals who came to him for confession, or who were flying from punishment. Certain brothers of Abingdon[2] confessed that owing to serious faults they had been expelled from the monastery. Lanfranc severely rebuked them, and on ascertaining that

[1] Epis. XXXIV (1086–9). Maurice was appointed Bishop in 1086.

[2] Epis. LV, addressed to 'Adelelinus'. An abbot of this name died at Abingdon in 1084.

they were ready to make amends, undertook to intercede for them. He wrote to the Abbot, asking him to forgive them and to receive them back into the monastery. Another fugitive said that he had been compelled to leave his native place and his parents and friends, on account of the Abbot's anger. The reference to parents and friends makes it clear that the petitioner in this case was not a monk, but nevertheless, Lanfranc gave him a letter of conciliation in which he asked the Abbot to treat the defaulter indulgently.[1]

Lanfranc moved cautiously amid the mass of delicate business which came under his hand. An Abbot once consulted him about the admission of a brother whose name is not divulged. Some unpleasant affair lay behind the matter. Lanfranc was inclined to lenient measures, but he did not wish it to be thought that he would condone a scandal, or suggest anything that might create a worse scandal, so he declined to give a definite opinion. He referred the Abbot to his Bishop, if he was accessible, and to the Prior Godfrey, and advised him to follow their advice.[2]

At the same time he did not shirk giving a definite decision just because the matter brought before him raised delicate points. In a letter to Abbot William,[3] he asked permission for the monk Rainald to go to live under Abbot Serlo at Gloucester for a year, for the good of his soul, as the monk hoped. Apparently Rainald sought the aid of a stricter rule of life than was possible at his own monastery,[4] although he said nothing to detract from William's monastery. Lanfranc begged that William would not be offended because the monk came to him, for, after all, he had appealed in his necessity to William's own friend. He was careful not to encroach upon the Abbot's authority, and left the matter finally in William's hands.[5] The movement of monks from one house to another was not usually permitted, and there

[1] Epis. XLVIII, addressed to Abbot B——, possibly Baldwin of S. Edmund's. Lanfranc says, 'Et quia putavit quod pro me multum facere debeatis'. This may refer to Lanfranc's action on behalf of Baldwin against Herfast. If so, the date of this letter was some time after 1073.

[2] Epis. LXI.

[3] Epis. LXII.

[4] 'Quod regularem locum petit.'

[5] 'Rogo te quantum rogare possum et debeo.'

can be no doubt that it was only the request to go to a monastery where the regular rule was in force that caused the Archbishop to sanction it in this case.

On the other hand, complaints which involved insubordination against the discipline of the revived Benedictine Rule called forth a prompt rebuke from Lanfranc. A letter to 'O . . . Abbot',[1] begins without even the usual kindly greeting, and continues

> We have forbidden brother Gregory your monk, who wanted to cross the sea. We have ordered him to return to his monastery, and have compelled him to do so. You have not done well by giving him permission to go wandering about outside his own neighbourhood. It is quite clear from this what sort of pastor you are, and what amount of care you see fit to bestow upon the souls committed to your charge.
>
> We demand therefore and order, and at the same time ask that you will receive him back with honour, and for the rest that you will shew him fatherly consideration as your son. We believe, indeed, that through the mercy of God, if you want to be careful for your order, you will be able to have advice and help from him in matters spiritual and secular. I am glad that he has reported that you fear God and are a good man, but he could not deny that through your simplicity you are negligent of our orders.

The Benedictine reforms were not allowed to go unchallenged. The bishops of Winchester and York and six other bishops introduced the secular canons into their monasteries. Walkelin went so far as to challenge Lanfranc's regulations at Canterbury (1072).[2] This was the beginning of a policy which had for its object the complete expulsion of the regulars from the cathedral churches of England,[3] and aimed a blow at the whole Benedictine movement in the country. At one time Walkelin appeared to have considerable prospect of success. He gained the adherence of several of the bishops, and even won the support of the King. His efforts were so successful that he did not anticipate that Lanfranc would raise any serious opposition.[4]

Walkelin's action was an attempt to secure a distinction between the functions and mode of life of a bishop with his

[1] Epis. LXIII.

[2] Eadmer, *Hist. Nov.*, p. 19.

[3] Epis. VI.

[4] Eadmer, *Hist. Nov.*, p. 18.

cathedral clergy and an abbot with his monks. The difficulty lay in the fact that bishops were sometimes abbots, as at Christ Church, Canterbury. This was emphasized in the complaint formally lodged against the Archbishop's reforms at Canterbury. It was alleged that the business of the metropolitan see could be more adequately discharged by seculars than by regulars, and it was contended that the primatial dignity would suffer if the cathedral community were a mere collection of monks.[1] It was suggested that the Archbishop should be surrounded by a staff of clergy well versed in secular business, with a far wider knowledge of men and places than was possible for the members of a Benedictine community.

But the motives of the objectors were not unmixed. We are told that behind the opposition lay the envy of the bishops. In Thomas of York and Herfast of Elmham, Lanfranc certainly possessed colleagues who, on account of previous differences, were by no means disposed to accept all his views; and although we do not read of any similar cause of antipathy between him and Walkelin of Winchester, he is specially singled out as being envious of the Archbishop's position and influence.[2] This is perhaps too severe a stricture. It comes, like all our records, from the pen of a monk, and reflects the narrow outlook of the monastic mind, but it is at least clear that Lanfranc's policy was accepted only after a good deal of criticism, and even open opposition.

Lanfranc had little difficulty in checking the efforts of Walkelin both at Winchester and Canterbury. The forty canons whom Walkelin had assembled at Winchester to replace the monks were sent back to their homes. Although the royal consent had been obtained for their installation, the consent of the Archbishop was regarded as essential to their appointment, and when this was refused, the affair came to an end.[3] In like manner, the Archbishop's authority

[1] Eadmer, *Hist. Nov.*, p. 19.

[2] Malmes., *G. P.*, p. 71.

[3] Eadmer, *Hist. Nov.*, p. 18. Alexander II wrote to Lanfranc and the Winchester chapter in favour of the regulars [cf. Epis. CXLIII and CXLIV (Migne, cxlvi)]

sufficed to ward off the attack upon his reforms at Canterbury,[1] but lest the question should again arise in the time of his successors, Lanfranc secured a papal ruling on the status and condition of the Christ Church monks. In his reply, Alexander II said :[2]

We have heard from certain men coming from your parts to the gates of the holy apostles Peter and Paul, that certain clerics, having secured for themselves the aid of the temporal power, filled with a diabolical spirit, are plotting to expel the monks from the Church of S. Saviour's which is the metropolis of all Britain, and to establish seculars therein. In addition to this nefarious plot, they are attempting to secure the extirpation of the order of monks in every episcopal see, as though the authority of religion were not valid in the case of the monks.

In regard to which matter, being compelled by the zeal of God, we ordered a scrutiny to be made of the privileges of the Churches, and there came to our hands a statute of our predecessor of blessed memory, Gregory the Great, with respect to the Churches of England, in which he commanded Augustine, the apostle of your nation, to place in the aforesaid metropolitan see, men of the same order to which he himself is known to have belonged. These commands of his, among others, are subjoined : 'Since', he said, 'your fraternity has been brought up in the rules of a monastery, it ought in the Church of the Angles—which has lately under God's providence been led to the faith—to institute this rule of life, which obtained at the beginning of the infant Church among other nations, in which, no one, possessing anything, called it his own, but the Church had all things in common.' No one doubts that this rule of communion is most suitable for the order of monks. Hence is obtained[3] the letter of Boniface, who was head of the Roman Church—over which by divine authority we preside, fourth after the blessed Gregory—addressed to Ethelbert, King of the Angles, and to Laurence your predecessor, in which he uses a censure of this kind, prefaced by anathemas : 'Glorious son', said he, 'that which thou hast asked from the apostolic see through our co-bishop Mellitus, we willingly grant, that is, that your benignity should lawfully establish for ever a habitation of monks, living by rule in the monastery, founded in the city of Canterbury, which our holy doctor Augustine, of blessed memory, the disciple of Gregory, consecrated to the same S. Saviour, and over which the present chosen head is our well-beloved brother Laurence. And we decree by apostolic authority that those monks, from whose preaching you are deriving salvation, should gather to their side

[1] Ibid., p. 19.

[2] Alexander II, Epis. CXLII (Migne, cxlvi) ; cf. Lanfranc, Epis. VI.

[3] 'Hinc habetur', i. e. from the records of the Chancellery.

a company of monks, and adorn their life with the morals of sanctity.'

The usual anathemas follow, together with a confirmation of the two decrees of Gregory and Boniface under the same anathema.[1]

Beyond checking the instigator of the opposition, Lanfranc took no steps towards enforcing the appointment of regulars at other cathedral foundations, which were not dependent upon Christ Church. Thomas of York was left free to make his own arrangements. He found only three of the seven canons in residence. The others had been compelled to leave when the city was sacked. These were now recalled and others were added to their number. Thomas first introduced the rule of Chrodegang of Metz, but when this proved unsuitable he organized the community upon a secular basis, and placed the canons in charge of their own prebends.[2]

At the close of the reign secular canons were to be found at eight of the cathedral chapters—York, London, Lincoln, Norwich, Salisbury, Chichester, Hereford and Chester. The rule of Chrodegang was in force at Exeter and Wells. Apart from the abbeys, where the Benedictine rule was developing, only five cathedral chapters observed the rule—Canterbury, Rochester, Winchester, Worcester and Durham. The testimony of these figures, supported by the tone of his letters, shows that Lanfranc was by no means a fanatical monk in his efforts on behalf of reform.

If the maintenance of episcopal authority over the monasteries acted as a check upon the complete application of the Cluniac theory to the English monasteries, the influence of the feudal organization of society exerted further restraint upon the reform movement. The King placed all the bishoprics and abbeys under military rule, and fixed the number of soldiers to be supplied to him and his successors during times of war. A roll, containing the names of bishops and abbots, together with their military quotas, was placed in the royal treasury.[3] This alleged act

[1] On the genuineness of this epistle cf. Appendix II.

[2] *Hist. of York*, ii, p. 108.

[3] Matt. Paris, *Hist. Ang.* i, p. 13.

of royal tyranny amounted to no more than the application of the feudal rule of knight-service to the spiritual tenants, as feoffees holding real property, and therefore standing under the same obligation to the King as the lay barons. The bishop or abbot in turn enfeoffed his knights with manors on the property of the Church, just as the barons provided for their vassals with grants of land.[1] Similar arrangements were made by Lanfranc at Canterbury, although the details are obscure.[2] The presence of a military bodyguard was frequently a necessity for the Norman bishop or abbot, at least at the beginning of the reign. Knights of fortune who came into England were frequently employed in this way under the title of stipendarii.[3]

To the military organization introduced by the King, Lanfranc raised no objection. He was not a whole-hearted monk like Odo of Cluny[4] or Peter Damiani, who were entirely absorbed by the claims of the monastic ideal. If he was swept into the movement it was, in the first instance, because the monastic life offered that seclusion for study and teaching which he was seeking when he left Pavia. His work at Bec and Caen resembled that of Abbo of Fleury and Gerbert of Rheims, the scholar abbots of the last generation. Moreover, his attitude to monasticism was always influenced by that independence of opinion and action characteristic of all his work. While the monastic revival in England was fostered and guided by Lanfranc, it was not the work of a Cluniac enthusiast prepared to sacrifice the whole ecclesiastical organization to the mere establishment of monastic houses, and to the observance of a rigid ascetic

[1] But the proprietary rights of the Church appear to have been more completely retained. The case is recorded (*Abingdon Chron.*, Rolls, ii, pp. 6–7) of certain knights of Abingdon who were sent into Normandy on the King's business. They were captured by pirates and were sent back scarcely alive with their hands amputated. One of them had not yet received a grant from the Abbot, who now refused to make it, doubtless on the grounds of the knight's disability for further service. But on the intervention of the King, in answer to the knight's appeal, a grant was made.

[2] Round, *Feudal England*, p. 300.

[3] *Abingdon Chron.*, Rolls, ii, p. 3.

[4] Died 942.

rule by all the clergy. If he was the refounder of English monasticism, he was also the refounder of the English Church. The work of overhauling the monasteries was only one feature in the larger reform, whereas the Cluniac movement was an attempt to reform the Church by impressing upon it the rigid discipline and severe ideals of monastic life. Lanfranc, like Theodore, revived the monasteries by means of the diocesan organization. The Norman abbots and bishops pursued the reverse process by attempting to revive the Church by means of the monastic organization. Lanfranc was not ordained until near the middle of life, and throughout the whole of his later career, whether as a monk or Archbishop, he retained a strong leaning towards the layman's view of the Church and its work. This partly explains the close relations maintained between him and the independent churchman, William the Conqueror. William's attitude on the question of his own marriage and the homage demanded by Gregory VII show that no mere monk would have been tolerated in the see of Canterbury. Lanfranc may have been the 'father and comforter of the monks',[1] but he loved other things more—a strong administration, and the episcopal organization. All the allusions to what he did for the monasteries of England and the Benedictine rule must be interpreted in the light of these facts, especially as the records were made by men who were monks, and who spent all their lives within the confines of the cloister. While every change made by him in the organization and material well-being of a monastery was made in the interests of the regulars, yet his zeal was tempered by an impartial consideration for the diocesan organization.

[1] Sax. Chron. (Peterburgh), 1089.

XI

LIFE AT CHRIST CHURCH, CANTERBURY

A COMPLETE picture of the reforms instituted at Christ Church has been left in the book of rules, sent by Lanfranc to Henry, the Prior of that house. The regulations were based upon the customs of the leading Benedictine houses, and especially upon those of Cluny,[1] but certain rules were added, and others were changed by Lanfranc, in order to create a special rule for Christ Church, which its dignity, as the primatial see, demanded.[2] At the same time he said that he had no wish to bind either himself or his successors to these rules, because, for various reasons, changes might be necessary. Moreover, no church could follow the rules of another in every respect. But certain things without which a soul could not be saved were to receive careful attention—faith, contempt of the world, charity, chastity, humility, patience, obedience, penitence, humble confession for faults, frequent prayers and the rule of silence. If these were observed, the rule of S. Benedict was faithfully kept, though other things might vary, such as the use of vestments and the times of the occasional offices. Discretion for the arrangement of these matters was left to the abbot, not to the bishop or archbishop, but he thought that if bishops took care of their charges in Christ, they could with good reason be regarded as abbots.[3]

Christ Church, Canterbury, was recruited in three ways. Boys (*infantes*) and youths (*juvenes*) were admitted at an early age to be trained for the religious life. Men who were past the age of adolescence came in as novices.[4] Members

[1] Cf. Migne, cxlix. [2] 'Propter primatem sedem.'

[3] *Lanfranci Decreta pro Ordine S. Benedicti*, Praefatio. A useful but somewhat discursive account of Lanfranc's Constitutions is given in Church, *Life of Anselm* (1870), pp. 43–68. Hook, *Archbishops*, ii, pp. 105–9, gives a disconnected summary.

[4] Ibid. xvii.

of other communities were received after performing special rites.[1]

A boy was led to the altar carrying the host and a chalice with wine, and was offered by his parents to the priest who was to celebrate Mass. Then they wrapped the boy's hands in the altar frontal and presented him to the Abbot, who formally received him. The parents read out a promise which had been written before witnesses, that the boy should never relinquish his vocation, nor be given anything that would kill him, and this written statement was placed upon the altar. The Abbot blessed a cowl, and taking some garment off the boy said 'The Lord take from thee the old man,' and placing on him the cowl, added 'May the Lord endue thee with the new man'. He was then taken out to be shaved and clothed with the habit of the order. His own profession did not take place until he had reached the age of manhood, when he took the vows like other novices.[2]

When the bell rang in the morning to rouse the monks, the boys, after saying their prayers, went into the cloister for their reading lesson. They read in turn with a low voice, remaining seated, and sufficiently far apart so that they could not touch each other with either hands or garments. No boy was allowed to beckon or speak to another, save in the presence and hearing of the master, nor was he allowed to rise from his place without permission. When they left the cloister, one master went out with every two boys, and on passing the senior monks the boys bowed to them.

No boy was allowed to receive anything save from the hands of the Abbot, the Prior or the master, although there were exceptions to this rule, when, for example, the Precentor handed books to him in the schoolroom or the choir. They made their confessions only to the Abbot or Prior, or to a confessor especially nominated by the Abbot in the chapter. The boys were flogged at their own chapter, and not at the ordinary chapter, where the monks received corporal punishment. At the midday hour of rest, they went to their beds, and remained quietly covered up without talking or reading. A senior monk, the oldest and

[1] *Decreta*, xx. [2] Ibid. xvii.

most discreet of the assistant-masters, was in charge. When called to bed at night the masters attended them with lighted candles, until they were covered up.[1]

A man who sought the novitiate was brought into the guest-house like other guests. After being questioned by the Abbot or Prior or some one deputed for the purpose, he was taken to the chapter-house, and then having made obeisance to the Abbot, lodged a formal application to be admitted to the community. The severity and difficulty of the life were brought before his attention, and if he still urged his request he was conducted into the nave of the church. At the close of the chapter he was handed over to a novice master, who saw that he was tonsured and shaved, and robed in the regular habit with the exception of the cowl. During his novitiate he was not allowed to communicate with other monks, though any monk might admonish or rebuke him with the master's permission. He could be chastised if necessary. He was expected to make frequent confession.

When the novice's conduct had been approved, formal application was made to the Abbot for his profession. This was granted after the rules had again been read, and a second warning, emphasizing the difficulty of the monastic life, had been given. After other ceremonies, his profession was made, and he was led into the choir, where he kissed the assembled brothers. But he did not become a full member of the order until permission had been granted to him to speak at a chapter-meeting. If he was a priest he was not allowed to celebrate for a year, unless he gave proofs of chastity while in the world.[2]

The chief duties of the day were performed in the choir, and minute rules for the proper conduct of the 'hour services' and of the Morning and High Masses occupy about one-half of Lanfranc's regulations.[3] At midnight, or in the small hours, the brothers were roused for Nocturns, which was followed after a short interval by Matins or Lauds (*matutinae laudes*). From 1st October to All Saints' Day, they again returned to their beds save on feast days and fasts, and were roused at dawn for Prime. But between

[1] *Decreta*, xxi. [2] Ibid. xvii. [3] Ibid. i. 1–12.

the festival of All Saints and the Wednesday before Easter they were not called usually for Matins until just so much time remained to say the office before dawn. The Prior made a perambulation of the whole monastery to rouse up any one who was sleeping. Meanwhile, the children remained in the chapter-house with lamps, and, if they had been aroused for a night office, were permitted to sit silently. At dawn, a small bell was rung, and the brothers sang Prime. After the office the children had their reading lesson in the cloister. Both seniors and juniors were still shod with slippers, which were not exchanged for sandals until the bell rang for Terce, when they returned to the dormitory, put on their sandals, received their knives, proceeded to the wash-house, and then into the choir to wait for the children, who were in the meantime in the wash-house. After Terce the Matutinal Mass was sung, and the daily chapter was held. At the close of the chapter all were free to converse in the cloister, while the children, who had held their own chapter separately, went into the cloister for a light meal.[1]

The office of Sext was followed by another opportunity for conversation in the cloister when the juniors had left the chapter, although this privilege was curtailed during Lent and Rogationtide.[2] High Mass followed Sext, and then the brothers remained quietly reading in the choir while some who could not be present at Mass had their meal. When these had finished, all went into the refectory for the chief meal of the day. In summer-time the midday hour of rest followed, when all went to their beds in the dormitory. This humane rule was necessary to compensate for the loss of sleep between Matins and Prime. The office of Nones was said in winter before the meal,[3] but in summer it followed the hour of rest.[4] The afternoon-hours were devoted to manual labour and other duties, which concluded when the bell rang for Vespers at five or six o'clock. A light supper was received in the refectory, and the day was closed by Compline and the rule of silence.

[1] *Decreta*, i. 1. [2] Ibid. i. 3, 5. [3] Ibid. i. 1.
[4] Ibid. i. 4.

A day or two before Christmas and Easter the brothers bathed under the surveillance of a senior monk of good character, who appointed servants of mature age to prepare the baths. Young men and novices were not allowed to go together, but with the seniors. After being shaved, and receiving a change of linen, each member entered a private compartment of the baths, and if he required anything more, called quietly to the attendant, who lifted up the curtain and quickly gave him what he needed. After bathing they returned to the cloister.[1]

On Christmas Day all the bells were rung before Prime. At the Invitatory four brothers wore copes. At each Nocturn, when the third portion of scripture was read, two priests, robed in copes, carried round two thuribles, first to the matutinal and high altars, then to the brothers sitting in the choir. The brothers who were appointed to say Mass went to an appointed place, where a big fire had been prepared together with basins, manutergia and warm water for washing the hands. On this occasion they combed their hair before washing. Then they returned to the church for Mass, which was sung, the officiants and servers all being festively robed. Two candelabra with burning candles stood before three novices and three chanters who were in the choir together with all the children. At the end of Mass the priest and servers disrobed, all the bells were rung, and Matins and Lauds were sung. Then after the commemoration of S. Anastasia all went back to bed. At dawn one of the big bells was rung, and the festive services proceeded until at Terce, at the words 'ipsum adoremus' every one genuflected to the earth.

On the feast of the Purification at Terce, when all were robed in albs, a carpet, upon which candles were placed, was laid before the altar. The priest clothed with the alb and stole blessed them, sprinkling them with holy water, and censing them. The candles were then distributed by the Custos to all present, and as the brothers began to light them the Precentor commenced the antiphon 'Lumen ad revelationem'. When this was finished and the 'Nunc

[1] *Decreta*, i. 2.

Dimittis', they proceeded through the large doors of the minster singing the 'Ave Gratia', and made the station before the cross. They returned to the choir singing the antiphon 'Cum inducerent'.[1]

After the interval for conversation in the cloister which came after Sext on Ash-Wednesday, the ashes were blessed. The priest wore the stole only, and after sprinkling holy water over them, scattered them over the heads of the brothers, saying 'Remember that ashes you are, and to ashes you return'. A procession followed, as on every Wednesday and Friday in Lent, until the Wednesday before Easter. On the first Sunday in Lent, after Compline, a cauldron was suspended between the choir and altar. On Monday before Terce, the crucifix, chandeliers, pyxes [2] and texts which possessed images or pictures of the Crucified, were covered. Before the brothers entered the chapter-house the Librarian gathered the books together on a carpet spread out in the chapter-house. The monks came in with the books which had been lent to them on the same day a year before. The Benedictine rules for the keeping of Lent were read and, after a sermon, the Librarian read out the list of books, together with the names of the brothers to whom they had been lent. As each man's name was mentioned he returned the book, and if any one had not read it, he prostrated himself, confessed his fault, and sought pardon. Fresh books were dealt out, and the names of the recipients were recorded.[3]

On Palm Sunday the Abbot, or some other priest, blessed the palms, flowers and fronds, which were placed on a carpet before the high altar. After being sprinkled and censed they were distributed by the Sacrist—palms to the Abbot, Prior and more important people, flowers and fronds to the others. A procession [4] was formed after the singing of the 'Pueri Hebraeorum', and while all the bells were rung it moved out of the choir. When one circuit had been completed the procession filed to both sides of a bier, containing the 'body of Christ'. The seniors were placed

[1] *Decreta*, i. 2. [2] *Capsae*. [3] *Decreta*, i. 3.

[4] The ordinary Sunday procession had taken place as usual after early Mass.

behind the boys, as in the choir, and each side faced the other. The 'Hosanna filio David' was sung by the boys, and at the end of each antiphon they cried 'Hosanna!' When the bier was moved forward again, each member on either side bent the knee as it drew level with him. The ceremony was repeated at the gate of the monastery, and at the crucifix in the church after it had been uncovered.

Minute directions were given for the ceremonial of Maundy Thursday. The high celebration did not take place until after Nones, and was followed by Vespers. At the celebration sufficient bread was consecrated to last over the next day. A meal of bread and water followed in the refectory, and the poor came into the cloister. Before being admitted the poor washed their own feet in warm water, under the directions of the Robe-keeper, and then entered into the cloister. The children came in with their masters; and before each poor man, was placed one of the brothers. At a sign from the Abbot the Prior struck three blows on the 'tabula' and all knelt down and adored Christ in the poor, and during the antiphon 'Dominus Jesus', washed the feet of the poor, dried them, and kissed them on mouth and eyes. The hands of the poor were then washed, and cups of cold water were given them to drink. A gift of money followed, and in this charity the poor relations of any brother who had died during the year were allowed to share. Later in the day the same ceremony was performed amongst the brothers, and Lanfranc points out that it was at the discretion of the Abbot to confine the ceremony of feet washing to members of the community.[1]

On Good Friday morning no bells were sounded, the brothers were roused for Nocturns by the beating of 'tabulae'[2] in the cloister, before the cellar and infirmary. After prayers and the recital of the fifteen psalms [3] the candles were extinguished. At Prime all entered the church with bare feet, and remained unshod all day, unless it was so cold that the Abbot gave permission for sandals, but even so the offices were said with bare feet. No conversation was

[1] *Decreta*, i. 4. [2] Wooden instruments used instead of bells. [3] The Gradual Psalms.

allowed in the cloister on this day. After Nones the altar was completely covered up with a sheet. No candles or censers were used. During the reading of the account of the Passion, at the words ' Partiti sunt sibi vestimenta mea ', two officiants drew aside in opposite directions two cloths which had been placed on the altar before the office, but the missal linen underneath was left. At Mass two priests took up the crucifix, which was covered, and approached the altar, and when the Sanctus was finished, uncovered it, and began the antiphon ' Ecce lignum ', and all genuflected. Carpets were placed before the altar, and the Abbot and officiants prostrated themselves, praying briefly, and followed in turn by all the others. They each kissed the foot of the Crucified and returned to the choir. If any wanted to adore the crucifix it was carried to them to a more convenient place, and if it passed the brothers in the choir they genuflected as it reached each of them.

The ' body of the Lord ' was censed in the place where it had been put on the day before. The host was brought to the altar, together with a chalice containing wine and water, and both were there censed while the brothers adored the elements. A particle of the host was dipped in the cup and administered, but without the kiss of peace. At the close of the service all went into the cloister, washed their feet in warm water and put on slippers. We are not told what happened in cases of frost-bite, although this humane provision must have saved many from that unpleasant malady. Vespers were said in the choir and all proceeded to the refectory and broke the fast, which had been observed all day, with a meal of bread, water and coarse herbs. Their regular food and drink was distributed by the Almoner to the poor. All the altars were then washed, first with water and then with wine, and the day closed with a drink of water and the loving cup [1] in the refectory.

On Easter Eve all the altars were decorated. The candles were collected and blessed. The date of the year was affixed to them by the Chanter, together with a cross, formed by pressing into the wax five grains of incense. Fire was

[1] *Decreta*, i. 4.

consecrated and was sprinkled with holy water. Live coals from this fire, together with incense, were placed in the censers. A candle was lighted and carried on a spear to the lamps, which were lighted, but no lamp was carried in the procession. From the consecrated fire all the fires in the kitchens, which had been previously extinguished, were relighted. The candelabra lights at the altar were relighted after the Litany, and a festive Kyrie and Gloria in Excelsis were sung at Mass. All the bells were rung at Vespers, which was followed by a procession to the crucifix.[1]

On Easter morning all the bells were rung before Matins, and a procession to the crucifix took place after Matins and Vespers. This ritual was repeated after Matins and Vespers throughout the whole of Easter week. There was a procession with copes at the Matutinal Mass. For the rest of Easter Day the ritual was so well known that Lanfranc did not think it worth while to repeat the directions.[2]

On Rogation days, after Matins and the office for the dead, the brothers might return to their beds if they liked, but the midday rest was not allowed on those days, nor were they roused by bells in the morning. The children were awakened by the masters as quietly as possible, and while they were reading in the cloister, the others got up. After Sext, during the time usually occupied with the midday rest, a very short interval was allowed, and then they came down from the dormitory with bare feet, washed their hands, and went into church to pray. A service was held, and a procession formed, which moved out of the monastery to visit a neighbouring church. As they left the minster precincts, staves were handed to them, Mass was sung in honour of the patron of the particular church to which they went. On returning to the monastery Nones was said.[2] The Whitsun festival resembled the other great festivals with some minor variations.[3]

[1] *Decreta*, i. 4. [2] Ibid. i. 5.

[3] Ibid. i. 6. The Constitutions (i, §§ 7–9) contain an elaborate list of festivals, drawn up by Lanfranc, divided into three grades, and forming a calendar for the year. This list contains the names of Augustine of Canterbury and Alphege, but omits that of Dunstan.

When the bell rang for the daily chapter all stood in the choir facing East, with no books in their hands. Then they

Attached to the Bosworth Psalter (cf. Gasquet and Bishop, *Bosworth Psalter*, 1908) is a calendar which contains the name of Dunstan, but omits that of Alphege. Dunstan was canonized soon after his death (988). Alphege was not canonized till after his death (1012) or more probably not till after the translation of his relics from London to Canterbury (1023). Thus the date of the Bosworth Calendar is 988–1023.

The Bosworth calendar resembles the calendar in the Leofric Missal which is based on an earlier Glastonbury calendar. The Leofric calendar does not contain the names of either Dunstan or Alphege, and Bishop assumes that Dunstan's name was not included in the earlier Glastonbury calendar (pp. 26 ff.). But the close connexion between Dunstan and Glastonbury throws some doubt upon this conclusion.

The problem is complicated by the existence of another calendar, Arundel MS. 155, which also exists in an extended form in Arundel MS. 60, and Cotton MS. Vit. E. XVIII. Bishop dates these three calendars approximately and respectively 1030, 1060, 1090 (p. 41 f.).

A comparison of Arundel MS. 155 with the Bosworth calendar proves that the former and not the latter calendar lies behind all the later Canterbury lists. Several omissions and a few additions appear in Arundel MS. 155, and the later calendars follow it. Although Arundel MS. 60 and Cotton Vit. E. XVIII are Winchester lists, yet Arundel MS. 155, which lies behind them, is pinned down to Canterbury by the inclusion of three lesser Canterbury saints, Blase, Austroberta and Salvius, which do not appear in the other Winchester lists (p. 59).

What is the relation of Arundel MS. 155 to the calendar in Lanfranc's Constitutions?

(*a*) On internal evidence: (1) The omission of Dunstan's name in both suggests the influence of Lanfranc. Lanfranc's conversation with Anselm in the spring of 1079; his omission of the Conception of the Virgin, and the alteration of the date of the Feast of S. Benedict in the Constitutions, all bear witness to his desire to reduce the list of English saints (p. 32). (2) But the admission of five Winchester feasts and three minor Canterbury saints suggests an earlier date because these eight feasts are absent from the list in the Constitutions in accordance with Lanfranc's principle of reducing the list.

(*b*) The earlier date for the Arundel MS. 155 is strengthened by external evidence: (1) Soon after Lanfranc's time there was a revival of the cult of S. Dunstan (cf. *Memorials of S. Dunstan* by Osbern the Canterbury writer), and the association of Dunstan's

proceeded to the chapter-house in the order of their conversion, headed by the Prior. If any name was called out, which a man shared with others, all of that name present arose, until the Prior signified who was designated, but some special designation was usually intimated when the name was called.

The sympathy of the chapter might be sought, though with a prescribed form for various objects, such as the necessity of going on a long journey, or before performing arduous work, or at the death of a relative of a new member of the convent, or, again, when any one sought the mercy of the chapter for a brother placed under discipline.

A brother who was about to receive judgement, or was about to be beaten with a heavy stick, fell prostrate. For a serious fault he was divested even of his undergarment, and remained nude, while he was flogged with birch rods at the discretion of him who presided. All the brothers meanwhile inclined their heads with fraternal compassion. No one spoke, and no one was expected to look at him save certain grave members, who could intercede for him. The discipline was meted out by any one whom the Abbot selected, save boys, youths or novices.

name with Lanfranc by Osbern (cf. *infra*, pp. 252–4) suggests that the revival was beginning before Lanfranc's death. Dunstan's name, therefore, would not have been omitted from a list drawn up after Lanfranc's death. (2) It is true that Lanfranc's conversation with Anselm shows that the former was compelled to revise his earlier attitude, and this is confirmed by the order given by Lanfranc for the development of the cult of S. Aldhelm (cf. *infra*, p. 189 n.). Moreover, we know that the relics of Blase and Austroberta were at Canterbury in Lanfranc's time (cf. Gervase, i., pp. 8, 10). Yet if Osbern's stories can be accepted it is difficult to account for the omission of Dunstan's name by Lanfranc in a fuller calendar drawn up by him towards the end of his life. Again, there is the possibility that the stories of Osbern are apocryphal, and in this case we should be driven to conclude that Lanfranc deliberately admitted five Winchester feasts and three minor Canterbury saints to Arundel MS. 155 in preference to Dunstan—a conclusion hardly credible. If Arundel MS. 155 is earlier than Lanfranc, as Bishop maintains, then the omission of Dunstan's name from the list proves that Lanfranc's principle was at work before his time, and therefore the additional omissions in the Constitutions were a mere development of a process already at work.

At a meeting of the chapter a speaker had to confine his remarks to useful objects, and while one spoke the rest remained silent. The speaker might not be interrupted save by the president, who could silence him if his words seemed superfluous or not useful. When the president spoke, every one, including the speaker, became silent.[1]

When the hour bell for an office rang, silence was observed by everyone throughout the monastery, including those who happened to be in the quadrangle and the infirmary, except at Compline, when those who had permission did not attend and were permitted to speak about needful things. So, during the offices, no one might eat in the refectory except at Compline, when permission was given to those whom duty kept from Compline, and also to brothers who came in from a journey. If they had not finished before the end of Compline they might go into the church for the blessing and then return to their meal.[2]

Certain religious forms were observed when the monks were shaved. The cowl was taken off before shaving and only the habit was worn, both by him who shaved and him who was being shaved. The guardians of the young men shaved them, and they in turn shaved their guardians. But if a guardian could not shave, he might obtain the services of some one else to shave his charge while he sat by. So also the masters shaved the boys and the boys shaved the masters if they were able to do so. When the bell rang for service a brother who was being shaved pulled his cowl over his head and went into church, but remained outside the choir, unless either his beard was completely shaved or was still intact. On these days the chapter was shortened, and the boys held no chapter.[3]

Special rules were drawn up to deal with the brother who was celebrant at the morning Mass if he overslept himself,[4] or if he permitted any of the sacred elements to fall on the corporal or on the ground,[5] also for those who had to be cupped[6] or who were going on a journey.[7]

[1] *Decreta*, xviii. [2] Ibid. xv. [3] Ibid. xi.
[4] Ibid. xiii. [5] Ibid. x. [6] Ibid. xii. [7] Ibid. xiv.

A whole series of offices were open to which a brother who proved worthy of promotion might be preferred by the Abbot in the chapter.[1] These included the office of Infirmarian who had charge of the sick,[2] the Almoner who carried relief to the sick poor in their cottages,[3] the Hospitaller who took charge of all visitors to the monastery. Permission to communicate with a monk was sought by the Hospitaller from the Abbot or Prior, and if this was not given the brother was not informed that a visitor had called for him.[4] The Cellarer had charge of all food and drink, and of the utensils and furniture for the buttery, kitchen and refectory.[5] The Robe-keeper had charge of all clothes, sandals, bedding, razors, scissors, towels and glasses, iron for shoeing horses and travelling requisites.[6]

A more important official was the Sacrist, who prepared the vestments and ornaments for the services and offices. He washed the chalices and corporals and prepared the host with the greatest care. Robed in alb and amice he selected grain by grain the corn which was contained in a clean sack. It was placed in an undamaged pan and given to a servant of good character to be ground. Before the selected corn was ground, other grain was passed through the mill, to make sure that no dirt was present. The flour was sifted in a round cauldron in a specially prepared place. On the day when the host was made, he and his assistants were again robed in alb and amice, except he who held the grid. After hands and faces had been washed, the dough was kneaded on the table, the cook's fingers being covered with nail-sheaths. A servant kept the fire supplied with wood, well-dried and prepared beforehand. Throughout the process psalms and hymns were sung.[7]

The Cantor superintended the services in the choir, and maintained discipline there. If any one failed to begin a response or antiphon he was ready to take it up. He notified the Abbot of the chants which the latter had to begin, but apart from this had no special function in the service, unless the Abbot was absent. He had

[1] *Decreta*. xix. [2] Ibid. ix. [3] Ibid. viii. 3. [4] Ibid. viii. 2.
[5] Ibid. viii. 1. [6] Ibid. vii. [7] Ibid. vi.

charge of the books in the library if he was sufficiently learned.[1]

The Prefects who invigilated the monastery were chosen from among those who could be trusted not to be spiteful or partial. They reported slackness and indiscipline in the chapter and were especially watchful at night.[2] The Prior was treated with a respect almost equal to that shown to the Abbot, whose place he took if the latter was absent from the monastery. His special duty was to minister to the sick in the infirmary. Some of his duties resembled those of the Prefects.[3]

According to Lanfranc's statutes all the brothers had a voice in the election of the Abbot. At the first chapter attended by him the keys of all places and offices in the monastery were laid at his feet. All the brothers bowed when the Abbot bowed at the beginning of the antiphon, or when his name was called in the chapter, or when any one made a mistake in the psalms, or at any place for which the Abbot's pardon was necessary. Whenever he went through the monastery the brothers rose. If he saw any misbehaviour he at once called the offender before him, and kept him standing, if necessary, so long as he thought fit, while the delinquent continued to ask pardon. But the Abbot was not to permit this to take place before secular men. No one presumed to sit near him, save at his request, and not until he had first bent the knee and kissed the Abbot's hand. When he entered the refectory, water and a towel were brought. While he was in the choir no one might correct a boy without his order. So long as he slept in the morning no noise was to be made. If the hour for rising passed, and the Prior's bell had not sounded, the master of the children roused them by tapping on their blankets with a stick, and after their customary ablutions and prayers they went to sit quietly in the school until the Abbot rose. All the arrangements of the monastery were under his control. When he died the nearest abbot or bishop was invited to come to conduct the funeral, and in addition to the usual burial rites of the community, the dead Abbot was robed in

[1] *Decreta*, v. [2] Ibid. iv. [3] Ibid. iii.

sacerdotal garments, and a pastoral staff was placed in his hand. Throughout the year following, the 'Verba Mea' was said for him, and a sum of money was placed daily on the table of the new Abbot to be distributed to the poor. The anniversary of his death was celebrated as a festival.[1]

Sickness was regarded as a divine visitation for sin. The sick man sought pardon from the Abbot before the chapter, and sought leave of absence from the brethren. If the sickness continued he was sent to the infirmary, and was allowed meat if necessary. So long as he continued to eat meat his head remained covered wherever he went, and he walked leaning on a stick. When he was recovered he shaved, went into the choir at the office before the chapter, but did not yet receive the sacrament. Then in the chapter he received formal absolution from the Abbot for having eaten food forbidden by the rule. But if he had not eaten meat during his illness the Abbot decided when he should return and what course was to be adopted for him.[2]

If a sick brother seemed to be near death and requested to be anointed, a procession was formed and the brethren came and stood round the bed in an orderly manner. The sick man was sprinkled with holy water, and after the religious rites had been performed, made his confession and was absolved by all, absolving them in return. Then he was kissed by all. The anointing followed, and the priest washed his hands, and threw the water into the fire or into the sacrarium. The priest then went into the church for the sacrament, and after washing the mouth of the sick man, gave it to him, unless he had already received it that day. Special Masses were sung every day for him until his recovery. If it appeared that he would not recover, two brothers remained with him night and day, reading the story of the Lord's passion and the gospels, and if he became unconscious or delirious they continued singing psalms, and saying the offices as they came round. When his end drew near a hair-shirt was spread out, a large sign of the cross was made with ashes, and the dying man was placed

[1] *Decreta* ii. [2] Ibid. xxii.

upon it. At the approach of his last agony the servant ran to the cloister with a 'tabula', and, violently and frequently smiting it, summoned the whole community. If the brothers were at Mass, or at one of the hours, they all rose and came to the dying man, saying the Nicene Creed with subdued voices. But the children and their masters, together with certain others, remained at their duties. The brothers engaged on special duties came as soon as they could. Special formularies were sung, and if he remained alive, some of the brothers continued singing psalms, but the whole community came back to him again before the end. At his death three bells were tolled at short intervals, and the body was carried away to be washed. But certain brothers, such as the priest for the week, those who served at the altars, the cooks for the week, the brothers who worked in the cellar or refectory, were not allowed to wash the dead. When the dead man was washed, a new or newly-washed woollen undergarment was placed on him, and a woollen amice was placed like a cap on his head, which was then covered by a cowl. Stockings made of cloth, reaching to the knees, and slippers, were placed on him, and his hands were covered with cowls, all being securely sewn on. Then the body was covered with a pall, and carried, accompanied by a procession into the church, where a cross was fixed at its head, and two candles, one at the head, and one at the feet, were left burning. The brothers whose duty it was to sing psalms stood by. The whole convent remained round the body at such parts of the day as were not occupied with religious or other duties. Watchers were appointed during the night, after Compline. Until he was buried no one spoke in the cloister. On the next day a festive Mass was sung, and the body was censed. On thirty successive days thirty special Masses were celebrated for him, in addition to the two ordinary Masses save on Good Friday. The burial usually took place after the chapter on the day after that on which he died. After the body was received into the grave by two brothers a written absolution was read and then placed on its breast. After the burial was over the procession returned to the monastery, the candles were extinguished and the bells ceased to ring. A funeral service took place in the choir.[1] If the monk died while away from the monastery he was brought back to it, and so far as was possible these rites were carried out.[2]

Lanfranc's regulations appear to be based upon the Constitution of Odo of Cluny,[3] and although the correspondence of Anselm suggests that less rigid rules were in force at Bec, yet many of these regulations must have been tested in practice when Lanfranc was at Caen and Bec. The influence of Cluny upon Bec and Caen was probably stronger than modern writers allow. But if not applied at Bec, it is clear that through Lanfranc's Constitutions the Cluniac system exerted a direct influence upon his reform in England. From Christ Church we have seen that they were introduced by Paul at S. Albans, and S. Albans became the model for many English houses. Probably Lanfranc realized that English monasticism was so completely decayed that nothing but the introduction of the Benedictine system in one of its most rigid forms would suffice to ensure its revival. It will be observed that no special reference is made to field labour in the Constitutions. Manual labour was strictly enforced by the Rule of Benedict, and this accounts for the large part it played in the daily routine at Bec under Herluin. In a Benedictine house, from five to nine hours daily[4] were devoted to field labour or to work in the stables, outhouses and kitchens, according to the season of the year, and there is no reason to suppose that the routine at Christ Church omitted this part of a monk's life. Yet the absence of direct reference to field labour in Lanfranc's Constitutions[5] may be an indication of the change which gradually came over Benedictine monasticism, transforming it from a community occupied

[1] *Decreta*, xxiii.

[2] Ibid. xxiv.

[3] Migne, cxlix. Doubtless the simpler English tenth-century rule, '*The Regularis Concordia*' (Migne, cxxxvii, cols. 475–502), was consulted by Lanfranc.

[4] Dom Butler, *Benedictine Monachism*, pp. 276–87.

[5] The vine-dresser and gardener are not mentioned, cf. *Constitutions of Cluny*, iii. 19, 20 (Migne, cxlix), which also contain a whole section (i. 30) on manual labour.

with work in the fields, into a learned body devoted to the writing of historical and contemporary records and the copying of manuscripts. The change had not indeed been completed in Lanfranc's day, for there is little reference to study in his Constitutions. The monks took only one book from the library each year, and even the Cantor was sometimes illiterate.[1] As in the original Benedictine Rule, learning held a subsidiary place in a monk's life. Study occupied only some three and a half to four hours,[2] and was distributed throughout the day between the duties of the choir and the field. No concentrated or sustained work was therefore possible. But the appearance at Christ Church, in the age which immediately followed Lanfranc, of a school of historical writers, of whom Eadmer and Osbern are well-known representatives, and the rise of the great school of writers at St. Albans where Lanfranc's Constitutions were introduced, illustrate not only the change which came over Benedictine monasticism, but show that Lanfranc's Constitutions were capable of ample development, as indeed the Preface intended.

Both Odo at Cluny and Lanfranc at Canterbury were faced by special difficulties. The great necessity in both cases was the revival of the religious life. Hence the characteristic feature of tenth- and eleventh-century Benedictinism was the concentration of the monk's attention upon the routine of the choir. Dullness was excluded by the frequent occurrence of festivals and fasts. The manifold details of ritual and ceremony extending from the altar to the choir, from the choir to the chapter-house and cloister, and on to the refectory and dormitory, prevented the lives of the brothers from becoming monotonous. Secure from the turmoils and dangers of an unsettled world, amid a pageantry of changing ritual, with days fully occupied, the years in a monastery, organized on these lines, must have passed rapidly, as always when time is clearly marked off into periods and busily engaged. To men of an artistic temperament this pageantry of the cloister must have made a strong appeal, and constituted, perhaps, the call which brought them into monastic life. In the long centuries between the decline

[1] *Decreta*, v. [2] Dom Butler, *Benedictine Monachism*, pp. 280, 281, 287.

of classical art and the dawn of the renaissance, when men could, none the less, feel the desire for the beautiful, though lacking inspiration and skill to mould it in sculpture or paint it on canvas, only two outlets for their yearning were afforded—the construction of the noble cathedrals and abbeys, and the pageantry of the altar and procession.[1] For many artistic minds the latter formed the most ready means to expression and enjoyment. They could always look forward to taking part in it, and might hope to be counted among those to whom it was permitted to add some individual detail of adornment which became incorporated in the regular ritual of a particular church.[2]

But monastic life, even at Christ Church, was not without its shadows. The monk was often a highly-strung individual, whose peace of mind was disturbed either by gloomy introspection or by wild outbursts of mental frenzy. The confined condition of his life sometimes rather intensified than relieved the temptations which perhaps had originally driven him to seek the refuge of the cloister. It is, therefore, not surprising to find him exhibiting mental and physical phenomena which, to-day, would form most interesting studies for the science of psychotherapy. Hitherto these stories have been discredited by serious investigators and almost invariably omitted from monastic histories, but the new science of psycho-analysis gives them new meaning and they appear to be natural accompaniments of the cloistered life of a Benedictine house.

A well-authenticated story illustrates some of these conditions at Christ Church, and supplies graphic details of Lanfranc's method of dealing with them.[3] A young monk,

[1] Illuminated manuscripts may be added.

[2] However necessary the Cistercian movement of the twelfth century may have been as a reform of decayed eleventh-century conditions, the plainness of the Cistercian ritual and architecture deprived the life of the cloister of much of its variety, and contributed to that weariness which is so often expressed by monks of the later period. If idleness invaded the Cluniac houses, it was not for lack of religious duties supplied by the Rule. Cf. G. G. Coulton, *Five Centuries of Religion*, i, for an erudite account of later conditions on the continent.

[3] Eadmer, *Hist. Nov.*, pp. 234–7; Milo, 47; Osbern, *Mem. of S. Dunstan* (Rolls), pp. 144–9.

named Egelward, was warned by the Archbishop to keep his mind free from evil thoughts, lest he should be attacked by an evil spirit.[1] One day when about to hand the paten to Lanfranc, Egelward saw certain terrible and devilish figures sitting near the altar, apparently about to attack him. Terrified by the sight, he shrieked out, 'Let Christ conquer, let Christ reign, let Christ rule!' and seized the Archbishop. The chaplains failed to remove him, and he was forcibly taken away by the military attendants.[2] When the Mass was over, Lanfranc ordered him to be brought to his private apartment, and after shutting the door, grasped the excited young man and persuaded him to confess his sins. The offender was then led into the chapter, but after receiving corporal discipline went to the feet of the Archbishop, and looking round on the brothers with wild and menacing eyes, threatened to reveal what they all did privately. There was among them another young man whom the Archbishop loved because there was good in him which might be cultivated. The demoniac reproached this brother, who was groaning and weeping inconsolably on account of what had happened. 'What have you to do with tears,' said the demoniac, 'your tears are vain and so are your prayers. The same place will have us, hell will hold us both.' Lanfranc, who was unwilling that the young man should be put to shame by the demented monk, hastily rose up, and taking him apart, prayed him to confess his sin lest the devil should get him into his grip. The young monk instantly confessed all the sins he could remember from his youth upwards, to the abundant joy of the Archbishop who repeatedly kissed his hands, and gave alms on that day to three hundred poor people.

Meanwhile the demoniac was led to the tomb of S. Dunstan, followed by the whole congregation, and after the Archbishop had exorcized him, he remained well and quiet for the whole day. But at sundown, while the monks were singing the psalms at the last service of the day, he attacked the Prior Henry. The Prior led him into the 'house of quiet' and ordered a watch to be kept upon him, while

[1] Cf. *infra*, p. 176.

[2] Milo, 47, says that Lanfranc caught him with his right hand by the hair, and brought him to his feet.

the young man continued to cry out in a distressing manner. When he heard of it the Archbishop said, 'I knew that unusual sadness would follow unusual joy, for the word of the prophet is true. "Before ruin the heart shall be exalted, and boasting comes before ignominy." Let him be taken back to the tomb of our Father Dunstan, and there let all make supplication that the same may cast out the wild demon by his power.'

In the morning he was accordingly seized by the strongest men, completely bound and carried to the tomb of the Saint, filling the church with shouts and cries. When ordered to say the creed, he blasphemed, and when ordered to say the Lord's Prayer he spat and cursed at every one. After remaining in this condition the whole of the day and the following night, he was carried to a cell where he remained under strict confinement for many days. When the attendants came to him he gazed upon them with wild eyes, and by making known their hidden sins, caused great shame to those whom he knew were sinful. But he was able to say nothing against those who had confessed their sins. He frequently called out the name of the other young monk and desired to see him. Lanfranc thereupon took this monk by the hand and accompanied by Albert the physician, and certain others, including Osbern, approached the cell of the demoniac. Before he could possibly see them, he cried out, 'Lanfranc, Lanfranc, and you Albert, and you, and you, and the young man in whose society I rejoice, I cannot see you, but I know you are coming to talk to me'. The Archbishop then presented the young man, but the demoniac completely failed to recognize him, and Lanfranc, who perceived that the demon was frustrated by the virtue of the confessional, said, 'Although you are a liar and a father of lies, you unwittingly own that this young man is not what you say he was, for by confession he is absolved from whatever he had committed by his own frailty or by diabolical assault'. Then the body of the demoniac was agitated by greater torments. This was followed by intermittent attacks, at one time he remained quiet and then raved with nonsense, sometimes weeping bitterly, and suddenly laughing ribaldly, at one time speaking softly, and then shouting vociferously.

At that time the new church was being built, and the body of S. Dunstan had to be transferred to a room attached to the refectory. It was being carried out in procession by the brothers singing a litany, and the demoniac, still bound to his bed, was brought to meet it. As soon as he saw the coffin, he cried out and blasphemed against God and all the saints, nor would he look at the body or hear the name of S. Dunstan. He burst some of his bonds and dragged the bed about with him. The seizures continued, and the evil spirit was seen moving in his body in the form of a tumour. Bishop Gundulf of Rochester [1] who was present said, 'Truly it jumps like a kitten'. The demoniac replied in the French tongue, 'Not like a kitten, but like a puppy'.[2] One of those present tried to put his hand on the tumour, and more blasphemous and unseemly threats followed.

At length the whole community repeatedly called on the name of S. Dunstan, and prostrated themselves on the earth. Then they carried the body of the saint, and the body of the demoniac, now half-dead, and placed them in the same room. A monk especially faithful to S. Dunstan was left behind to watch. This brother took S. Dunstan's staff and placed it on the madman, praying for the help of the saint. He at once became quiet, and after one more seizure remained as one dead. The monk unfastened his bonds, and the sufferer rose up and embraced the staff, and returned thanks to the monk and to S. Dunstan.

The story records an incident which cannot have been uncommon in the artificial life of a monastery, and among a number of highly emotional and often unbalanced young men. But it is of more importance as an indication of the necessity for reform in the morals of the monks, a point to which Eadmer [3] draws attention in his version, and as an illustration of the importance attached by Lanfranc to the confessional as a means of training young monks.

[1] Milo, 47. As Gundulf was not Bishop before 1077, and Christ Church was finished by 1077, the incident took place in 1077, if Milo's statement is correct.

[2] Eadmer, *Mem. of S. Dun.*, pp. 236–7.

[3] Ibid. p. 236.

XII

LANFRANC'S FRIENDS AND PUPILS AT BEC

THE reforms at Christ Church and Rochester were carried out by monks who had been trained at Bec and other Norman houses. The letters which passed between Lanfranc and Anselm were generally concerned with the training of the neophytes at Bec. Sometimes valuable gifts were brought over by the Archbishop's messengers.[1] When Lanfranc came to England he appears to have taken with him his nephew and namesake.[2] After a year or two spent at Christ Church the younger Lanfranc was sent back to Bec and committed to Anselm's care. In a letter [3] written soon after the return from Rome (1071) Lanfranc referred to his difficulties in England and to the depraved state of the country, and continued:

The letter which you sent through master Robert I have joyfully received, and more joyfully read. Indeed I cannot tell you with what great joy in reading I ponder over it, and in pondering over it, I read it again, because in it there is written that you have received with extreme happiness the dearest son of my brother, whom I love as my own soul; that you have conceived from this event greater trust in my love for you, and especially and above all, that the burden of the Prior's office, which formerly seemed unbearable to you, has been lightened by his coming. Concerning him I give you my brief and true opinion. If he has hitherto lived among heathen people, then I love him more than other unbelievers, and would do anything to advance him in this world. For these things I return thanks to God, to the lord Abbot and to you, because whatever I want I gather you always bring about for me, and for all who are loved by me.

But because on account of approaching the service of God, and

[1] Anselm (Migne, clviii), Lib. I; Epis. XII and XLI, Lib. II, Epis. I and II, cf. Lib. I, Epis. I. Anselm acknowledged the receipt of some gold to provide a chalice, but he returned the gold beaten into a chalice.

[2] Anselm, Lib. I, Epis. IV and VII, addressed to Gundulf in England, refers to the younger Lanfranc. The *Vita Gund.* (Migne, clix, col. 818-19) refers to the receipt of these letters by Gundulf at Christ Church.

[3] Lanfranc, Epis. XLIX.

especially on account of his youth, he is inwardly torn by many and various temptations, through the suggestions of evil spirits, and troubled within and without by promptings of the flesh, it is especially necessary that you make him a frequent participator in your conversation, and that you order, so often as possible, all those whose teaching can be healthy for him, to talk to him.

When he was leaving me, by my request I commanded him, and by my commands I requested him that during this year he should read nothing in the refectory or chapter-house or monastery, until he possessed a knowledge of the psalms and some experience of his order. But he has altogether despised my wish, and has obtained from you permission to read, by the excess of his tears. Therefore I had arranged to send a very sharp letter to him, but having seen your other letter, I have left out the bitter hastiness of mind which I had conceived against him.

But the nephew's delinquency was not allowed to pass entirely without rebuke. At the close of a letter to the younger Lanfranc and his friend Guido, in which warnings against spiritual pride were uttered, Lanfranc said: [1]

Since providentially, as I believe, you have loved each other in the world, I beseech that you will pray to God, that with His help you may love each other in that holy life which you have assumed. May the one be a solace to the other in tribulation. May the one receive from the life of the other an example of pious behaviour. Shew humility to all. Restrain your tongue from questioning any wholesome rebuke, and if any brother who speaks maliciously against you, shall refuse to refrain, after you have corrected him, cease to have any conversation with him. If any of the brothers extravagantly praise you for having given up for God's sake, parents, possessions and carnal delights, always look into your consciences, and realise that you are always sinners, and by constant prayers, ask that God will be propitious to your sins.

I had conceived great anger of mind against you, dearest nephew, because you apparently transgressed the command, the first I gave you concerning your order, but through the intervention of father Anselm, whom I desire to obey as God, I indulge this fault with a sincere heart, though I warn you not to offend again, because the more weightily I love a friend, the more anger do I conceive against him for a small fault. May Almighty God protect you by his grace, and mercifully absolve you from all your sins.

The kindly allusion to the special temptations of youth, suggests that Lanfranc's severity was due rather to hastiness

[1] Lanfranc, Epis. LIII (*c.* 1072).

of mind than want of sympathy. Severe though his restriction was, perhaps it was not altogether uncalled-for as a test of vocation in this special case. His nephew was devoted to books, and may have sought the monastic life mainly on account of the facilities which it offered for reading, so that some such test as Lanfranc proposed may well have been needed. As a discipline, Anselm thought it too severe, if not injurious. The more the young man's mind was filled with thoughts unconnected with himself and his immediate surroundings, the better would it be for his welfare. But Lanfranc seems to have estimated his nephew's character more accurately than the indulgent Prior. In later years, the younger Lanfranc, secretly and without consulting Anselm, who was then Abbot of Bec, accepted an invitation to go to Fontenelle as Abbot. This was directly contrary to the wishes of Anselm.[1] Yet the reports of Anselm upon his conduct and progress were consistently favourable.[2] He kept away from those who were to be shunned, so that no one in the community could find fault with him. He practised a kindly humility, with quiet attention to silence and prayer, so that his lovable disposition won the good opinion of all.[3] But there was one trouble which appeared to be sent by Providence, but which Anselm could not see without being moved to pity. For several months the younger Lanfranc was disturbed by headaches, so that the community had been compelled to do without his cheerful company, and all reading and study were impossible for him.[4]

At one time the younger Lanfranc's tutor at Bec was Gilbert Crispin, the author of the Life of Herluin, and who afterwards became Abbot of Westminster. Lanfranc wrote to him about his nephew.

The brothers, dearest brother, whom I sent to you especially to be taught letters, and to be instructed in good behaviour, I understand from the account of certain people, are being

[1] Anselm, Lib. II, Epis. XLII; cf. D'Achery, note to Lanfranc, Epis. XLVII.

[2] Anselm, Lib. I, Epis. XIX, XXIV, XXXI, LVII.

[3] Ibid., Epis. XXXI.

[4] Ibid.

honestly trained according to my will, wherefore I offer my thanks for your kindness. I desire that you will go on with what you have begun, and if you are deficient in admonition, then admonish. I commend especially to your love the beloved son of my brother—for he is indeed your brother—beseeching, as a most pleasant son, and as my brother ought to be besought by me, that you will love him with the great amiability of your soul, and that you will not fail to train him, with your strength, to a praiseworthy life. Indeed I have called him your brother because, truly, I wish and greatly desire him to be, for truly, your venerable mother, as I have been told, thought him worthy to be called her son, although she came of a most excellent stock, and he was born in a humble place. Doubtless she will receive her reward from him who said, 'Whoever humbles himself shall be exalted.' I send a cross with relics for you to look upon as you celebrate Mass, and this I desire to be a token of perpetual friendship between thee and him.

I am filled with joy because you say that the promise made in your boyhood has been preserved by the divine mercy through youth, and if you carry it on unbroken to the end, I have no doubt that you will be able to gaze securely upon a judgment terrible to others. May Almighty God deign to come into your heart through the inspiration of His Holy Spirit, so that you may always love me, as in boyhood and youth you used formerly to love me. May He himself bless you, and being propitiated, absolve you from all your sins.[1]

The younger Lanfranc died in 1091, soon after being made Abbot of Fontenelle.[2] The members of religious

[1] Giles, Epis. LI and D'Achery Epis. XLV (Migne, cl., col. 540, and col. 616, where the letter is wrongly numbered XLVI), address this letter to Gundulf, though D'Achery, col. 616, does so with hesitation, since it was addressed to 'G. . . .' Armitage-Robinson, *Gilbert Crispin*, p. 9, n. 4, thinks it was sent to Gilbert on the ground that Gundulf left Bec with Lanfranc; that the 'G' addressed is still 'in juventute', and because of the reference to his mother. The Dean's argument is confirmed by the following facts. Gundulf was originally ordained at Rouen. He vowed himself to the monastic life during a perilous voyage back from Jerusalem. The vow was fulfilled at Bec in the same year that Anselm arrived (c. 1059). Thus he was long past youth when Lanfranc became Archbishop, and he was not at Bec as a boy. In England Gundulf was Lanfranc's confidential agent for much important business. He could not have found time to become tutor to Lanfranc's nephew (cf. *Vita Gund.*, Migne, clix., col. 815–20). The Crispins were a noble family (cf. Ord.), so that Gilbert's mother was probably noble too, and Lanfranc's reference to a lady 'of a most excellent stock' would suit Gilbert's mother.

[2] D'Achery (Migne, cl., col. 617, quoting a manuscript Chron. of

houses were frequently overcome by sickness. The rigorous and unnatural life of the communities, the unhealthy and insanitary sites sometimes selected for the monasteries, and perhaps the weak constitutions of some of the inmates which may have originally caused them to seek the shelter of the cloistered life, all provide an explanation of the sickness frequently mentioned in the correspondence. Besides reporting on the illness of Lanfranc's nephew, Anselm referred to the case of Maurice, afterwards Bishop of London, who had been severed from an undesirable friend by the Archbishop and placed under Anselm's care at Bec. Anselm, while deferring to Lanfranc's judgement, pointed out that at least the love between the two friends was a virtue. He then referred to Maurice's headaches and asked that the physician Albert might be consulted on his behalf.[1] Gilbert, also, at one time suffered from attacks of illness, and called forth a letter of consolation from Lanfranc.

I perceive from your letter that you are greatly troubled by illness, on account of which I charge you not to be downcast, but to rejoice—rejoice in your Creator who has care for you, and offer up unwearied thanks because the Scripture says, ' Freely will I glory in mine infirmities ' and ' The Lord chastises every son whom He receives '. He would not indeed smite you with affliction in this world, unless after this world He intends to leave you free from affliction. Remember yourself, recall your most recent faults, and confess your sins. If you do this you will either obtain bodily health from God, or you may look for death, which is feared by others, without fear, and this will be for you the end of evil and the beginning of good.[2]

Lanfranc sent a drug[3] especially recommended by physicians for this infirmity, together with directions for its use. D'Achery says that this drug was given in cases of

S. Wandrille); Anselm, Lib. II, Epis. XLII, and D'Achery's note to Lanfranc, Epis. XLVII.

[1] Anselm, Lib. I, Epis. XXIV; Lanfranc, Epis. L. Several letters are concerned with Maurice's sickness and recovery, viz. Lib. I, Epis. XXV, XXVI, XXXII, XXXVI.

[2] Lanfranc, Epis. LII, addressed in Giles and Migne (Epis. XLVI) to Gundulf.

[3] *Diaprasium magnum,* to be taken like *Sylvestris nucis* three times daily.

phthisis.[1] But if Gilbert was suffering from this disease, his constitution was able to throw it off, or else the symptoms were misunderstood.

The Christ Church monk and writer Osbern [2] was trained at Bec. When Lanfranc sent for Osbern to assist with the revival of the Benedictine Rule at Christ Church, Canterbury, Anselm thought it necessary to refer to his faults,[3] but said that he felt parting from him severely, and when Osbern left Bec he wrote to the Prior of Canterbury, urging him to deal gently with him lest any harsh treatment might ruin the work of grace which had begun in his heart.[4]

Another young monk to whom Anselm became especially attached was Guido, the friend of the younger Lanfranc,[5] who while still a neophyte, went over to England. Anselm begged for his return.[6] Guido was probably the successor of Scolland at S. Augustine's, and in that case Anselm's wishes were not conceded. A similar disappointment was in store for him when Gilbert left Bec for England. Anselm wrote to Lanfranc asking that Gilbert might be allowed to return soon, but after a few years he was promoted to the Abbey of Westminster.[7]

The correspondence with Anselm was maintained to the end.[8] No sense of dignity on the part of the Archbishop hindered its freedom. On one occasion Lanfranc consulted Anselm about the practice of abstinence by monks. Anselm quoted a passage from the Epistles of S. John, and said that it exhorted abstinence for the sake of assisting the needy and not merely as a discipline.[9] On another occasion,

[1] Migne, cl., col. 616.

[2] To be distinguished from another Osbern who at Bec played practical jokes on Anselm, but was won over by the Prior's mildness. He died soon after (Eadmer, pp. 323–6).

[3] Anselm, Lib. I, Epis. LVII.

[4] Ibid., Epis. LVIII. This correspondence took place soon after Lanfranc's arrival in England. Lib. I, Epis. IV and VII, addressed to Gundulf when at Christ Church, before the younger Lanfranc returned to Normandy, refer to Osbern and the younger Lanfranc.

[5] Lanfranc, Epis. LIII.

[6] Anselm, Lib. I, Epis. LXVI.

[7] Ibid., Lib. II, Epis. XIII.

[8] Ibid.; Lib. II, Epis. LIII.

[9] 1 John iii. 17; Lib. I, Epis. XLI.

Anselm made the curious complaint that Lanfranc did not address him properly, at least not so as to please him.[1] This was an indication of Anselm's excessive humility. In the only copy of a letter from Lanfranc to Anselm which we possess, written while the latter was still Prior at Bec, the Archbishop addressed him as ' master, father, brother, friend ', while he simply alluded to himself as ' Lanfranc the sinner '.[2]

A similar confidence characterized some letters concerned with the literary work of the two friends. Lanfranc wrote asking for his own commentaries on the Epistles of S. Paul. Anselm sent them off and requested that they might be returned, or a copy of them, because he possessed no other copy than the one which Lanfranc desired.[3] At another time, Anselm sent over one of his own works,[4] and asked that if the Archbishop was too busy to read it, he would have it read to him.[5] Later on, Lanfranc found time to read the work, and returned it with his comments and certain corrections, begging Anselm not to take offence. The latter replied good-naturedly, and said that while he had adopted some of the corrections, he could not alter certain other points referring to the doctrine of the Trinity.[6]

In the correspondence between Lanfranc and the inmates at Bec there are few references to Herluin. In a letter to William, Abbot of Caen, Lanfranc suggested that Herluin and Anselm should be consulted before a Prior was appointed at Caen.[7] There is also no allusion to Herluin in Anselm's letters. However, there is on record a visit of Herluin to Lanfranc, which appears to have been undertaken solely with the object of gratifying the Abbot's desire to see his former Prior. On the way to England Herluin visited the wife of Count Eustace at Boulogne. When the ship had put to sea, a stranger was found among the company, and all

[1] Anselm, Lib. I, Epis. XLVIII.

[2] Lanfranc, Epis. XLIX.

[3] Anselm, Lib. I, Epis. LVII.

[4] In a Brit. Mus. MS. (XIV Burn, 286) this letter is included with Anselm's work the ' Monologion ' (cf. Longuemare, p. 217).

[5] Anselm, Lib. I, Epis. LXIII.

[6] Ibid., Epis. LXVIII.

[7] Lanfranc, Epis. LIV.

attempts to discover his identity failed. The sea was rough and the sailors thought they saw monsters in the rolling waves, but the stranger succeeded in pacifying them, when they immediately asked whether he had paid his fare or not. At Dover he disappeared. He was probably a guide sent by Lanfranc to take care of Herluin during the voyage. Canterbury was reached five days after landing at Dover. Gilbert says that the great Archbishop, who exercised apostolic authority in the churches 'beyond the seas', submitted himself to his former Abbot like any monk. Lanfranc took the second place everywhere, except when celebrating the Mass. He kissed Herluin's hand before receiving anything from him, unless Herluin snatched it away. He forgave delinquents their faults at Herluin's request. The longer the Abbot stayed at Lanfranc's palace, the greater was the crowd of prominent people, both clergy and laity, who came to it, and the more deference Lanfranc delighted to show him before them all. People marvelled, and especially the English, that the Archbishop of Canterbury should so humble himself before any one.[1]

In the year before Herluin died, Lanfranc paid his final visit to Bec when he crossed over to attend the dedication festivals at Caen and Bec. The ceremonies began at Bayeux and Évreux, where churches were dedicated to S. Mary. The distinguished company, which included William and Matilda, their sons Robert and William, together with a large assembly of bishops, nobles, clergy and commons,[2] then passed on to Caen, where Lanfranc's former abbey-church of S. Stephen's remained undedicated. The sister church of Holy Trinity, founded by Queen Matilda, had been dedicated shortly before the Conquest.[3] Some preliminary consecration of S. Stephen's possibly took place in 1073.[4] But if this was the case, the official dedication was left until

[1] *Gilbert Crispin*, pp. 100–1. Although written in a legendary strain there is nothing improbable in such a visit.

[2] Ord. v. 2 (ii, p. 305).

[3] 18th June 1066.

[4] The dates 1081 and 1086 are also given for the consecration; cf. Freeman, *N. C.* iii. 108, n. 2.

the autumn of 1077. The ceremony was performed by John, Archbishop of Rouen, assisted by Lanfranc.[1]

The Church of S. Mary at Bec had been completed four years before, and was formally occupied on the feast of All Saints (1073). Everything for the use of the brothers had by that time been gathered together, and on the eve of the festival, they left their old cells singing in procession, 'O beata Trinitas', to the new church, where the feast was joyously kept. On the next day while the Mass was being sung, the Abbot ordered a crowd of poor people to be gathered together in the new buildings and abundantly supplied with food and drink. As at Caen, this was a preliminary consecration until a more convenient day should arrive for the official ceremony.[2]

In 1077 Lanfranc either went straight to Bec on his arrival in Normandy,[3] before the dedication at Caen, or at least arrived at Bec some days before the ceremony took place there.[4] On reaching the slope on one of two hills between which the monastery lay, he took off the episcopal ring from his finger, and while he remained in the Abbey did not replace it, except at the celebration of the mysteries.[5] Memories of former days were racing through his brain as he gazed down upon the beloved haunts by the stream, and the sight of his old master coming to meet him revived earlier feelings of filial respect, for we are told that when he approached the Abbot, who was bent down with age, Lanfranc attempted to kneel on the ground in order to kiss him. The Abbot in his turn tried to do the same, and some moments were spent by the two grey-headed men in this contest of humility, though in the end neither succeeded in doing what he desired.

After he had embraced many old friends, Lanfranc assembled all the brothers in the cloister, young men, old men and the boys, and there interviewed them singly,

[1] Orderic says that Thomas of York was present.

[2] Milo, 22. Not reported by Gilbert.

[3] Ibid.: 'veniens, primo accessit ad ipsum monasterium'.

[4] Two phases of the visit are indicated by Gilbert, p. 105.

[5] Milo, 22. Not reported in Gilbert.

exhorting each one according to his condition. He sat at table with the brothers on either hand, and shared with them the same cup and platter.[1] He had come back as a monk to his monastery, and wanted to be treated as a monk, for in church he was unwilling that an episcopal throne should be prepared for him. He went into the Prior's stall, saying that he was formerly Prior, and had not given up the office.[2]

Gilbert then records a curious incident. Lanfranc was seemingly unwilling to consecrate the church, perhaps from the desire to take his old place as Prior of the community on the day of its great festival. But under the compulsion of all, and being indeed prepared to give way to them, he sought permission to go to the court, in order to ascertain the King's will. He found the King and talked the matter over with him. A day for the consecration was fixed, and he returned, charged not merely with the name of one who was to perform the ceremony, but with orders to do it himself.[3]

The day of the dedication, 23rd October, so long expected,[4] remained vividly in the recollection of those who were present as a time of singular happiness and jubilant exultation. It was within the octave of S. Luke, and S. Luke's summer shone out with all its autumn beauty on that clear and smiling morning. The Abbot had been indisposed for eight days previously, but owing to the mercy of God he was well again. The King, who was detained by business, could not be present, and Queen Matilda, though unwillingly, was also kept away by royal duties.[5] But a goodly assembly of bishops, abbots, clergy and nobles came together from all the neighbouring regions, among them being Odo of Bayeux, Gilbert of Lisieux, Gilbert of Evreux, Robert of Séez, and Arnold of Le Mans.[6] Large gifts, including those sent by

[1] Gilbert, p. 105.

[2] Milo, 22. Not in Gilbert's account.

[3] Gilbert, p. 105.

[4] Gilbert, p. 106; *Annals of Bec* (Porée, 1883), p. 3; Milo, 23; Robt. of Torigny in the Chron. of William of Jum. But in his own Chronicle (p. 41) Robert gives 22nd Nov., and this date was copied by Ralph de Diceto, i, p. 210.

[5] Gilbert, p. 106, and Milo, 23.

[6] *Ann. Bec.* (Porée), p. 3.

William and Matilda,[1] were handed over to the monastery by the illustrious men and women from France, Normandy and England.

A procession was formed for the commencement of the great act of the day—the dedication of the Church of S. Mary by the Archbishop, who had laid the second stone [2] of the building, after Herluin had laid the foundation stone,[3] sixteen years before.[4] The voices of the choristers were scarcely heard on account of the noise of the people thronging around, but at so great a gathering, no one felt any offence, for the disturbance did not hinder the proceedings. When the procession was over, the bishops were scarcely able to enter the church without collision, for the people, after breaking open all the doors, rushed in—though without injury to any one—so far as the space of the church would admit. An altar to be consecrated was provided for each of the visiting bishops, but the high altar was left for the Archbishop. A great celebration was made throughout the whole church, accompanied by a certain pious rivalry. Even the choristers could hardly hear their own voices on account of the multitude of those who were crying out. Many in their jubilation did not know what they said, and paid very little attention to what they were singing. The older monks, who could not be present on account of the crowd, fulfilled the solemnity of the occasion with tears and devotion of heart. The festivities closed with a great banquet which went on far into the night. Crowds of people kept on refilling the tables of the refectory. A multitude of visitors was accommodated, not only in and around Bec, but at distant places, which were supplied with provisions by the monastery. The feasting was maintained for several days. The Abbot repeatedly asked the servants, who went hither and thither, what they were doing, and whether the supplies were holding out, and when he heard from them that they abounded, repeatedly said,

[1] Gilbert, p. 106; Milo, 23.
[2] Ibid.
[3] Gilbert, p. 106; Mirac. de Sanct. Nich. Evreux, MS. Lat. 96.
[4] Gilbert, p. 106.

'What shall I return to the Lord for all His benefits to me?'[1]

Lanfranc did not protract his visit. On the third day he took his farewell from the brothers.

All burst into tears, and the boys could not be consoled. Wisely he hastened his departure, so that they might restrain their weeping. The venerable Herluin, who loved him above all mortals, and was beloved by him, went with his departing friend for two miles—the friend who would never return to his sight in this life. What bitterness of heart! What tears at the final farewell, at the final parting! After his return to the monastery he sat alone in his cell, with the one who was most familiar to him, and giving vent to his falling tears said, 'Lord now lettest thou thy servant depart in peace since mine eyes have seen, for that I might see him before I died very greatly did I wish, and constantly did I pray to Thee for this. What I desired is fulfilled. Now will thy servant come to Thee happy, at whatever hour shall please Thee.' So he ceased speaking, but he was not able to check the flow of his tears, until the brother who was speaking with him could stand it no longer, and began a discourse about another matter.[2]

Herluin's health failed rapidly after the dedication festival. On the following 19th August he was unable to rise from his bed. He could take no food and was unable to sleep. Three days later he gave orders for the last rites to commence. The psalms were sung amid the sobs of the assembled community, and at the confession he and they broke forth into tears. After this ceremony was over and the brothers had left with his blessing, he instantly checked any sign of emotion on the part of those who waited upon him. On the Sunday morning Anselm had stolen quietly into the cell, but not without Herluin's notice, for at the hour of Matins he invited the Prior to say the office with him. The host was obtained from a priest who was celebrating on Herluin's behalf, the brothers were assembled again,

[1] Gilbert, p. 107.

[2] Ibid., p. 108. Porée, *Hist. de l'Abbaye du Bec*, i, p. 141, says that Lanfranc revisited Normandy in 1082. His signature is found on a charter, given in favour of Holy Trin. and S. Steph., Caen, in that year. Porée quotes Gallia Christiana, xi, cols. 68, 72. He says that Lanfranc also signed a charter for the foundation of the Abbey of Lessay, 1056–64 (Gall. Christ. xi, col. 224).

according to the custom of a Benedictine house,[1] and were finally dismissed by him with signs and nods. But Herluin lingered throughout the whole day, and towards evening began to be delirious. 'Why do our lords not come?' he said, and Abbot Roger, although not quite grasping his meaning, humoured him by saying that they were in the cloister praying for him, and would come when he desired their presence. At length after Vespers he quietly passed away on the evening of 26th August. The people from the neighbouring villages attempted to break into the monastery and through the cloisters, but were restrained by Abbot Roger. The funeral sermon was preached by Gilbert, Bishop of Évreux.[2]

After the death of Herluin, when Anselm became Abbot of Bec, he paid a visit to England, in order to do some business connected with the property of Bec in England. Of course the two old friends met, and had much discussion upon matters of interest to them both. Anselm was at once made to feel at home, not only with the Archbishop, but with the whole community. He went among them and 'became one of them'. Eadmer, who was then a boy at Christ Church, vividly remembered Anselm's kindness to him on that occasion. Each day, either in the chapter or the cloister, Anselm gave a beautiful discourse. One of these, on charity, is reported by Eadmer.[3]

One day Lanfranc consulted Anselm upon a point which had long troubled him. Eadmer says that the Archbishop had not yet been able to accustom himself to some of the religious practices of the English. Some customs he had already changed and, through the ecclesiastics appointed by him in different parts of the country, was investigating the validity of the cultus of saints beatified by local Saxon feeling. At Evesham, Abbot Walter, Lanfranc's nominee, doubted the sanctity of the relics of S. Wistan, and claiming the authority of Lanfranc, placed them in the fire as a test. According to the tale S. Wistan was vindicated, for when the head of the saint was removed from the fire it was found to

[1] Lanfranc, *Benedictine Decreta*, cap. XXIII

[2] Gilbert, pp. 108–10.

[3] Eadmer, *Vit Ans.*, pp. 348–9.

be perspiring.[1] Lanfranc was particularly doubtful about the case of his predecessor Alphege, who was indeed a good man. The English counted him not only among the saints, but among the martyrs, whereas he died not through confessing the name of Christ, but because he refused to redeem himself by a large sum of money, which could only be raised by the spoliation of his people.

Anselm replied that it was plain that he who did not fear to die rather than commit a light offence against God, would still less fear to die rather than anger God by a serious sin. It was clearly, in his opinion, a more serious offence to deny Christ than to anger an earthly lord by refusing to gain freedom for himself at the cost of a sum of money raised upon his men. But that which was less Alphege had declined to do, and still less would he have denied Christ, if He had been the cause for which the mad lord had threatened death. Whence it was given to be understood with what wonderful strength his breast was possessed of righteousness, for he preferred rather to give his life than, having spurned charity, to scandalize those nearest to him. Wherefore that woe was far from him, which the Lord threatened against him through whom scandal arose. Not without merit was he counted among the martyrs, he who was truly reported to have undergone death for so great a righteousness. The blessed John the Baptist was credited and venerated by the whole Church of God, not because he was killed for refusing to deny Christ, but because he was not willing to allow truth to be silenced. Moreover, when, by the testimony of the sacred word, as Lanfranc well knew, Christ was called truth and righteousness, then he who died for truth and righteousness, died for Christ. He who died for Christ was, by the witness of the Church, held to be a martyr. The blessed Alphege suffered as much for righteousness as the blessed John for truth. Why therefore should there be any more ambiguity about the martyrdom of the one, than of the other, when an equal justification detained both in the passion of death? So far as he could see, reason itself showed that these arguments were reason-

[1] *Chron. Evesham* (Rolls), p. 335.

able, but it was open to Lanfranc's wisdom, if he felt otherwise, to correct him, and to demonstrate his view to the Church of God.

Lanfranc replied that he recognized the subtle perspicacity, and strongly approved and venerated the perspicacious subtlety of his mind, and, instructed by his powerful reasoning, said that he would henceforth worship and venerate from his heart the blessed Alphege as a truly great and glorious martyr of Christ.

The Archbishop kept his word. He placed the name of Alphege in a calendar drawn up for Christ Church and ordered the story of Alphege's life and passion to be studiously put together, and when it was written, gave orders, not only that it should be read aloud, but put to music. The monk Osbern had charge of both the biography and the musical composition.[1] The worship of the martyr received such signal attention at Canterbury, that no martyr in those parts was glorified in the same way.[2]

The story brings into strong contrast the habits of thought of the two men. Lanfranc's legal mind, bound by loyalty to an accurate interpretation of tradition, was fearful of demeaning itself by breaking the rules, even from a generous motive. But Anselm's kindly charity, assisted by philosophic insight and logical clearness, enabled him to penetrate to the real merits of the case, and to brush aside the legal sophistries of the traditionalist, without surrendering principle. Like all purely critical thinkers, Lanfranc was not quite sure of himself, but the constructive mind of Anselm perceived by intuition, as much as by reasoning, the inwardness of the case. But that Lanfranc was open to conviction on the question of the Saxon saints is proved by another story. On hearing of the cure of a boy at the tomb of Aldhelm at Malmesbury, Lanfranc ordered Aldhelm to be worshipped as a saint throughout England, and ordered a fair to be held on his anniversary.[3]

[1] Hamilton in Malmesbury, *G. P.* (Rolls), p. 33, n. 2, says that Osbern wrote the life in 1080.

[2] Eadmer, *Vit. Ans.*, pp. 351–2.

[3] Malmes., *G. P.*, p. 428.

Before leaving Canterbury, Anselm was one night returning to bed after Matins, when he found in his possession a gold ring. After making the sign of the cross, lest it should be a trick of the devil, he found that the ring was no illusion. He showed it to all in the monastery who were in responsible office, and when he failed to find the owner, sold it for the benefit of the brethren. When Lanfranc heard the story, he remarked that it was a sign that Anselm would succeed him as Archbishop of Canterbury.[1]

In the year 1080 Lanfranc received a visit in England from Mainer, Abbot of S. Evroult, another Norman friend. In earlier years some disagreement had arisen between them.[2] But in 1077, at the consecration of S. Stephen's, Caen, he sent Mainer a present of twenty-four pounds of English money and two marks of gold. Later on another present of forty pounds was sent from Canterbury.[3] So, when Mainer came to England, to accept an invitation often given to him by the King, he did not fail to visit Lanfranc, to whom, says Orderic, he was greatly attached.[4]

[1] Milo, 51.

[2] Cf. *supra*, p. 34.

[3] Ord. iii, 12 (ii. pp. 128–9)

[4] Ord. vi, 5 (iii, p. 18

XIII

PRESTIGE IN IRELAND, SCOTLAND, AND NORMANDY

LANFRANC has been described as 'Patriarch of the West'.[1] There are several letters in the correspondence which supply foundation for the flattering address. In 1073 or 1074 the Archbishop received a communication from Donnell, the 'Bishop of Ireland'.[2] The Irish Bishop asked for information and instruction on certain points of doctrine relating to the reception of the body and blood of Christ by infants, and although Lanfranc replied at some length, with quotations from the Old and New Testaments and from Augustine, he apologized for giving an inadequate answer because the Irish messenger was unable to wait until the necessary books had been procured. Certain other points, relating to secular literature, Lanfranc declined to answer, on the ground that he had long given up such studies, because they were not compatible with his pastoral functions.

In 1074 another letter arrived from Gothric, the King of Dublin,[3] and the clergy and people of the church in that city, asking that the bearer of the letter, a monk[4] named Patrick, a man of recognized standing and culture, well-learned, orthodox and devout, might be made their Bishop.[5] Patrick was consecrated by Lanfranc in S. Paul's, London, and signed a declaration of obedience to Lanfranc and his successors.[6] He took back with him to Ireland, two letters

[1] Hook, *Archbishops*, ii. 149. Gervase (ii, p. 318) speaks of Lanfranc's influence in Ireland, Scotland and Wales. Cf. *supra*, p. 182.

[2] Lanfranc, Epis. XXXV; cf. *Chartularies of S. Mary's Abbey* (Rolls), ii, p. 249. The bishop, who is called Dunanus, died in 1074.

[3] *Chart. of S. Mary's, Dublin*, ii. p. 249.

[4] Lanfranc, Epis. XLIII.

[5] Ibid., Epis. XXXIX.

[6] *Chart. of S. Mary's*, ii. p. 249. Cf. Giles, i. p. 356.

from the Archbishop, one addressed to Gothric and the other to Turlough, the suzerain of Gothric.[1]

Although the Archbishop had received a good report of him, he urged Gothric to preserve his loyalty to the holy Roman Church, to live a life consistent with his faith, and to rule justly. He drew his attention to the abuse of the law of marriage, which was common among the Irish and Scots of that day,[2] as it had been in England in former times. Three abuses are mentioned—unions with their own near relations or those of deceased wives; divorce on account of mere whim; and the exchange of wives. Gothric was advised to seek the counsel of Patrick the new Bishop, and to be guided by him.

The letter to Turlough reflects the troubles in East Anglia of 1074, when the rebellion of Ralph and Roger was brewing. Lanfranc said that God sent no greater blessing than when He put the government of souls and bodies in the hands of those who love peace and justice, especially when temporal power was entrusted to good kings. From this source came peace, discord was lulled and the forms of religion were observed. These benefits the Irish people secured when Turlough was appointed to rule by Providence. The Archbishop placed every confidence in him because of the good report of him which had been brought by Patrick. But the King's attention was drawn to irregular marriages, episcopal consecrations and baptism. People were divorcing their lawful wives without due cause, and were marrying either complete strangers, or the relations of their divorced wives, or those whom other men had deserted in a similar

[1] *Chartularies of S. Mary's, Dublin*, ii. p. 250. Lanfranc makes no distinction between Turlough and the sub-king of Dublin. He addresses Turlough as 'magnifico Hiberniae regi' (Epis. XLIV) and Gothric as 'glorioso Hiberniae regi' (Epis. XLIII). Possibly Lanfranc was unacquainted with the details of the Irish polity which divided the country into a number of kingships comprising local or sub-kingships. The date of both letters (1074) is fixed by the Chartularies.

[2] Cf. letter of Gregory VII to Lanfranc (1073) (Jaffé, *Mon. Greg.*, p. 520) in which the Pope urged Lanfranc to warn the Scots not to desert or sell their wives.

way. Episcopal consecrations were being carried out by one bishop, not by the canonical number, and several bishops were being consecrated to the same rural or town see. Infants were being baptized without the consecrated chrism. The bishops received payment for administering the rite of ordination.

In 1084 Patrick and his suite were drowned in the Irish sea.[1] A monk of Patrick's community named Donagh was elected by Turlough and the bishops, clergy and people of Ireland, and was sent to Lanfranc for consecration. The consecration took place at Canterbury in the next year,[2] and Donagh made a profession of obedience to Lanfranc and his successors.[3]

The Irish letters, besides supplying interesting details of the episcopal organization of Ireland, reveal the widespread influence of Lanfranc's reputation as an ecclesiastic and scholar whose orthodoxy and learning made him an obvious referee upon uncertain points of doctrine and practice. They also bear witness to the predominance of Canterbury in popular imagination as the chief metropolitan church in the British isles. Although York was within more easy reach of Dublin, the messengers were not sent to Thomas. But these letters cannot be regarded as evidence for any recognition of the metropolitan at Canterbury by the Irish Church outside the city of Dublin and the region ruled over by Turlough. The Church of Dublin represented rather the Danish immigrants who had established themselves in that city, than the tribesmen and churchmen of the native community. The greater part of Ireland still observed the old methods and practices of the days when Irish bishops were little more than presbyters set apart to perform episcopal functions, subject to the authority of the monastic community to which they belonged, and possessing no recognized territorial status. Lanfranc's reference to irregular episcopal consecration shows that the Danish community had been influenced by this system, and while

[1] 10th October.

[2] *Chartularies of S. Mary's, Dublin*, ii. p. 250.

[3] Giles, *Op. Lan.*, i, p. 356.

the appeal of the Church of Dublin to him may have been caused by racial rivalry and the exclusiveness of the Danish conquerors towards the rest of Ireland, it also implies that it had become doubtful of the orthodoxy of the native Irish Church.[1]

Freeman has pointed out that the relations with Dublin were partly inspired by William, who was beginning to look towards Ireland as a field for further enterprise, and that he was anxious to occupy that country by peaceful means if possible.[2] We have no evidence, beyond the casual allusion of one chronicler, that the King had any such ambition.[3] That Ireland might be regarded as a lawful field for occupation by William would have been a natural consequence upon the connexion of the family of Godwin with that country, and might have been prompted by an apprehension lest the sons of Harold should use it as a base of operations against his rule in England. But while this danger was in existence we read of no attempt made by William to counter it by an expedition to Ireland. At the same time the correspondence of Lanfranc with the Church of Dublin undoubtedly marks the beginning of the policy which ended in the establishment of Norman barons in Ireland under Henry II.

An even more definite testimony to Lanfranc's commanding position in the west is forthcoming in the letter of the Archbishop to Queen Margaret of Scotland. Margaret

[1] Lanfranc's exhortation on the marriage customs might also have been applied to conditions throughout the whole of Ireland, and, on a cursory reading of the letters, appears to show that the Danes in Dublin had completely embraced the customs of the native Irish. But these irregularities had been prevalent among the Danes in all western lands a generation or two earlier. They were found in Normandy and East Anglia, as well as in Ireland and Scotland, and although the Irish and Scots were equally casual in their conception of the law of marriage, the existence of these customs in Dublin during Lanfranc's time proves nothing more than that the Church and people of Dublin had not yet abandoned the ancient practice of 'Danish marriage'. Thomas of York consulted him on the question of divorce (Lan., Epis. XIII).

[2] Freeman, *N. C.* iv. pp. 526–30.

[3] Sax. Chron. (Peterborough), 1087.

was the daughter of that Edward the Atheling who had come back to England from Hungary, at the request of the Confessor and his Witan during the latter days of Edward's rule, as a candidate for the English crown. She was therefore a granddaughter of Edmund Ironsides, and a sister of the Atheling who figured in the Conqueror's reign. Any natural antipathy towards a representative of him who had displaced her father's house from the succession, and prevented her brother's election as King of England, does not appear to have entered her mind. She was brought up at the court of the saintly Stephen of Hungary, and seems never to have developed any patriotic feeling for England, or family pride in the succession of England. While in Hungary she acquired that veneration for the organization and life of the holy Roman Church of the West, which she was now so successfully introducing into Scotland, as the consort of Malcolm Canmore. Her application to Lanfranc [1] for assistance was part of the policy which rapidly brought into Scotland not only the organization of the Western Church, but several leading churchmen from the south. Eadmer, the Canterbury writer, and firm supporter of Lanfranc, was nominated for the see of S. Andrews, and on his refusal, after some delay, Turgot, a member of the Church of Durham, who had been the Queen's confessor, became the first Catholic Archbishop of S. Andrews (1109).[2] The nomination of Eadmer was doubtless influenced by the connexion established by Lanfranc between Canterbury and Scotland before his death (1089), although the nomination of bishops for Scotland had been left in the hands of the Archbishop of York at the settlement of 1072.

In his beautiful *Life of S. Margaret,* Turgot, playing on the meaning of the Queen's name, speaks of her as a pearl. 'A pearl she was to me, to Christ, to us all,' and Lanfranc, like all who had communications with her, was infected by the Queen's saintliness and simplicity. In none of his epistles was the Archbishop moved to write in so spiritual

[1] Lanfranc, Epis. XLI.

[2] David Patrick, *Statutes of the Scottish Church* (Scottish History Society, liv), p. xvii. This was after the death of Margaret (1093).

a tone as in the letter sent to Queen Margaret. He uses language peculiarly like that of Turgot, especially with reference to the influence of the Holy Spirit on the life and conversation of Margaret. At the same time a spirit of humility lay beneath all Lanfranc's outward peremptoriness of attitude and action. It only required a correspondent like Margaret or Anselm to bring it to the surface.

Lanfranc, the unworthy Primate of the holy Church of Canterbury, to Margaret, the illustrious Queen of Scots greeting and benediction.

The small compass of a letter is insufficient for declaring with what joy you have filled my heart, O Queen, well pleasing to God, by your excellent epistles which you have sent me. With what pleasantness do your words flow forth, proceeding from the inspiration of the Divine Spirit. I believe indeed that what you have written is said not by you but for you (by Divine inspiration). Truly by your mouth has He spoken who said to His disciples 'Learn of Me, for I am meek and lowly of heart'; from this teaching of Christ it has proceeded that, born of royal ancestors, royally educated and nobly wedded to a noble King, you choose me, a man of foreign extraction, vile, ignoble, involved in sins, as your father, and pray me to consider you as my spiritual daughter. I am not what you think me to be, but may I become so! Lest you remain deceived, pray for me that I may be worthy as a father to pray to God and to be heard for you. May there be between us an interchange of prayers and benefits. I bestow little indeed, but I hope to receive much myself. Hence, therefore, may I be your father and you my daughter. I send to your illustrious husband and to yourself our dearest brother Master Goldewin and two other brethren, according to your request, because he himself would not be able to accomplish alone what is requisite for God's service and your own. And I beg and intreat that you may endeavour quickly and perfectly to complete what you have undertaken for God and your own souls. If you are able, or are desirous to finish your work by means of others, we greatly desire these our brethren to return to us, because they are very necessary to us in the offices of our Church. Your will, however, be done, since in all, and for all things, we desire to obey you. May the Almighty God bless you, and mercifully absolve you from all your sins.[1]

The arrival of Turgot at the court of Margaret was not an isolated incident creating a relationship between the two Churches. An application was made by Earl Paul of the Orkneys, to Thomas of York, for the consecration of the

[1] Hook's translation (*Archbishops*, ii, p. 152).

bearer of the letter to the episcopate of those islands. The application was made to Thomas partly because he occupied the metropolitan see nearest to the Orkneys. However, the logic of facts made necessary a reference of the case to Lanfranc, and once again, as throughout the whole course of the York controversy, the actual circumstances of the two primates gave Lanfranc a *de facto* predominance. The only suffragan of York was the palatine Bishop of Durham. Thomas was therefore compelled to apply to Lanfranc for assistance with the consecration. He asked that the Bishops of Worcester and Chester might be sent to assist with the consecration of Earl Paul's nominee. It is significant that these were two of the bishops over whom Thomas had originally claimed authority.[1] But he promised that if permission were given he would not, on any future occasion, regard the visit as a precedent for reviving his claims. Lanfranc accordingly wrote to Wulfstan of Worcester and Peter of Chester, ordering them to appear at Thomas's cathedral city, and sent verbal instructions for the date of the visit.[2] But in view of the possibility of a revival of Thomas's claim in the future, he warned the two bishops carefully to preserve the copies of Thomas's letter in their archives. It is also significant that Lanfranc referred only to Thomas's right to consecrate for the Orkneys, and not for the whole of Scotland, as had been agreed.

Lanfranc, by the grace of God, Archbishop of the holy Church of Canterbury, to his venerable brothers Wulfstan, Bishop of Worcester, and Peter, Bishop of Chester, greeting.

Our venerable brother Thomas, Archbishop of York, has intimated to us that a certain clerk from the Orkneys has come to him, whom he states to have been chosen to the episcopate of that country, at the nomination and recommendation of Earl Paul, and since, of ancient custom the right of consecrating the

[1] Milo, 31.

[2] Lanfranc, Epis. XV. Written after 1075 (cf. Milo, 43, 'Post haec', i. e. council of 1075) and before 1086, the date when Robert succeeded Peter at Chester. The Saxon Chron. (*Lat. Acta*) gives 1077 as the date of the letter, although this may be equivalent to 1076 in our reckoning, cf. *supra*, p. 116, n. 1. Haddan and Stubbs, ii. p. 162, follow Wilkins, who quotes a MS. (Cott. Vesp. E. 4), which gives the date 1073, Indiction XI.

bishops of those islands is his, he has begged me to send him two of my suffragans that they may be able with him to celebrate so great a sacrament. We intreat and commend you, therefore, to proceed thither without any delay, and in pursuance of our order, as is proper, complete so solemn a mystery. For it is not fitting that one coming hither for consecration, and with all humility requesting it, should, through want of coadjutors, depart from such a realm as this unconsecrated. The term of this consecration the bearer of these presents will point out. And that you may not be solicitous in thinking that either he or his successors should from this precedent, at some time or other, endeavour to seize prelatical jurisdictions over your churches, having regard to the future, I have taken care to transmit to you the letter which he sent to me, and I charge that this, as well as the present which I send to you, be preserved among the archives of your church for future reference.[1]

While Lanfranc was extending the influence of Canterbury by means of his correspondence with Ireland and Scotland, he was constantly consulted by high ecclesiastics in Normandy. The letters to the Archbishop of Rouen show that he found great difficulty, amid a host of duties in England, in maintaining a frequent correspondence with the churchmen of Normandy,[2] and the difficulty was increased by the fact that it was not easy to find trustworthy bearers of the letters. But whenever an opportunity for writing occurred, and a suitable messenger was forthcoming, Lanfranc dealt faithfully with correspondence covering business of all kinds.

In 1067 Lanfranc had declined the see of Rouen in favour of John, the Bishop of Avranches. Soon after his appointment to Canterbury, John consulted him upon certain points of ritual and ceremonial.[3] Lanfranc agreed with John's suggestions concerning the wearing of the stole, apparently with special reference to the consecration of a church. But he did not agree that the Bishop should on that occasion

[1] Hook's translation (*Archbishops*, ii. p. 153).

[2] Lanfranc, Epis. XVIII, XIX.

[3] Epis. XVI. Lanfranc's reply makes no reference to the disturbances at Rouen (1073), which occupy space in Epis. XVII and XVIII. The date of Epis. XVI is therefore probably 1071–2, after Lanfrancis return from Rome (1071). The opening paragraph suggests a recent parting from Normandy.

wear the Mass vestments and chasuble, except during the celebration of the mysteries. He expressed amazement [1] that John regarded this usage as an episcopal privilege. He could not remember ever to have seen it done. He had been present at the consecration of churches in different dioceses, and had taken special care to notice what took place. Although there were some differences in detail, yet all were robed in the cope without the chasuble, until the celebration of the Mass began. This was the practice observed by the Pope when he consecrated a church at Remiremont.[2]

A second question was concerned with the ritual at the ordination of a sub-deacon. John contended that the handing over of the maniple [3] was a special feature in that rite, and should be reserved for the sub-deacon only. Lanfranc asked him to quote an authority for this usage. He had indeed heard of the practice, but he could not remember whether it had the sanction of canonical authority or not. On the other hand, many held that the maniple was part of the vestment of all officiants, like the alb and the amice. In monastic communities the lay brothers were robed with the alb, and by an old custom of the fathers, carried the maniple.[4] In the codes concerning episcopal rank, which he had collected from various quarters, customs on this point apparently varied. In some cases the sub-deacon received from the archdeacon the urceolus with aquamanile and manutergium. In other cases the aquamanile only was allowed.[5] But John confused the aquamanile or manile with the maniple, and Lanfranc asked for his authority for thus placing the grant of the maniple between that of the urceolus and manutergium, and also for insisting that the

[1] *Valde stupui.*

[2] D'Achery (Migne, cl, col. 586). During the synod of Rheims (1049). Not far from the Moselle in the Vosges Mountains.

[3] D'Achery: 'quae sinistro aptatur brachio, ad humores e naribus atque oculis defluentes extergendos, accipitur'.

[4] But this custom had been abolished by Pascal II after the Council of Poitiers. D'Achery (Migne, cl, col. 586).

[5] The urceolus was a large vessel containing water, which was poured into the aquamanile for cleansing the hands at the celebration of mass. The manutergium was a small towel.

maniple was handed to the sub-deacon by the archdeacon, and the other things by the bishop, and for interpreting the maniple in this way. He declared that the fourth council of Carthage was quite ambiguous on the points raised by John. The sub-deacon did not receive the imposition of hands at his ordination. The ritual acts consisted in the reception of the empty chalice and paten from the bishop, while the urceolus with water, and the aquamanile and manutergium were received from the archdeacon. But the symbolism was quite clear. It had reference to the sub-deacon's duties as a 'server', according to the epistle of Isidore on ordination rites. It was the duty of the sub-deacon to carry the chalice and paten to the altar, and to minister to the deacons.[1] He also held the other vessels and handed them to the bishop and priest and deacon for washing their hands at the consecration.

The course of the reformers was no more easy in Normandy than in England. The sequence of events is not altogether clear. At an ecclesiastical synod held at Rouen, the Archbishop of Rouen passed decrees against the married clergy. An uproar broke out, and John was assailed with stones, and compelled to fly from the Church crying out 'O! Lord, the heathen are come into thine inheritance'.[2]

A contemporary writer, who was a member of the community of S. Ouen at Rouen, records another disturbance which took place on the festival of S. Ouen in 1073.[3] It was customary for the Archbishop to celebrate the mass on that day, and he had never allowed any other duty to keep him away from the festival or to cause him to be unpunctual for it. On this occasion the Conqueror was either at Rouen or in the neighbourhood, and summoned the Archbishop and Nicholas, the Abbot of S. Ouen into his presence. John sent word that he would be back in time for the festal celebration, and the service was delayed. But after a time, when the monks calculated that he would be

[1] *Levitis*.

[2] Ord. iv. 9 (ii, p. 241).

[3] Migne, cl., cols. 587–90. The date is fixed by *Chron. S. Steph. Cad.*, Duchesne (Maseres, *Hist. Ang.* 1807, p. 359) and Matt. Paris, *Hist. Maj.* ii, p. 11.

already on the road, they began the office, lest by further delay indignity should be offered to their patron saint. A large part of the service had been recited when the Archbishop appeared. He at once gave way to resentment, abused the monks and excommunicated them, drove the Abbot of Séez, who was celebrating, from the altar, and prepared to complete the office himself. The brothers were divided into two sections, influenced on the one side by respect for the episcopal dignity, and on the other by jealousy for the prestige of their house. But one of their number went up into the tower, rang the great bell of the church, and rushed out shouting that the Archbishop was about to transfer the glebe of S. Ouen's to the cathedral church of Rouen. The monks came out of their cells, and seizing swords, axes and anything that came to hand, broke into the church. John fled into the cloister and barricaded himself with forms and chairs. The disturbance was quelled by the appearance of a vapoury cloud above the resting-place of the saints in the sanctuary, which overawed the unruly monks, but the Archbishop was not safe until the Sheriff of Rouen arrived.[1]

A report of the dispute with the monks was sent by John of Rouen to Lanfranc. In his reply the Archbishop of Canterbury condemned the behaviour of the monks as an unwarrantable refusal to show deference to the episcopal authority.[2] Although a reformer on Cluniac lines, Lanfranc

[1] These stories reflect, in the one case, the resentment of the seculars against the new marriage rules, and in the other the resentment of the regulars against the tightening up of episcopal control, which on this occasion appears to have created apprehension lest the monastic lands should be secularized. The trouble arose from the viciousness of the ecclesiastical situation. The Church was being reformed on monastic lines, but by bishops who, though frequently monks, were also dignitaries attached to the secular sphere of the Church's organization. Because the monastic houses formed part of the diocesan organization, the regulars frequently found themselves compelled to submit to interference from the bishops whom they regarded as mere secular clergy. Thus the seculars resented the reforms because the bishops were monks, and the regulars resented them because the monks who had charge of reform were bishops.

[2] Lanfranc, Epis. XVII.

showed the same care for the episcopal authority in Normandy as in England.

Having seen your letter in which you have been careful to make clear the undignified and proud rashness of these wretched men against the Lord and the episcopal dignity, I sorrowed as I ought to sorrow, and I could not rejoice in the same sorrow. I grieved because a thing has happened to your excellence, which we do not read ever occurred to a bishop before, from the time of the pagans onwards.[1]

After the dispatch of this letter by the hand of Robert, a monk of the house of Bec, Lanfranc received two more communications from John, one by the hand of John's chaplain, Hugh, and the other by a layman in the service of Queen Matilda.[2] These details are mentioned in the Archbishop's second letter to John, and he continued:

In both (letters) the contents were the same, in both you show forth most clearly the episcopal office, by manifesting patience towards rivals, and innocence against the terrible rashness of the reprobate community, which cannot escape punishment. In both there is cause for praise and thanksgiving to God that you have done what you ought to have done in respect of the episcopal dignity. These men, on the contrary, delivered by the just judgment of Him, into a reprobate mind, have done that to which they should have been provoked by no impulse or injury whatsoever, giving a most certain indication of their depravity to those who do not know them, and by this indicating more clearly how they are to be estimated in the sight of God by every one.

We learn from the S. Ouen writer that the offending monks were sent into exile, and Lanfranc appears to refer to this disciplinary action in his letter to John. While it is possible that Lanfranc was genuinely indignant at the breach of monastic discipline at Rouen, he stressed the importance of maintaining the episcopal dignity so strongly that this appears to be the predominant thought in his mind. There is no trace of disapproval of John's high-handed attitude towards the monks There is but a mild allusion to that hastiness of temper which was characteristic of the Archbishop of Rouen. He urged him to cast aside all rancour of heart and not to grieve more than was necessary, but to devote his whole attention to punishing the dishonour done

[1] Lanfranc, Epis. XVII.

[2] Epis. XVIII.

to God and His Church. It was indeed a cause for grief that the monks might have been his sons if they had wished. But as regards himself he had only cause for joy and exultation that he had earned the blessing promised to the apostles, since he had suffered this evil on behalf of the Son of Man, whom he loved and honoured, and into whose love and honour he wanted to draw them.[1]

Another point of significance is Lanfranc's promise to communicate with the King on John's behalf.[2] The relations between Lanfranc and William in ecclesiastical affairs were very close. William maintained a careful control over the affairs of the Church in Normandy as in England, which Lanfranc did not question. If popular approval constituted him the patriarch of the West, he never attempted to become its pope. In all disputable cases he was anxious to have the royal support. On the other hand, William was guided by Lanfranc's advice in ecclesiastical affairs, and since the Archbishop of Canterbury now asked that John's injury might be vindicated by the royal authority, the statement of the S. Ouen writer, alleging that William fined John in an open court and finally drove him into banishment, is open to doubt, although William expressed his disapproval quite unmistakably.[3]

Further evidence of the decay of monastic discipline is supplied by the second letter of 1073.[4] A monk asked for permission to leave the monastery on account of a dream. Lanfranc agreed with John's decision, and said that no vision was to be regarded as proceeding from God, which prohibited the monks from remaining in the monastery where they had devoted themselves to God's service, and where they had made their profession. Christian burial was not to be denied to a monk who had been struck by lightning, but only to those who died under sentence of excommunication.

Some time after 1076 Lanfranc wrote again to John of Rouen.[5] Mischief-makers had attempted to sow discord

[1] Lanfranc, Epis. XVII.
[2] Epis. XVII and XVIII.
[3] Epis. XX; *infra*, p. 205.
[4] Epis. XVIII.
[5] Epis. XX. The date is suggested by the allusion to the marriage decrees of 1076.

between the two friends. Lanfranc acknowledged the receipt of another letter from John, and apologized for his delay in replying; he had been hindered by business, and a suitable messenger had with difficulty been found. The Archbishop continued:

> You say that it has been reported to you that I criticize some of your actions, and particularly that I maintain that you have ill understood the rules of the holy Fathers concerning the preservation of clerical chastity, and that I assert that you do not properly hold the reins of ecclesiastical discipline. Your beatitude ought to have remembered, and occasionally to have warned those who are in your presence by word of mouth, and those who are absent by letters, that there are many full of detestable envy who desire in turn to separate us, so that they may be able the more freely to go their evil ways, whose part it is always to invent something new and unheard of, and lightly and injuriously to propagate, and so far as in them lies, to publish false reports, to reverse things said well and advisedly. Indeed in my conscience I am aware of none of these things, nor do I remember ever to have said anything against your praiseworthy life, or to have expressed any approval for saying anything which, if it were necessary, could not have been uttered in your presence with safety to your peace of mind. Yea, provoked by your example and that of the venerable Fathers, I have prohibited throughout the whole of England, any one of canonical rank from receiving a wife, and married priests and deacons from receiving promotion unless they have first abandoned their wives.

As a protagonist of reform, John may well have been dissatisfied by this reply. His zeal on behalf of the celibacy of the clergy was eulogized on his epitaph.[1] His prohibition against clerical marriage had been put on record in the acts of the synod of Rouen (1072).[2] The news of Lanfranc's London decrees of 1076 may easily have caused him surprise and chagrin, without the intervention of malicious tongues.

Lanfranc continued his letter with an account of a monk named Robert Pultrellus, who had crossed the sea without John's permission, but who had brought letters sealed with the Archbishop's seal, and in which, if genuine, John had commended him honourably to Lanfranc, and desired him to help the bearer, so far as possible, to secure the assistance of Abbot Baldwin for his infirmities, and also to aid him, if an opportunity occurred, from his own funds. All these

[1] Ord. v. 4 (ii, p. 313). [2] Ibid iv. 9 (ii, p. 240).

things Lanfranc had carried out, for on account of his love for John, he had faithfully received Robert, had kept him with him for three weeks, and had commended him to Abbot Baldwin with petitions and promises. Then he spent money liberally, in order that he might be able to return. But the Archbishop's mind was not easy about the case. The possibility of forgery occurred to him, but he asked John how it was possible for a forger to have obtained his seal.

Lanfranc refused to make a pronouncement upon a question raised by the Bishops of Bayeux and Coutances concerning an archdeacon. The matter was left to John's prudence. He reported that he had consulted the King upon John's affairs—probably the question in dispute at Rouen—so far as it was fitting and necessary, for it was not easy to obtain a hearing against those who embittered John's life. Lanfranc's words are significant. We learn from William's punishment of Thurstan of Glastonbury that he did not approve of ruthless treatment of the monks. Moreover, Rouen was the capital of his duchy, and he was anxious not to offend the clergy there. In some manner which has not been recorded William had made his displeasure known to John.

The correspondence with John of Rouen throws a strong light upon the conditions of diocesan and monastic life in Normandy at that day, and brings out the contrast between conditions in England and in that country. The Cluniac reforms were being more zealously introduced into Normandy, but the indiscipline revealed by the letters shows that the older communities were not altogether favourable to the new ideas. As in England at Glastonbury and S. Augustine's, so in Normandy, at S. Ouen, at least, the monks rose in rebellion against the introduction of Cluniac measures. At the same time the Norman reformers appear to have been less considerate for the feelings and comfort of the monastic clergy than the English bishops. We read of no outbreak against an English prelate to be compared with the revolt against John, and Lanfranc's milder regime stands out in contrast with John's both in method and results.

Lanfranc's Norman correspondents were not confined to

those who had been on terms of intimacy with him in earlier days. On one occasion he acted as an intermediary between Manasseh of Rheims [1] and the papal court, and appears to have exercised a kind of legatine authority. The Archdeacons of Bayeux communicated with him concerning the case of a priest who had committed murder in his own defence and that of his father. They asked whether he should be permitted to celebrate Mass. Lanfranc displayed his usual caution before making reply. He thought it dangerous to give an opinion until he knew something of the life of the defendant. He counselled the Archdeacons to inquire into the priest's past and present life, in accordance with the authority of their office, in order to discover if he was humbly penitent, if he was sorry and was grieving for his action, and especially to take care that he promised to preserve the rule of chastity to the end of his life. These would be indications of penitence, and if they discovered them, licence for celebrating the Mass might be given, but otherwise it would be dangerous and pernicious for the defendant to presume to consecrate the body and blood of Christ with polluted hands.[2]

In the year 1085 the dispute between Gregory VII and Clement III, the antipope set up by the Emperor Henry IV, had almost divided the Church into two sections. There were two parties at Verdun, headed by the Bishop and Abbot respectively. Thierri, the Bishop, was a bitter partisan of Clement, and persecuted Rudolf the Abbot. Rudolf and some of the monks left the monastery and took refuge with the community of S. Benignus of Dijon.[3] But they became anxious about the validity of their action. Rudolf wrote to Lanfranc asking whether it was lawful to leave the monastery in which he had made his vows. He desired to please God, but feared lest he might end by displeasing Him. Lanfranc replied :

If, I, Lanfranc should depart by my own action from any monastery, which I had sworn not to leave, because it did not seem possible to save my soul there, I should not be guilty of

[1] Lanfranc, Epis. XXXIII. [2] Ibid., Epis. XLII.
[3] D'Achery, note to Epis. LX (Migne, cl, col. 622).

perjury. He who is bound to God for God can be released from his vow, unless it is to oppose Him. But then he is scarcely released against Him, who on account of his love for Him, and in order that he may be pleasing to Him, departs from the sons of discord, pride and slackness, yea from the sons of the devil, to the sons of peace, humility, hope, yea to the sons of God. For does not he who so removes himself fly from the abode of the devil to the abode of God? Who can say that he is to be condemned by God who flies to Him as to a father, a lord, a friend? Therefore he who so removes himself, does not go from the church to the church, for there are not many churches, but one which is spread all over the world, and serves the one God everywhere, and fights for the one thing. Finally the blessed Benedict, who ordered the monks to stay in one place, commands that a monk coming from one monastery to another, shall be received, and if he is a man of good life, he shall be persuaded to take up his permanent abode there.[1]

The reply is characteristic of Lanfranc's reasoning. The point in question awakened his sympathy. He had been faced by a similar difficulty at Bec. But Rudolf was an Abbot, and so the ruling may have been prejudiced. At the same time, Lanfranc never raised any objection to the removal of a monk from one house to another if a reasonable cause existed, and especially if it was for the individual's spiritual welfare.[2]

On the death of Bishop Thierri in 1090 Rudolf returned to his abbey at Verdun and turned out certain new-comers whom he found there, who had disorganized the community. Before his death Thierri retracted his support of Clement, and was absolved from excommunication by Gerard, a monk sent to him by Rudolf, under the authority granted to him by the Papacy for dealing with the case. In the absence of a strong Archbishop like Lanfranc, the Cluniac movement in Normandy was aggrandizing the power of the abbots at the expense of the diocesan bishops. The English abbots in like manner had the support of the Papacy, but the power of the great Archbishop prevented any English bishop from undergoing the indignity suffered by John at Rouen, and made unnecessary the issue of delegated authority to an abbot as in the instructions sent to Rudolf of Verdun.

[1] Lanfranc, Epis. LXVI.

[2] Ibid., Epis. LXII.

XIV

LANFRANC AND WILLIAM

THE success of the Conquest was safeguarded by the friendship existing between the heads of Church and State. To other men the King was often scarcely civil. To the Archbishop he was invariably affable.[1] Whenever Lanfranc entered the council chamber, no matter what business was being transacted, William at once relaxed the sternness of his countenance, and became friendly and amiable, to the amazement of all.[2] At one of the great feasts when the King was accustomed to wear his crown, Lanfranc was sitting beside him, and a guest, seeing William resplendent with gold and gems, cried out 'Lo! I see God; lo! I see God!' Lanfranc urged the King to have the man beaten. William gave the order, because, says the chronicler, he did not wish to appear to be like Herod.[3]

The extent of Lanfranc's influence upon the scheme of the Conquest remains unknown. As the Duke's counsellor in Normandy[4] he must have been aware of William's ambitions. The results of the Hastings campaign must have been discussed at Rome during Lanfranc's visit of 1067, although we are expressly told that William's negotiator at Rome was Gilbert of Lisieux.[5]

Considerable doubt also exists concerning his official status after the Conquest in English political affairs. Before his arrival in England, the control of the administration during the absence of the King had been left in the hands of William's half-brother, Odo, supported by William Fitz-Osborne.[6] During the revolt of 1075, when William was again absent from England, the royal forces were commanded by William of Warren and Richard of Bienfaite, to whom

[1] Malmes., *G. P.*, p. 72.

[2] Eadmer, *Hist. Nov.*, p. 23.

[3] Milo, 45.

[4] *Gesta Abbat. S. Alb.* i, p. 46; Milo, 16.

[5] Ord. iii, 11 (ii. p. 122).

[6] Ord. iv, 1 (ii. p. 167), Flor. 1067. Malmes., *G. R.* ii, p. 334, describes Odo as 'vicedominus sub rege'.

Orderic[1] gives the title of 'Justiciar', and they were supported by Odo and Geoffrey of Coutances. But the correspondence between Lanfranc and William suggests that Lanfranc was the supreme representative of the King during that period. To him Roger and Waltheof made their submission. This is confirmed by Milo, who says that when the King was in Normandy, the Archbishop remained in charge as guardian of the secular affairs of the country, with control over all its resources for the defence of the kingdom and the conduct of public business, together with supervision over the barons and royal officials.[2] Lanfranc certainly complained of the burden of secular business during this period.[3] But his dispatches to the King need prove no more than that he was the only medium of communication with William of Warren and Richard of Bienfaite at a time when the civil officers were unlettered men. Lanfranc held no executive office so clearly defined as the functions

[1] iv. 13 (ii, p. 262).

[2] Milo, 48.

[3] Lanfranc, Epis. XIX; cf. Epis. LVI. Certain writs in the *Liber. Eliensis* (cf. D. J. Stewart (1848), i, pp. 256–60) have been quoted as evidence that Lanfranc held the formal office of Justiciar. (Stubbs, *Constitutional Hist.* i, p. 375.) But with Lanfranc's name are coupled those of Geoffrey of Coutances and Robert Mortain, who were probably deputed to watch the royal interests, while Lanfranc took care of ecclesiastical interests. The writs contain nothing to show that Lanfranc, Geoffrey and Robert were more than presidents of the court of inquiry. The Ely writs appear to have little more significance in support of Lanfranc's lay functions than three charters addressed to him by the King containing grants for the Abbey of Ramsey (*Cart. Mon. de Ram.* (Rolls), i, pp. 233–4; *Chron. Abbat. Ram.* (Rolls), pp. 205–6, 208). A similar charter was addressed to Wulfstan, to William son of Osbert and all the barons and ministers of Gloucestershire and Worcestershire (*Hist. and Cart. Mon. Glouc.* (Rolls), ii, p. 107; iii, p. 263). His name of course frequently appears among the signatories of William's grants to the Abbeys. Cf. Matt. Paris, *Hist. Maj.* vi, p. 34; *Cart. Ram.* ii, p. 98, with duplicate in *Chron. Abbat. Ram.*, p. 204; *Hist. and Cart. Glouc.* i, p. 387; ii, p. 186; *Reg. Malm.* (Rolls), i, pp. 326–7; *Mem. of S. Edmunds* (Rolls), i, p. 349. In one of the Ramsey charters Lanfranc signs after Maurice the Chancellor (*Cart. Ram.* ii, p. 98). But cf. *Chron. Abbat. Ram.*, p. 204, where he is the first ecclesiastic to sign the same charter.

of Warren and Bienfaite, but his peculiar relationship to William, his status as Archbishop, his tried experience in secular affairs, gave him a position of general supervision over the administration whenever the King left England.

The powers of Lanfranc as an administrator were put to the fullest test during the East-Anglian troubles of 1075.[1] The Bridale of Norwich was the first outbreak of the Norman baronage against the settlement of William. The Conquest was barely ten years old. The Norman followers of William were by no means satisfied with the arrangements made by the King on their behalf. They regarded themselves as co-legatees with the King of the heritage which had been won by the slaughter of Harold and the landowners of England. The right of the sword, rather than the hereditary claim put forward in the negotiations between William and the Confessor, was regarded by them as the deciding factor in the Conquest. A failure to check the rebellion of Roger of Hereford and Ralph of Norfolk might have led to a general break-up of the stability of the settlement, and might have necessitated a new Conquest, in which William would have been supported by the tardy adherence of Anglo-Saxon England, against a combination of the discontented Norman barons, supported by Scots, Danes and Welsh. This calamity was obviated by the effective measures taken by Lanfranc in collaboration with the executive officers of the King. Information had reached him that dangerous designs were being planned. He opened a correspondence with the young Earl Roger of Hereford.[2]

> Our Lord the King of the English greets you and all of us as faithful men in whom he has great confidence, and commands that, so far as we are able, we shall take care of his castles, lest (and may God prevent it) they are handed over to enemies. Therefore I beg of you, as I ought to beg a most beloved son, whom, by the witness of God, I love with my whole heart, and desire to serve, and whose father [3] I have loved as my own soul, that in this matter, and on account of your loyalty, you will pay such attention to our Lord the King, that you may receive commendation from him and from all good men.

[1] Florence, followed by Ralph de Diceto (i. 209), says that the rebellion broke out in 1074.

[2] Lanfranc, Epis. XLV.

[3] William Fitz-Osberne.

Keep in your mind always how your glorious father lived, and how faithfully he served his lord, and with what activity he acquired large possessions, and with what great honour he retained them.

The King commands that his sheriffs shall not hold pleas on your lands, until he has crossed the sea, and has heard the disputes between you and his sheriffs.

Willingly would I speak with you, and if you are willing, command me at what place we can meet and have a talk concerning your business and that of the King. Really I am prepared to come to meet you whenever you command.

I beg that you will do justice to the bearer of this letter, Berengar, against those men of whom he complains that they have secretly taken away his horse. May Almighty God bless you, and dispose your life towards every virtue.

Besides revealing Lanfranc's vigilance in taking action before serious events had happened, and his tactful dealing with discontent, the letter emphasizes one of the causes of revolt. The royal administration was coming into collision with baronial rights. This was an inevitable result so soon as the royal power began to check and restrain the privileges of the feudal magnates. In the interests of justice and order, it was essential that the sheriffs should occasionally conduct cases within the geographical limits of baronial jurisdiction. But the baronage were sure to regard the tendency as derogatory from their own dignity and power, more especially as they looked upon their perquisites in England as the independent rewards of their own prowess. The abuse of baronial rights and the slackness of feudal jurisdiction are illustrated by the allusion to the theft, for which the bearer of the letter could obtain no redress without Lanfranc's intervention. The necessity for even sharper oversight upon the part of the sheriffs is clearly established.

The young Earl made no response to Lanfranc's advance. The Archbishop interpreted this attitude as a sign of guilt, especially as reports of Roger's disloyalty continued to come in. He wrote to Roger again.[1]

Having heard things concerning you which I do not want to hear, I grieve more than I can say. It is not seemly that a son of Earl William, whose prudence and goodness and fidelity to

[1] Lanfranc, Epis. XLVI.

his lord and all his friends have been noticed in many lands, should be called disloyal and should stand open to any infamy on account of perjury and fraud. It is better rather that the son of so great a man should stand forth as the imitator of his father, and should show an example to others of every virtue and fidelity. Therefore I beseech you, most dear son and beloved friend, as much on account of God as your own honour, if you have committed any fault, that you will return to a right understanding, or if you have not, that you will show that you have not by incontrovertible documents. However the case stands, I beg that you will come to me, secure, you need have no doubt, that neither in coming nor going you will suffer any hindrance through my own or the royal officers. May Almighty God bless thee.

Lanfranc thus tried to bring the matter to a head, either one way or the other. But he failed again. The Bridale at Norwich took place, when a match forbidden by William was consummated between Roger's sister Emma and Ralph of Norfolk. Waltheof was present. The rebel earls then separated. Roger went off to raise the west, and Ralph began to levy forces in East Anglia. The earls were summoned to appear before William of Warren and Richard of Bienfaite.[1] On their failure to appear Lanfranc issued excommunication against Roger. The Earl then apparently became uneasy, and begged for an interview, but being under excommunication this could not now be granted without the royal permission.[2]

I grieve for you, how much I cannot say, since by the witness of God I loved you, and I wanted to love you and serve you. But since by prompting of the devil, and by the advice of evil men, you have undertaken that which you ought never to have done, compelled by necessity I have changed my mind, and have converted my love not so much into hatred as into vexation of mind and just severity. Indeed by messengers and letters, once and again I invited you to come to me, in order that you might accept counsel for your soul from me as from a spiritual father and sincere friend, and that through my better counsel you might desist from the stupid plan you had conceived. But you refused to do it.

Therefore by canonical authority I have imprecated and excommunicated you and all your helpers, and I have separated you from the boundaries of holy church, and the society of the faithful, and I have ordered this to take effect throughout the

[1] Ord. iv. 13 (ii, p. 262). [2] Lanfranc, Epis. XLVII (1075).

whole of England by pastoral authority. From this bond of anathema I cannot absolve you, until you ask for the mercy of my lord the King, and do justice to him and others for things which you have wrongfully committed.

You say moreover that you want to come to me. This I should willingly desire, except that I fear that the royal anger would break out against me, but I will notify him by a messenger and by letters of your penitence, humility and prayers, and I will help you as much as I am able, saving my fidelity to him. Meanwhile I beg and advise that you will remain quiet, lest anything that you attempt to do may incur great anger from him.

The excommunication took effect. Although standing under arms, Roger made no attempt to cross the Severn, which was guarded by Bishop Wulfstan, Abbot Ethelwig, and Urse, the Sheriff of Worcestershire. No reference to any hostilities conducted by Roger appears in Lanfranc's dispatches to William.

The extent of Waltheof's complicity is doubtful. Although married to Judith, the Conqueror's niece, he was certainly present at the hilarious gathering at Norwich when the conspiracy was hatched. But after the wedding festivities had ended, while Roger went west and Ralph remained in East Anglia to begin operations, Waltheof went to Lanfranc and revealed the plot. The Archbishop took a lenient view of the matter at this point. He probably regarded it as the result of the drunken revel at Norwich, although the fact that the marriage had taken place in defiance of the King's orders was indicative of serious trouble to come. But no open act of rebellion had yet taken place. So Waltheof received episcopal absolution, after promising to fulfil certain acts of penance, and on condition that he went over sea and confessed his share in the plot to the King. No attempt was made to incarcerate him. If the meeting at Norwich took place before Lanfranc excommunicated Roger, it is possible that the Archbishop received definite information from Waltheof about the other conspirators, which made him still more eager to secure a meeting with Roger, but the sequence of events is not clear.

We read of no attempt made by Lanfranc to restrain the third party in the conspiracy, and it is significant that the only one of the three against whom active operations were conducted was Ralph of Norfolk, who appears to have had no dealings with Lanfranc. Ralph moved towards Cambridge, the place where he had arranged to join forces with Roger. He came into contact with the royal troops under William of Warren, Robert Malet, and the Bishops of Bayeux and Coutances at 'Fagadun',[1] and after meeting with a defeat retreated to Norwich. Lanfranc immediately announced this victory to the King, without waiting for the issue of the operations.

Willingly would we see you as an angel of God, but we do not want you to cross the sea, because you would be doing us great dishonour if you were to come for the sake of repressing such perjurers and robbers. Ralph the earl, yea Ralph the traitor, and his whole army have been put to flight, and our men with a large number of French and English are following them, and in a few days, as our chiefs have notified me, either these perjurers will fly from our country across the sea, or they will have them alive or dead. For the rest I commend this monk to you, whom you can confidently trust, since he is faithful to me. May Almighty God bless you.

Ralph did not wait to stand a siege at Norwich castle. He fled to Denmark leaving the castle in the hands of Emma, his bride. Emma withstood the royal forces for a time, and received honourable terms at the surrender of the castle, which Lanfranc was soon able to announce to William.[2]

Glory to God in the highest, by whose mercy your land is purged of the filthiness of the Bretons. The castle of Norwich is restored. The Bretons who were in it, and who had lands in England, having had life and limb granted to them, have sworn to leave your kingdom within forty days, and never more to enter it without your license.

Those who served the traitor Ralph and his friends without land, but for money, have requested with many petitions, the space of one month for effecting this.

In the same castle Bishop Geoffrey, William of Warren and Robert Malet have remained, with three hundred men at arms, including slingers and many operators of the machines. All the sound of war has ceased in England. May Almighty God bless you.[3]

[1] Ord. iv. 13 (ii, p. 262), possibly Beecham or Beechamwell.
[2] Lanfranc, Epis. XXXVII.
[3] Ibid. XXXVIII.

Lanfranc, who had effectively neutralized two of the conspirators, was bound by his pastoral office to act as an intermediary with the King, if the offenders gave him an opportunity. His mediating policy is revealed in the second letter to William. No reference was made to Roger, who was either still under arms, or in hiding, or under restraint awaiting trial, and was at least guilty of having plotted in Ralph's treason, and of having marched an army to the banks of the Severn. Moreover, Lanfranc attempted to cover the Norman and English followers of Ralph by concentrating the King's attention upon the Breton auxiliaries.[1] From the wording of the letter we might suppose that the rebellion had been nothing more than a Breton outbreak headed by the Breton Earl Ralph. Lanfranc even attempted to cover these men by pointing out that they had already suffered the consequences of their treason. The one rebel who stands out in the dispatch undefended was Ralph. He may have given personal offence to the Archbishop by ignoring him altogether, and by a provocative attitude of which Waltheof and even Roger were not guilty. Lanfranc may have regarded him as the arch-traitor because he had effected the forbidden marriage. Possibly he attempted to make him and his Bretons the scapegoats for the Normans and English who were concerned. However, the Archbishop's policy was designed to avoid bloodshed in any judicial proceedings which had to follow. He did everything possible for Waltheof, and is reported to have heard his confession before his death. The hurried proceedings at the execution made this almost impossible, but he always maintained that Waltheof was innocent of the crime for which he suffered.[2]

Lanfranc's anxiety was not confined to the movements in East Anglia and Herefordshire. He feared renewed disturbances in the north, and especially another invasion by the Danes. The threat from Denmark really created more apprehension in the minds of King and Archbishop than the baronial outbreak. Danish rule in England,

[1] Cf. Epis. XXVIII, to Walcher of Durham, in which Bretons only are mentioned.

[2] Florence, who reports the confession made to Lanfranc.

particularly in the north, had been fondly remembered since the days of Canute. A large proportion of the East Anglian population was Danish, or of Danish descent. The Danish invasion of 1069, when York was captured, had shown that the Northmen were still enemies to be feared. After receiving William's reply to his final dispatch, Lanfranc wrote to Walcher, Bishop of Durham, congratulating him that no outbreak had taken place in the north, but warning him to look to his defences.[1]

I am made joyful by those things which have been reported to me by you. I have learned from your letters that you have peace which, frightened by the reports of many, I believed to be far from you. We indeed, having expelled the Bretons, and having settled all the wars, live in so great tranquillity, that we do not recollect that we lived so peaceably since the King crossed the sea.

The fortune [2] of our lord the King is in the greatest prosperity, and soon, be it known to you, he will cross over to us. The Danes, as the King has warned you, will surely come, so cause your castle, by watchful care, to be fortified with men, arms and stores. May the Almighty Lord defend you from all evil.

The King's return was hastened by the threatened approach of the Danes. Earl Ralph had been in communication with them,[3] and after the flight from Norwich he proceeded to Denmark, and hastened the arrival of the Danish fleet which took place before the year was out. They came with two hundred ships, but after again entering York, where they plundered the church, they sailed back to Flanders.

Lanfranc did not bear lightly the burden of responsibility. Beneath the calm self-confident exterior revealed in his first dispatch to William,[4] a sign of inward disturbance appeared. He 'longed to see the King as an angel of God'. The same uneasiness and weariness appears in a letter written about this time to Archbishop John of Rouen.

Since I have omitted, during a long interval of time, to get in touch, by means of a letter with your fraternity, whom, by the witness of God I love, and hold in great reverence, I beseech, indeed I beseech greatly, lest you interpret me to have done

[1] Epis. XXVIII. [2] *res.*

[3] Sax. Chron. (Peterborough), 1075 (Worcester), 1076.

[4] Epis. XXXVII.

this from any sinister motive, and lest you may think the cause and beginning of this has been some vexation or disapproval. Put it rather down to this, as is indeed true, that, as you from your experience are well able to understand, the condition of my life is disturbed by many preoccupations, and by much distressing business. I know not by what judgment of God I undergo incessantly so many and so great difficulties in temporal affairs, sustain so many anxieties of mind without ceasing, both from my own and from other people's business, and so many troubles do I think, from a consideration of present conditions, are coming in future, that an opportunity for dictating or writing is very rarely afforded, or if it is provided, then either those who can carry the letters are wanting, or the persons who might do so I do not consider suitable to justify my sending an account of my troubles by letter.[1]

Throughout the correspondence there are frequent traces of mental fatigue and desire for rest, but no complaint ever appears against the King, or against the constant supervision over all departments of national life maintained by him. Even in ecclesiastical affairs Lanfranc did not regard himself as a free agent, nor did he allow it to be assumed that he could overrule the royal judgement.[6] William kept

[1] Lanfranc, Epis. XIX.

[2] Ibid. LVIII and LIX. The extent of William's careful supervision of the details of ecclesiastical administration is illustrated by the Ely writs. The sac and soc of five hundreds in Suffolk were granted to Abbot Simeon of Ely (Stewart, *Lib. Eli*, p. 123). Remi of Lincoln was not to be allowed to obtain any new customs in the Isle of Ely (ibid., p. 124). The charters of Ely were to be examined to discover the conditions attached to the consecration of the Abbots of Ely. The advice of the Bishops of Coutances, Winchester and others who had knowledge of the grants made to Ely was to be taken. The inquiry was to be carried out carefully, briefly and quickly (ibid., p. 125). A careful investigation was to be made into Remi's right to consecrate the Abbot of Ely, and other points relating to Remi's demand for wine and his destruction of a mill (ibid., p. 127). But no invasion of the rights of Ely was intended, its former customs were to be preserved, and its lands left intact. We have a letter which appears to refer to some of this business. It had been reported that Remi's case was being damaged at court by slanderous tongues. Lanfranc wrote (Epis. LVIII) saying that the King had not entertained the slanders, but had rather defended the Bishop, and suggested that he should come to the Archbishop and settle the matter by word of mouth, since it would otherwise involve a lengthy correspondence.

a firm hand upon all branches of the administration. Even in an ecclesiastical council the Archbishop was not permitted to make new canons or to modify or repeal old ones without the sanction of the King.[1] No baron or royal minister might be excommunicated even for incest or adultery without the royal permission. No bishop might go overseas without the King's permission. No Bishop of Rome might be recognized as apostolic in England without William's consent, and no letter from him might be received without first being submitted to the King.[2]

At the same time these restrictions are to be interpreted in the light of the conditions of the day. On the one hand the bishops and abbots were territorial magnates, and on the other the lay lords were subject to the ecclesiastical discipline of an authority which had its centre outside the boundary of the royal dominions. Consequently, unless careful supervision was exercised over the ecclesiastical authority at Canterbury, and a careful watch kept upon the relations of the Papacy with the English bishops, who were territorial lords, the feudal organization and administration of the country could at any time be upset by an unscrupulous Pope. The King realized that he must be King in his own kingdom. There is no evidence that William wished to interfere unduly with ecclesiastical affairs, but he realized the dangers of ecclesiastical influence when it was so closely bound up with the civil constitution of society as in the Norman body politic. Lanfranc appreciated accurately these conditions, and accommodated his ecclesiastical policy to the needs of the dynasty and the kingdom. He realized that both were one. The safety of the country and of the Church depended upon William.[3] He was wise enough to perceive that his own freedom and initiative should be confined within certain clearly-marked limits. He was big enough not to feel that any indignity was thereby

[1] In a Charter of Matilda making a grant to the abbey of Maldum, signed by Lanfranc, the Archbishop is authorized to excommunicate any one who invaded the privileges of the charter. *Reg. Malm.* i, p. 327.

[2] Eadmer, *Hist. Nov.*, p. 10.

[3] Lanfranc, Epis. III.

offered either to the Archbishop or to the Church. Moreover, he realized that if William's hand was firm it was just. Lanfranc always knew exactly where he stood in the royal estimation, and could rely upon the methodical operation of William's actions and the just conclusions of his mind. With such a lord it was always possible to forecast probabilities. Friction was thereby avoided and friendship grew.

Lanfranc never challenged the royal supremacy as the final source of appeal, even in ecclesiastical matters, and William was always open to conviction when a good case was presented to him. The importance of this alliance, both for the country generally and for the Church, cannot be over-estimated. During a period when life and property necessarily became very insecure in Saxon England, it was most important that the chief confidant of the King should be an adviser who, though appreciating Norman strength and Norman peremptoriness at their fullest value, none the less was not a man who recklessly counselled resort to the sword. That all the Norman churchmen were not men of this stamp is proved by the case of Odo of Bayeux, and to a less extent by that of Geoffrey of Coutances, who were ready to join in any military expedition, like the youngest Norman warrior. Any breakdown of the harmonious relations between William and the Church must have made the Conquest less decisive, and therefore more provocative and burdensome for the people of England.

XV

RELATIONS WITH GREGORY VII

THE correspondence of Lanfranc with Ireland, Scotland, and Normandy shows that the commanding influence of the Archbishop of Canterbury in western Europe sprang from the recognition of his personal qualities and experience. A cursory perusal of the letters of Gregory VII, the antipope Clement III and Urban II creates the impression that the Papacy sought his assistance on similar grounds. But if the friendship and support of Lanfranc are courted in this correspondence in no uncertain terms, it was because the Papacy was faced by the necessity of securing the assistance of the King of England, not only for the general scheme of ecclesiastical reform, but against its secular opponents on the Continent.

Gregory perceived quite early that if the reform of clerical life and discipline was to become widely spread and firmly established the theory of papal supremacy must be strengthened, and that recognition must be secured for it from the royal authority in all western lands. The theory of feudal proprietary rights had given to the lay magnates control of the parishes, and the Benedictine movement centred its main battle round the demand for freedom from lay interference in the election to ecclesiastical offices and in the control of ecclesiastical affairs. In the early years of his papacy Gregory attempted to counter the same influence by claiming prior proprietary rights, based upon the old figment of the grant of western lands to the chair of S. Peter. In 1074 he laid claim to suzerainty in Hungary as a papal fief based upon a grant of S. Stephen of Hungary.[1] In 1077 similar claims were made over Spain and Corsica,[2] based, apparently, upon the old forged donation of Constantine. He was driven into this device because he was unable to rise above the feudal conceptions of the age, which vindicated the fictitious basis of the papal claim.

A second stage in the development of the Hildebrandine

[1] Jaffé, *Mon. Greg.* ii. 13.

[2] Ibid. i. 7 ; iv. 28,

theory was reached through the conflict with the Emperor Henry IV of Germany. In this conflict also Gregory was driven forward by the force of circumstances. His application of the Benedictine reforms was not at first accompanied by coercive measures. Although raised to the Papacy in 1073 he did not declare ordination at the hands of a simonist bishop to be illegal until 1078. The decree against lay investiture was passed in 1075, but it was not enforced by rigorous action until the opposition of Henry IV, and particularly of the German bishops, became active. It is doubtful whether the humiliation of the Emperor at Canossa (1077) would have been demanded if Gregory had been sure of the German bishops. Gregory was rather a practical reformer, keenly sensitive to the ordinary abuses of the day, than an idealist like Cardinal Humbert, who was prepared to wreck everything for a theory.[1]

By 1080 the quarrel with the Emperor had become so acute that an antipope had been elected in the person of Clement III.[2] Hitherto Gregory had relied upon the assistance of the Saxon magnates in Germany and the Normans of South Italy, but when the imperial army marched against Rome he was compelled to seek for more vigorous assistance. Moreover, the theory of papal supremacy needed to be developed. Events since Canossa had shown that the prestige even of the reformed Papacy was inadequate to restrain attack by a recalcitrant king. But Gregory did not attempt to apply the theory of the Isidorian decretals and the donation of Constantine to Germany.[3] He realized that some development of the idea of papal supremacy, along the lines of the spiritual authority granted by Christ to S. Peter, was necessary. So he turned his eyes towards England.

Here was a friendly King who owed his conquest partly to the friendship of the Papacy, and an Archbishop who had

[1] Cf. Prof. J. P. Whitney, *Church Quarterly Rev.*, July 1910, p. 432.

[2] Elected at Brixen, 26th June.

[3] Cf. Whitney, *Ch. Quar. Rev.*, July 1910, pp. 422–4, and Crutwell, *Saxon Church and the Norman Conquest*, pp. 175–8, for an account of the decretals.

long been the protégé of the chair of Peter. In a letter dispatched to Lanfranc in 1073 Gregory had spoken of William as 'The beloved King and singular son of the Roman Church'.[1] In replying to a letter of congratulation from William on his own accession to the Papacy, Gregory had said that he esteemed William above all other Kings.[2] In 1077, although unable to accede to a request made by William on behalf of the deposed Bishop of Dol, Gregory expressed unusual deference to the wishes of the King.[3] In 1078 he again wrote to William saying that his loyal support of the Roman Church caused him to stand out among the other kings of Europe.[4]

In April 1080 Gregory opened the negotiation which was to pave the way for a more general recognition of the supremacy of the Papacy than any which had hitherto been put forth. In a letter sent to William, by the hands of the royal ambassadors, he reminded the King of the services he had rendered to him at the papal court before the conquest of England, and of the calumny which he had suffered in consequence. He then alluded to the difficulties of his position and asked for the King's obedience in certain matters which would be revealed to him by the bearers of the letter.[5] On 8th May this was followed by another letter in which the Pope claimed the support of William, not because of assistance rendered in the conquest of England, but upon the general ground of the superiority of the spiritual over the temporal authority. The apostolic and the royal dignity were created by God for the government of the world and were compared with the two great lights, the sun and moon.[6] In this passage, under the designation of the sun, the supremacy of the spiritual over the temporal authority is clearly claimed. The letter was carried to England by the legate Hubert, and Hubert was entrusted with the duty of carrying verbally to William, Gregory's demand for fealty.[7]

[1] *Mon. Greg.* i. 31. [2] Ibid. i. 70. [3] Ibid. iv. 17.
[4] Ibid. v. 19. [5] Ibid. vii. 23. [6] Ibid. vii. 25.
[7] Cf. Z. N. Brooke, *Eng. Hist. Rev.*, April 1911, and Boehmer, *Kirche und Staat*, p. 134. Mr. Brooke's chronology has been followed.

Homage was declined by the King in an emphatic letter which has been preserved.[1] Consequently, Gregory's attempt to secure a moral victory over Henry IV, by obtaining through William an opportunity for publishing throughout Europe a general declaration of the supremacy of the spiritual over the secular arm, failed, and the triumph of the Emperor and the death of Gregory in 1085 followed by regular stages.

The attitude of Lanfranc to Gregory now falls into its place. Like Gregory, Lanfranc, while being a firm supporter of the reform policy, had not submitted entirely to the influence of Cluny. An early letter of Gregory reveals the same sort of confidence in Lanfranc as that in which the Pope originally held the King. Gregory confided to Lanfranc the difficulties of his new position, and the dangers besetting the apostolic see.[2] But in the same year the Pope found occasion to offer a mild reproof to the Archbishop for his lack of severity towards Herfast, Bishop of Elmham, who was encroaching upon the rights of the Abbey of S. Edmunds.[3] Gregory expressed surprise that Lanfranc had been so silent against a bishop who perchance had said ' I have placed my chair in the North, and I will be like unto the Highest '.[4] Whether as the result of the Pope's letter or not, Lanfranc wrote to Herfast about this time;[5] but while rebuking him severely for his secular mode of life, he sanctioned Herfast's exercise of the rights of his predecessors over S. Edmunds. This was a clear case where the two reformers differed as to the detailed application of the reform programme. The papal attitude was that monasteries were to be immune from episcopal control, whereas Lanfranc, although a monk and a founder and reformer of monastic houses, upheld the authority of the diocesans over the monasteries within their jurisdiction. But the letter is not to be interpreted as a sign of fundamental divergence between Lanfranc and Gregory on the question of policy.

The correspondence between Gregory and Lanfranc of

[1] Lanfranc, Epis. X.

[2] Jaffé, *Mon. Greg. Epis. Coll.* i (1073).

[3] Cf. *supra*, p. 143.

[4] Jaffé, *Mon. Greg.* i. 31.

[5] Lanfranc, Epis. XXVI.

1079–82 cannot be easily arranged. In 1079 the Pope wrote complaining that since his own elevation to the Papacy Lanfranc had not troubled to visit him at Rome.[1] This implies previous communication with the Archbishop on the same matter, which has not been preserved.[2] Gregory suggests that Lanfranc's delay was due either to fear of the King or his own culpable neglect. There is no record of a reply by Lanfranc to this letter.[3] About a year later, in May 1080, Gregory sent his demand for homage to William, by word of mouth, through the legate Hubert, and at some time between this date and the peremptory letter to Lanfranc of 1082, he appears to have written another letter to the Archbishop, which has also been lost, in which he complained that since Lanfranc's elevation to the episcopate, the Archbishop had lost his earlier respect for the holy see. That some such letter was written appears to be made clear by Lanfranc's reply, in which the point was taken up : [4]

I have received, with due humility, the letter which your excellence caused to be conveyed to me by the learned Hubert, sub-deacon of your palace. The purport of the letter was, with paternal kindness, to find fault with my conduct, for that having been advanced to the honour of the episcopate, I have no longer that respect for the Holy Roman Church, and for yourself in particular, which I professed before my elevation to the post of honour, for which, as is well-known, and as I do not deny, I was indebted to the apostolical see.

I ought not to misrepresent your words, venerable Father, neither do I wish to do so, but I must say that I cannot understand what absence or distance of place, or exalted station, be it ever so great, can have to do with this matter. I am ready to yield obedience to your commands in everything according to the canons, and, if by God's blessing, I shall have at any time the pleasure of conversing with you personally, I will endeavour to make it evident, by deeds rather than words, that my affection for you, instead of being diminished, has, on the contrary, increased, although yours, excuse me for saying so, is evidently not towards me what it once was.

I did what I could for your legation and legate. I laid the

[1] Jaffé, *Mon. Greg.* vi. 30, 25th March 1079.

[2] Ibid. viii. 43. Gregory refers to frequent requests for Lanfranc to come to Rome.

[3] Unless Lanfranc, Epis. XI, was a reply.

[4] Lanfranc, Epis. XI.

case before my lord the King. I advised him to comply with your wishes, but I did not succeed. The reason why he utterly rejects your proposal he has himself made known to you, by word of mouth to your legate, and by letter to yourself.[1]

Whether Lanfranc's letter was sent together with William's refusal is uncertain, but it is clear that his attitude to the Pope was influenced by William's attitude, and also by William's dislike for visits to Rome. His promise of obedience is qualified. He will yield obedience in everything, but according to the canons. The last paragraph of the letter is not to be taken literally as an indication of Lanfranc's private opinion of the papal demand. It was probably a diplomatic communication following up the royal letter, which can have had no influence upon Gregory's interpretation of the King's refusal, and was intended to obviate further complication of a delicate matter by seeking to free the Archbishop from any share in Gregory's disapproval of the King's action. The statements are substantially quite correct. Lanfranc was the head of the papal administration in England, and as such it became his duty to advise the King to comply with Gregory's wishes, whether he personally approved or not. William may well have understood the situation, and may have tacitly accepted the advice in the manner in which the Archbishop offered it. Both King and Archbishop appear to have had their tongues in their cheeks, especially as the legate was probably present on the occasion referred to in the letter.

No reply was made by Gregory to the King's refusal, nor does he allude to it in his next letter to Lanfranc, but the Pope now wrote peremptorily to the Archbishop, demanding

[1] Hook, *Archbishops*, ii, p. 140. The date of this letter cannot be fixed with any certainty. If it was not a reply to Gregory's letter of 1079, but to some subsequent epistle, it is not likely to have been sent until after the King had received Gregory's demand for homage in the spring of 1080. In his next letter, written probably in the spring of 1082, Gregory makes no reference to Lanfranc's reply, so that Lanfranc's letter was probably received some time before, and was allowed to pass unnoticed. (Cf. Z. N. Brooke, *Eng. Hist. Rev.* April 1911.) In that case the latter part of 1081 is a possible date for this letter.

his appearance at Rome within four weeks, by All Saints' Day, under pain of suspension from his episcopal functions. Through pride or negligence Lanfranc had disregarded his repeated appeals. No canonical reason had been given for his refusal to come. No excuse on the ground of fatigue or the difficulty of the journey could be accepted, because it was well known that invalids, though scarcely able to rise, had, when summoned, hastened to Rome, being carried there on vehicles.[1]

Whether Lanfranc complied with his demand is very uncertain.[2] There can be little doubt that he had no particular desire to go to Rome at this juncture. He approved of the royal action, and in any case, in iew of the strained relations between Gregory and William, such a visit at this time would have been impolitic. The conditions of Gregory's dispute with the Emperor Henry in 1080 made Rome a very undesirable place, save for avowed partisans of the Pope. Towards the end of 1082 the imperial troops were still round the city, or had only just retreated. In either case the roads were uncertain save for professed partisans of the Emperor. Moreover, Gregory's epistle suggests that Lanfranc feared the fatigues of the journey, and was suffering from some physical trouble, possibly from the ailment which finally ended his life. But although Lanfranc does not appear to have complied with the Pope's demand, Gregory did not issue the sentence threatened against him. This also can be explained by the troubles of Gregory in Rome during this period. The Emperor besieged the city every year from 1081 until 1084 when Gregory finally left Rome.

[1] Jaffé, *Mon. Greg.* viii. 43.

[2] Boehmer, *Kirche und Staat*, p. 138, n. 3, and Z. N. Brooke, *Eng. Hist. Rev.*, April 1911, quote Jaffé-Lowenfeld 5255–6, in support of a visit to Rome at the end of 1082, in company with William of Durham, whose business was the revival of the monastic life at Durham. But Boehmer admits that it is doubtful whether Lanfranc accompanied William. The southern writers know nothing of such a visit, and Symeon of Durham does not say that Lanfranc accompanied William. Gregory's letter on the Durham business, addressed to William and Lanfranc, makes Lanfranc's visit almost impossible.

But more can be explained by the policy of Gregory. Lanfranc had not been guilty of any act of disloyalty either to the reform programme or to the Pope personally; it would not have been in keeping with Gregory's general moderation if he had taken active steps against the Archbishop, especially as by this time the evil results of Canossa for the Papacy were manifest.[1] Gregory reserved extreme action for extreme cases of recalcitrance, and then resorted to it only when the well-being of the Church was at stake. Neither William nor Lanfranc adopted the attitude of the German King and bishops. Soon after the oath of fealty had been refused, Gregory received fresh evidence that in purely ecclesiastical affairs the King and Archbishop were willing to be guided by his advice.

The reform of the cathedral clergy was being introduced at Durham. William of S. Carilef, who succeeded Walcher as Bishop of Durham[2] in 1080, proposed to eject the secular clergy and to introduce a community of regulars. Before taking this step the Bishop consulted the older clergy of his diocese, and referred to a book on the life of S. Cuthbert,

[1] By accepting the penance of the Emperor at Canossa, Gregory was compelled to restore him to favour. But he did not thereby win over the malcontents in Germany. He sent Henry away incensed at the degradation to which he had been submitted. Gregory gained only a formal victory.

[2] Elected in 1080, consecrated 3rd January 1081 (Sym. of Dur., *H. D. E.* iv. 1). The reform of the monasteries in the see of Durham was commenced by his predecessor Walcher (1071–80). Aldwin Prior of Winchcombe, the deacon Alfwin, and the lay brother Regenfrith were brought from the south, and were established at Monchester, the future Newcastle. Aldwin was moved to Jarrow (1074), Regenfrith was moved to Whitby (*H. D. E.* iii. 21) which was refounded, and then to York when the Abbey of S. Mary's was founded (1078) (Sym. Dur., *H. D. E.* iii. 22; *H. R.*, § 165); Aldwin and Turgot were afterwards established at Wearmouth (*H. D. E.* iii. 22). This was after they had spent some time at Melrose. In 1080 Walcher founded the monastery of Tynemouth under his friend and adviser Ligulf. Ligulf was murdered through the jealousy of Leobwin, the Bishop's chaplain. Before the year was out, the Bishop, Leobwin and Gilbert, Ligulf's murderer, were killed by friends of Ligulf (Sym. of Dur., *Hist. Reg.* § 166). A punitive expedition under Odo of Bayeux was dispatched by the King (*H. D. E.* iii. 24).

and to Bede's Ecclesiastical History of the English. From these authorities it was ascertained that S. Cuthbert had established a monastic community at Durham. The Bishop then consulted William and Matilda and Lanfranc.[1]

The King declined to issue any independent opinion, and, supported by the advice of his counsellors, sent William of S. Carilef to Rome to lay his case before Gregory (1082–3).[2] The embassy was also intended to palliate the Pope's feelings which had been ruffled by the King's refusal to do homage. The result of the embassy was not likely to be doubtful, and the Bishop speedily obtained the Pope's consent to the scheme.[3] Gregory agreed that the monks from Wearmouth and Jarrow should be concentrated in the reformed community at Durham, because the poverty of the diocese could not support three monasteries. A formal letter, containing his decision, together with an anathema against any who might oppose the scheme, was dispatched to William and Lanfranc, by the hands of William of Durham. The letter was received at a council, at which the King, the Queen, Lanfranc and the chief barons were present, and license was readily given for the changes at Durham.[4]

Further evidence for Lanfranc's attitude to the papal claims, and for their bearing upon his relations with the King, is to be found in the letter to a partisan of Clement III.[5]

I have received and read your letter which you sent to me through the bearer of mine. I do not approve of your disparage-

[1] Sym. of Dur. *H. D. E.* iv. 2. No reference was made to Thomas of York. This may have been due to the special status of the palatine Bishop of Durham, who regarded himself in some measure as independent of the metropolitan. It may have been due to the fact that Thomas had continued to secularize the clergy at York, and was therefore not likely to favour the changes proposed at Durham. But as Durham was especially designated as a suffragan see of York (Gervase, ii p. 366) at the conclusion of the York dispute, the Bishop's appeal to Lanfranc was a testimony to the primacy claimed by the Archbishop of Canterbury.

[2] Jaffé-Lowenfeld 5256.

[3] Sym. of Dur., *H. D. E.* iv. 2.

[4] Ibid. This letter has not survived.

[5] Lanfranc, Epis. LXV (1084). Clement was nominated Pope by Henry IV in March 1084. But Lanfranc speaks of a striking victory. This refers to Gregory's final departure from the city (1084).

ment of Pope Gregory, and of your designation of him as Hildebrand, and of his legates as quibblers, and of your constant and extravagant advocacy of Clement. Indeed it is written that a man should be neither praised nor condemned in this life. What men are now, is unknown to men, and also what they will be in the sight of God. Yet I believe that the Emperor would not have attempted to take so great a step without good reason, nor do I think that without the help of God he would have been able to achieve so great a victory.

I do not recommend your coming to England unless you first obtain the permission of the King of the English. Indeed our island has not yet rejected the former nor decided whether it should obey the latter.[1] When both sides have been heard, if events so happen, it will be possible to arrange more clearly what ought to be done.

The letter is characterized by Lanfranc's usual caution. William's attitude is of course reflected. From the beginning this had been altogether clear. Whenever purely spiritual or ecclesiastical points were raised, William offered full and loyal support to the Papacy and to the reforming bishops and monks. But so soon as the royal power or dignity was challenged, William assumed the defensive in no uncertain terms. The attack upon the imperial power must have been seriously regarded in England, and only the unsatisfactory character and conduct of the Emperor and the German bishops can have prevented William from making his attitude more clearly known. It was a distinct gain for the imperialists that William acted as though the controversy were an open question. For Gregory it was a set-back.

But the letter is especially interesting in its bearing upon Lanfranc's attitude to the Pope on the one side and to the King on the other. It would be too much to conclude that Lanfranc was entirely under the influence of William, and that his policy as Archbishop of Canterbury was solely a reflection of the will and action of the Conqueror upon ecclesiastical affairs. Lanfranc undoubtedly respected the King's advice in matters relating to the Church, but if he, like William, adopted an independent line on the question at issue between Gregory and Clement, and Gregory and the Emperor, it was because his position all through was

[1] i. e. decided between Gregory VII and Clement the anti-Pope.

characterized by the isolation and independence of a man who had moved about the world a great deal, who possessed a most varied experience of life, and who had won his way to influence by the sheer weight of his own ability, and the success of his own achievements. This independence and self-confidence were clearly revealed in his estimate of the Emperor in the letter to Clement's agent, and explain far more completely his attitude to the papal claims, than the suggestion that he acted solely as the King's agent. Moreover, by this time he must have been aware that the royal power and dignity in England would suffer a decline on the demise of William, while the history of the Papacy made it equally clear that no succession of popes who could compare with Gregory, either in ability or moral force, was to be expected. Thus neither to the imperial nor the papal theory *qua* theory was he likely to give entire assent. By experience and by temperament he was led to rely upon the personal factor in all these matters. What was sufficient for the day was all that could be achieved.

On the other hand if his policy was, by the pressure of events, and especially on account of his own experience and character, that of an individualist, he was well aware of William's own attitude, and clearly recognized the limitations which this imposed upon his own position and on his relations with the Papacy. So, in this letter to Hugo, he kept the royal wishes well in view. Whatever course was adopted to win England to a decision for or against the claim of Clement, it must remain dependent upon the royal will. If the reform of the English Church at the Conquest was the work of Lanfranc, and if he laid down a *via media* policy which only began to be abandoned for a more whole-hearted acceptance of the dictates of papal policy when Anselm opened his dispute with William II, this was largely the result of William's own influence upon the general scheme of reform.

The results achieved by the Hildebrandine reforms in England were only partial, and were confined almost entirely to the inner life of the Church. The regular monastic rule was revived. The episcopate was reorganized. Simony was uprooted,[1] though we hear nothing of the details. Clerical marriage was restrained, but piecemeal, and not ruthlessly. The investiture question which had thrown Germany and Italy into turmoil was not yet raised. The famous Roman decree of Gregory VII (1075), prohibiting lay investiture, was not put into operation in England during Lanfranc's time. There is some ground for thinking that the Archbishop did not publish it.[2] Throughout the reign of William, all the bishops were invested with the pastoral staff by the King, with two exceptions—Ernest and Gundulf of Rochester.[3]

The Hildebrandine reforms were introduced gradually, with due regard to local conditions and the necessities of the Conquest. The Norman settlement of the English Church was a compromise, but a compromise working by experiment, and conceding more and more to the ecclesiastical claims of the Papacy, as one opportunity after another was supplied. But on the question of the royal homage, not an inch was conceded. England was never recognized by the King or by the Archbishop as a papal fief.

[1] Alex. II to William, Epis. LXXXIII (Migne, cxlvi).

[2] Boehmer, *Die Falschungen*, p. 65.

[3] Eadmer, *Hist. Nov*,, p. 2; cf. *supra*, p. 130.

XVI

ACCESSION OF RUFUS AND THE DURHAM LAW-SUIT

THE arrest of Odo of Bayeux in 1084 was the last occasion when we read of Lanfranc and William working together. Odo's ambition caused him to attempt to secure the accession to the papal chair after the death of Gregory.[1] He persuaded a number of English and Norman knights to concentrate in the Isle of Wight. As they were about to embark, William and his Court came down upon them. Among the charges of general oppression brought against Odo was one of cruelty during the punitive expedition to Durham in 1083. The King asked for the opinion of his lords on Odo's conduct, and when no one dared to give advice, ordered him to be seized and imprisoned. The barons remained inactive, and William himself seized the Bishop. Odo promptly claimed ecclesiastical privilege and appealed to the Pope. The astute brain of Lanfranc at once brought assistance to the King. At a hint from the Archbishop, William replied: 'I do not arrest the Bishop of Bayeux, but I do arrest the Earl of Kent. I arrest my Earl whom I appointed over my kingdom, and I demand from him an account of the office I entrusted to him.' Odo remained in prison until William released him, under extreme persuasion, on his death-bed.[2]

That Lanfranc was always at hand to advise William in such matters as the plan of the Great Survey and the taking of the oaths at Salisbury is certain, and doubtless he was left in charge of the government when William crossed over to Normandy in 1087. When the great King passed

[1] Odo bought a palace at Rome, and bribed the Roman magnates. Ord. vii. 8 (iii, p. 189).

[2] Ord. vii. 16 (iii, pp. 247–8). Odo was imprisoned at Rouen and Gregory VII wrote to William demanding his release. Jaffé (*Mon. Greg.*, p. 518) suggests that the date of this letter is 1083. Cf. Gregory's letter to Hugh of Lyons (ibid., p. 570).

away Lanfranc was still in England. Although it was known that the end was near, no attempt was made to bring Lanfranc over in order to receive the wishes of the dying Conqueror. His place was in England, where it was necessary that some personage of outstanding authority should be present when the King died. As a spiritual counsellor at his death-bed William probably preferred the holy Anselm, who through sickness was unable to offer the last ministrations which Lanfranc might have looked forward to performing. We read of no personal message sent to Lanfranc, and as William was a brief correspondent, it is unlikely that the letter concerning the succession sent by him to Lanfranc contained very much that was of this nature. Putting two contradictory statements of Orderic together,[1] it appears that William, while moved during his last moments to thoughts of penitence and perhaps misgiving, intimated a preference for Rufus. This is confirmed by the departure of Rufus from Normandy, carrying a letter addressed to Lanfranc, before his father was actually dead. The final onus of selection may, by the terms of the letter, have been left with Lanfranc, but its tenour, and the fact that Rufus was the bearer, must have clearly intimated the wishes of the King. Lanfranc was so overcome on the receipt of the news that Eadmer and others present thought he also would die.[2]

There is no record of any formal election by the Witan, such as the Conqueror thought it necessary to secure.[3] Lanfranc's uneasiness of mind was manifested at the coronation. He knew Rufus as well as any one. At one time

[1] In his lengthy account of the Conqueror's last moments, Orderic reports that William declined to name any successor to the throne of England, vii. 15 (iii, p. 242). But in his report of the interview between the King and Henry, he makes the Conqueror refer to Rufus as his successor in England, vii. 16 (iii, p. 244).

[2] Eadmer, *Hist. Nov.*, p. 25.

[3] On the constitutional question of the election cf. Freeman (*Rufus*, i, p. 12; ii, p. 459), quoting the Sax. Chron., *Lat. Act.*, 'Lanfrancus in regem elegit'. He tries to prove that an election was made by Lanfranc. But Lanfranc had no authority on a constitutional point.

William had been his pupil,[1] and Lanfranc had performed the religious rite when he was knighted.[2] At the coronation,[3] which was conducted with maimed rites,[4] in addition to the usual oath promising to rule justly and with mercy, to promote the interests of peace, and to respect the rights of the Church, Lanfranc exacted from William a promise to follow his counsel in everything.[5] But though the Archbishop might well hesitate, partly on account of his knowledge of Rufus, partly on account of the great responsibility which he was himself undertaking, by promoting the accession of the Conqueror's successor, it is difficult to see that he could have supported any other candidate. Robert's claim could not be considered. Henry's claim had not yet come into existence. Though William's character was doubtful, his capacity was well known, and he might become completely changed by the dignity and responsibility of his new function. But the deciding factor with Lanfranc was the receipt of the dead King's letter, and the Archbishop's attitude was the deciding factor in the election of the new King. One writer states that William was willingly accepted by all the provincial districts of England.[6] But another writer says that without the consent of Lanfranc no one could have obtained the throne of England.[7]

At the beginning of the new reign Lanfranc's influence played a large part in rallying English support to the side of Rufus during the baronial revolt of 1088, and his counsel contributed largely to William's success during the campaign. He pacified the barons who were disposed to support the claims of Robert, and it was by his advice that William called the nobles together, and by secret promises won over Robert Montgomery. Then, at Lanfranc's suggestion the

[1] Malmes., *G. R.* p. 360. The Conqueror is reported to have advised Robert to be guided by Lanfranc, Ord. v. 10 (ii, p. 379).

[2] Ibid. Malmes. says that Lanfranc knighted William. Ord. viii. 1 (iii, p. 267), says that he also knighted Henry. But the Sax. Chron. (1086) and Florence (1086) says clearly that the King knighted Henry. Lanfranc performed the religious rite on both occasions.

[3] 26th Sept. 1087, Sax. Chron. and Florence. Orderic, 29th Sept.

[4] Matt. Paris, *Hist. Ang.* i. p. 35.

[5] Eadmer, *Hist. Nov.*, p. 25.

[6] Malmes., *G. R.* p. 359.

[7] Eadmer, *Hist. Nov.*, p. 25.

King put into operation the principle 'divide et impera'.[1] The Archbishop's zeal in the royal cause was the more pronounced because his old enemy Odo was now again in the van of the revolted baronage. But we have no details of the part played by Lanfranc behind the scenes during that important campaign. Our record of his administrative career closes with the recital of his conduct of the famous Durham case, when the old lawyer is seen once more using his characteristic faculty for acute decisive argument and clear-headed cautious handling of a difficult proposition. This last public act in his life rings truly to type. His career had been a series of migrations, interspersed with disputes. But he was always successful. In Italy, in Normandy, in England; in matters legal, or ecclesiastical or constitutional, he ever resorted to his most powerful weapon—a lawyer-like capacity for penetrating to the heart of a case, won during his early experiences in the schools and courts of Pavia, which made him the most formidable antagonist of the day, whether his opponent was theologian or king, baron or bishop or pope. The dramatic unity of his career was most fittingly completed by his action in the case of William of Durham.

The cause of the royal displeasure with William of S. Carilef remains obscure. The southern writers agree in making the Bishop of Durham a secret collaborator with the revolted barons, and hold up his action to execration on the ground that he had been one of the special friends of Rufus.[2] An entirely different account is offered by the Durham writer, in which the Bishop appears as an innocent victim of William's aggression. If he was not one of the original promoters of the revolt, yet the Bishop did not sufficiently actively declare himself on the royal side during its early stages, and on this ground Lanfranc appears to have taken up the royal case against him. The dignity of the see of Canterbury was not at stake, and William of S. Carilef had, by instituting regular clergy at Durham,

[1] Matt. Paris, *Hist. Ang.* i., p. 36.

[2] Sax. Chron. (Peterborough) 1087, (Florence) 1088; Malmes., *G. R.* p. 360

clearly shown his deference to the wishes of the primate.[1] It is unlikely that Lanfranc would have proceeded against him so definitely without good ground for suspecting his loyalty. The Archbishop was well aware of certain defects in the King's character which were likely to lead him into acts of oppression. It is therefore improbable that he would have missed the opportunity of checking the new King's action, if his treatment of the Bishop was the result of mere arbitrary caprice. A precedent would have been created which would have seriously hindered Lanfranc's action. None the less S. Carilef had a good case, and ably made the best use of it.

According to the Durham writer the Bishop was disseised of his lands and those of his church on 12th March 1088, before the rebellion had actually broken out. He appears to have aroused suspicion by leaving the court without permission. An order for his arrest was issued, but S. Carilef was able to reach his castle at Durham with safety.[2] From Durham he wrote to William asking that his lands and dependants might be restored, since the case had not been tried in any court.[3] William's reply was to grant the forfeited lands to other barons in the presence of the Bishop's messenger.

After further negotiations, during which the Bishop's lands were ravaged, S. Carilef came to London under the protection of a safe-conduct, but no agreement was reached, and he returned to Durham and established himself firmly upon its rocky fortress, while his lands were again spoiled by the royal troops.[4] Another safe-conduct was arranged at Durham, and the Bishop appeared at a court convened under the presidency of Lanfranc at Salisbury.

S. Carilef based his case from the beginning of the proceedings, both at the London meeting and at Salisbury, upon ecclesiastical privilege. With this object in view he urged that all the bishops should appear in their robes, but Lanfranc declined with the remark that 'clothes do not

[1] Sym. of Dur., *H. D. E.* i. 21.
[2] Sym. of Dur,. *De Injusta Vexatione*, i.
[3] Ibid. ii.
[4] Ibid. v.

hinder truth'.[1] The Bishop then attempted to forestall the royal charge by claiming to be reinvested with his lands before the case proceeded. Lanfranc denied that he had been disseised, or that he had seen a writ ordering him to be disseised, and when the Bishop referred to the confiscation and devastation of his property which had already taken place, by the King's orders, and at the hands of men present at the court, the Archbishop maintained that his demand was absurd. 'First give satisfaction to the King and afterwards demand from him that which you now demand.' The laity vociferously agreed.[2]

S. Carilef held to his point. The King and some of the earls intervened and expressed surprise at his claims, when Roger Bigod contended that William should at least state the substance of the royal charge. The Bishop then relented to the extent of agreeing that he would plead if canonically advised so to do. Hugh de Beaumont, at the command of the King, thereupon presented the royal case:

The King alleges against you that when he heard that his enemies were coming upon him, and that his men, Odo of Bayeux, and Earl Roger, and many others wished to take from him his kingdom and crown, and he himself at your counsel rode against them, he summoned you, in my hearing, to ride with him. You replied to him that you yourself and the seven knights whom you have here, would willingly come, and that you would speedily send to your castle for many others, but afterwards you fled from his court without his permission, and took some of his household with you, and so in his necessity you deserted him. Now he desires that on this account you shall do to him what this court shall judge, and if necessary, afterwards he will charge you with many things.

No impression was made upon the stubbornness of the Bishop's defence, and another uproar followed his refusal to submit. But the case began to go against him when Geoffrey of Coutances proposed that a committee of bishops, assisted by some lay lords, should settle the preliminary difficulty whether the Bishop should be reinvested before pleading or not. Lanfranc accepted the suggestion, but insisted that S. Carilef and his following should withdraw,

[1] Ibid. ix.

[2] Ibid. x. Lanfranc is styled 'Primate of all England'

leaving the point to be settled by those who remained. As the Bishop left the court Hugh de Beaumont shouted: 'If to-day I am not allowed to judge thee, thou and thy order shall never more judge me.' [1]

When S. Carilef returned it was announced to him by Thomas of York that he must plead before being reinvested, and Lanfranc gave formal expression to the finding by saying: 'This court decides that the King ought not to reseise you with anything, until you first do satisfaction to him.' The Bishop so far relented as to ask permission to take canonical advice upon the point. Lanfranc replied that as the judgement was lawful he must submit; moreover, because the bishops were judges he could not have them as counsel.[1]

S. Carilef gave way and accepted the royal permission to consult his own following, but brought the case to a head by making an appeal to Rome:

> The judgement which is given here I repudiate, since it is uttered contrary to the canons and to our law. I was not canonically cited, but I am present, driven by the force of the royal army, and I am compelled to state my case, while despoiled, outside my territory, of my bishopric, with all my local supporters absent, and in a lay court, and my enemies, who deny to me counsel and speech, and the kiss of peace, having brushed aside my statements, judge me concerning things which I have not said, and are at once my accusers and judges. In our law I find it prohibited that I should receive such a judgement as in my folly I am disposed to accept. My Archbishop and Primate ought to curb me charitably from this presumption, from respect for God and my order. And since through the hatred of the King I feel you are all my enemies, I appeal to the apostolical see, to the holy Roman church, to the blessed Peter, and his Vicar, in order that by his arrangement I may be worthy to receive a lawful opinion concerning my business, to whose discretion the ancient judgements of the bishops, and the authority of the apostles and their successors have resigned major ecclesiastical disputes.

Lanfranc made some further attempt to distinguish between S. Carilef's status as a lay lord and a bishop. 'We do not judge thee concerning thy bishopric, but concerning thy fief, and in this manner we have judged the Bishop of

[1] Sym. of Dur., *De Injust. Vex.* xi   [2] Ibid. xii.

Bayeux concerning his fief, before the father of this King, nor did the King call him Bishop in that case, but brother and Earl.' But S. Carilef turned the argument round, and with equal logical force replied that he was not concerned with the lay fief but with the bishopric. 'I have made no mention to-day of a fief.' Lanfranc then gave an opinion upon the facts of the case. 'Even if I never hear thee speak of a fief, I none the less know that you have held a great fief, and we have judged thee concerning this.' S. Carilef again asked leave to withdraw, and on his return Hugh de Beaumont delivered, as the judgement of the court, the opinion that the Bishop's refusal to plead, and his appeal to Rome, constituted a ground for forfeiture.[1]

The case then entered its second stage when the King demanded the surrender of Durham castle before ships and a safe-conduct to the continent were supplied. The Bishop was technically justified in maintaining that this was not mentioned in the Durham compact under which he had come to Salisbury. Lanfranc expressed the opinion that the King might arrest the Bishop if the castle were not surrendered, on the ground that he had himself broken the pact of Durham, and had cast reflections upon the royal officers. But the Archbishop modified his severe view of the Bishop's action when the three earls who had signed the pact of Durham agreed with the Bishop's contention. Lanfranc said that if S. Carilef, while not submitting, yet admitted the legality of the court's decision, a safe-conduct to the Continent would be granted, and when the Bishop still demurred, tried to force him into giving an answer 'Yes!' or 'No!' But not until the King had again intervened did S. Carilef agree to surrender the castle.[2]

The question of the revenue to be allowed to him was then raised. Lanfranc retorted with indignation: 'To the damage of the King, and to the discredit of us all you are going to Rome, and shall he charge his land for you? Remain in his land and he will restore to you your bishopric which is beyond the city, on condition that you will give satisfaction to him in his court, by the judgement of his

[1] Ibid. xiii.

[2] Ibid. xiv.

barons.' S. Carilef refused to revert from his decision to go to Rome, but asked for permission to purge himself from the charge imputed to him. In the course of his petition he entered what was practically a plea:

Up to the present you have said nothing to him (the King) favourable to my necessity, but whatever pleases you, you can well say, but before I depart I am prepared, before all those barons, to purge myself from all crime and perjury, and to defend myself by all means, since I have neither done nor sought, to my knowledge, any loss to the King concerning his person or his realm, nor have I pledged or received a pledge from anyone in that connection. When, before this, I perceived his difficulties, I fortified him against them as speedily as I was able, and I helped him faithfully against his enemies, and I will shew that I did this lawfully. I will shew that at Dover and Hastings, which he had then almost lost, I was detained, faithful to him. Also at London, which had already rebelled, I remained quiet, faithful to him, and more than twelve citizens of that city I conducted to him, in order that through them he might the more readily put life into the others. And that I did this I will prove by the testimony of his barons, if he will give them permission. I beg him earnestly that he will accept the purgation which I have now uttered, and afterwards that he will permit me to shew my service lawfully, and, if it shall please him, and he is willing to give kind permission to them, I can produce many witnesses from among these bishops for making this purgation.

This permission the Bishop earnestly and repeatedly sought, but the King altogether refused to grant it. Lanfranc urged entire submission. 'You would do better if you threw yourself on the King's mercy, and I would willingly come to your assistance at his feet.'

After some further discussion between the Bishop and Lanfranc, William agreed to supply transport to the Continent, if the Bishop promised not to plot against him oversea, and not to allow his brother to retain the ships. S. Carilef maintained that this also was not in the Durham pact, and the Sheriff of York supported his contention. The King then became angry and cried: 'By the holy face of Lucca you shall not cross the sea this year, unless you now first give the pledge which I require for my ships!' The Bishop then submitted,[1] and after an attempt was

[1] Sym. of Dur., *De Injust. Vex.* xv.

made by William of Merlao to claim damages for an attack made upon the property of Geoffrey of Coutances by the Bishop's men, during the safe-conduct, a charge which Lanfranc refused to sanction on the ground that S. Carilef now held nothing of the King,[1] the case ended, although the three earls had to make a further appeal to the King before S. Carilef got away from Southampton.[2]

The precedent for the trial was the case against Odo of Bayeux. The actual words placed in the mouth of the Conqueror on that occasion may have proceeded from Lanfranc, but the subtle distinction then drawn, and now made the basis of the royal case against William of S. Carilef, was well apprehended by the men of that day. Even Hugh of Beaumont's taunt does not prove that the laymen objected to a separate ecclesiastical jurisdiction. It rather points the other way. If the bishops recognized lay jurisdiction in lay cases, the barons were ready to recognize ecclesiastical jurisdiction in ecclesiastical cases. All the relationships of the time, even those controlled by the growing body of the canon law, were based upon fictions, which necessarily resulted from the fundamental feudal principle upon which all tenure of property and all public and private service were based. No matter what a man's special functions and privileges might be, if he held property of the King, or was invested with it by the King, he could always be isolated from the implications of those privileges, and made subject to the royal will.

But in William of Durham Lanfranc met with an opponent of very different calibre from Thomas of York, or even Odo of Bayeux. Possibly Lanfranc's sublety had been sprung upon Odo, and gave him no time for a reply, and doubtless William of Durham's case was carefully prepared beforehand, as the compact with the three Earls shows, and was prepared with the recollection of Odo's case in mind; but throughout the trial at Salisbury, although point after point went against him, he maintained his own position intact to the end, and in mere argument was never overmatched by Lanfranc. The Bishop turned Lanfranc's argument

[1] Ibid. xvi. [2] Ibid. xvii–xx.

against him. If it was true that a bishop as a lay lord might be condemned by a lay court in a lay plea, it was logical that he could not be condemned, nor was he amenable to a lay court on an ecclesiastical charge, especially in view of the Conqueror's separation of the two jurisdictions. S. Carilef indeed made no reference to the Conqueror's arrangement. This was probably because he based his case upon deductions from the canon law, which were being worked out by the Hildebrandine party. His refusal to plead before being reinvested was a direct appeal to the pseudo-Isidorian principle 'Spoliatus ante omnia debet restitui'.[1]

At the same time the case resulted in a practical victory for Lanfranc. The King secured more by the Bishop's departure than if the latter had consented to plead without raising the question of reinvestiture. The sentence of forfeiture in that case would not have been passed.

No fresh light is thrown by the trial upon Lanfranc's attitude to the bishops in their relation as territorial magnates. As he had always consistently supported the territorial claims of the Conqueror, so he continued to support Rufus in his capacity as chief landlord of England. Nor is anything fresh revealed in his attitude to the papal claims, although his arguments on this occasion, if the minutes quoted by the Durham writer can be trusted, demonstrate his position more clearly. No exception was taken to the appeal to Rome as such. Odo of Bayeux had already appealed to Rome under similar circumstances. Nor was any objection raised on the ground of the appeal being a breach of the royal authority, though indeed this appears to be suggested by Lanfranc's ruling that the appeal to Rome constituted a justification for forfeiture because of the damage done to the King. The appeal was really resented because the Bishop refused to admit that the procedure of the trial and the findings of the court were in order. Lanfranc seemed willing to allow the appeal to Rome if the Bishop admitted these points.[2] Provided no encroachment

[1] Maitland, *Collected Papers*, ii, p. 249.

[2] Sym. of Dur., *De Injust. Vex.* xiv.

was made upon the royal authority he was prepared to entertain the Hildebrandine claims. The trial of William of S. Carilef made it unreservedly clear that he was not among the advanced reformers of the papal school. With him theory was always subservient to practice, and policy gave way when necessary to expediency. He gave no blind adhesion to doctrinaire shibboleths. Although he was the author of the *De Corpore et Sanguine Domini*, yet he was really on the side of Berengar, as the latter knew. John the Scot, not any forerunner of S. Thomas, was the spokesman of men like Lanfranc, and although the Middle Ages had to run out before the older nominalism finally routed the revived realism of the Schoolmen, Lanfranc's attitude was that of Henry VIII. He would have had an even more famous place than he occupies in the history of England if he had lived in the sixteenth century, and if he had lived in the twentieth we might look for the successful solution of some problems which baffle the doctrinaire statesmen and ecclesiastics of the day.

XVII

LAST DAYS

Details of practical administration continued to occupy Lanfranc's attention to the end of his life. In 1087 he consecrated Gosfrid to Chichester, and in July 1088, John of Tours to Wells.[1] He became involved in a dispute with Rufus over some Rochester property. The Conqueror had granted the manor of Haddenham[2] in Buckinghamshire to S. Andrew's, Rochester, for the period of his own life. The Archbishop suggested to Rufus that the grant should be made permanent. The King informed Lanfranc and Gundulf that he would agree on receiving a payment of one hundred pounds. They replied that they could not pay this amount. Two of William's friends, Robert, son of Haimo, and Henry, Earl of Warwick, then suggested that the sum should be reduced to forty pounds, and that Gundulf should build a castle for the King at Rochester. The bishops replied that they would rather see the manor at the bottom of the sea, than place such a burden on the monastery, for the monks would be compelled to keep the castle in repair. Earl Henry answered that he had hitherto thought Lanfranc was one of the wisest of men, and although he did not now say that he regarded him as a foolish man, or lacking in the wisdom that he had possessed a short time before, yet he could not see what burden there was in undertaking to build a castle at the King's desire, and to pay forty pounds in addition. The transaction would be made known to the Earl of Kent, or the Sheriff, or any others whom the King might choose. It would be demonstrated to all concerned that the monastery was free from further charges in the matter. The King sought no occasion for

[1] Stubbs, *Reg. Sac. Ang.*, p. 23, quoting the Cant. Profession Rolls and Gervase, ii, p. 367. But the Sax. Chron., *Lat. Act.*, dates both consecrations 1088.

[2] Cf. *supra*. p. 142. The story is printed in *Ang. Sac.* i. pp. 337–8.

future service from the Bishop, but desired rather to deliver the community from it. Lanfranc gave way, Gundulf built the castle, and forty pounds were paid to the King.

The story is probable. Gundulf would scarcely have undertaken such a work so near his cathedral unless some kind of pressure had been exerted. Rufus seldom granted a favour without some material return. But the story shows that according to popular tradition the relations between King and Archbishop were not what they had been in the Conqueror's time.

In the year 1080 Lanfranc began to regulate the affairs of S. Augustine's, Canterbury. He was assisted by people whom Thorn[1] calls accomplices. He often cunningly obtained his wishes through his friendship with Abbot Scolland. He urged Scolland to come with all his monks to the synods in order to hear him preach, and to add to the dignity of the synod. The Abbot frequently delayed on account of the opposition shown by the monks, who declared that if they went at all, they would only go for the sermon. But in the end they had to give way. The monks of S. Augustine's thought that the dignity of their house was thus impaired. The quarrel over this point went on for some years, until in 1086 Lanfranc gave further annoyance by forbidding the S. Augustine's brethren to ring their bell before the Christ Church monks had rung theirs. The brethren wanted to carry the dispute to Rome, but Lanfranc forbade them to ventilate it outside the cloister.

In 1087 Scolland died,[2] and Lanfranc determined to appoint Guido, one of the Christ Church monks, possibly Anselm's friend from Bec, in order to keep the S. Augustine's brethren in order.[3] He applied to the King for permission to make the appointment, and claimed the right on the ground of ancient precedent.[4] Rufus replied that he desired to hold the pastoral staves in England in his own hands,[5] but the S. Augustine's writer says that he declined when the monks of that house appealed to their privileges.[6]

[1] Thorn (Twysden), *Decem Scriptores*, a late authority.
[2] Thorn, *X. Script.* [3] *Hist. S. Aug. Cant.* (Rolls), p. 345.
[4] Gervase, i, p. 71. [5] Ibid. [6] Thorn, *X. Script.*

Lanfranc did not press the point, on the grounds of expediency, but sought and obtained permission from the King to promote Guido, his own candidate. The new Abbot made a formal declaration of obedience to him at the altar of Christ Church.[1] But the monks of S. Augustine's still held out, and refused to accept Guido, not because he was consecrated in Christ Church, nor because he had taken an oath to Lanfranc, but because they claimed the privilege of selecting their own candidate.[2] Lanfranc then repressed them with harsh and caustic words, and they gave way,[3] though only after refusing to be bribed by him with money and promises of future assistance. They feared 'the snake in the grass, and could not trust him for the future because of the past'.[4] On the day following the appointment of Guido, Lanfranc, accompanied by Odo of Bayeux, went to S. Augustine's to ask the monks whether they would accept Guido as their lawful Abbot and pastor. They replied that they had no desire or intention of receiving him. Lanfranc thereupon ordered that all who would not obey should at once leave the monastery. Almost the whole community left, and Guido was installed, with due rites, into the monastery and church. The Prior Alfwin and some other ringleaders were imprisoned in the castle at Canterbury. The rest of the seceding monks took up their abode in S. Mildred's church, and Lanfranc sent to them a message saying that if they returned by the hour of Nones, all would be well, but if they refused, they could only be admitted as fugitives who had unlawfully left the house. Some of them returned when the hour of refection arrived, and made their submission, taking oaths of obedience to Guido. The refractory monks were then distributed among other religious houses in England, and were placed under discipline. One of the fugitives named Alfred, with some of his companions, was captured in Canterbury, and charged with plotting against Guido. They were put into irons, and placed under rigorous discipline for some time. Meanwhile the other monks, who had been sent to different houses,

[1] Gervase, i, p. 71.
[2] Ibid.
[3] Ibid.
[4] Thorn, *X. Script.*

soon became penitent, and were allowed to return to S. Augustine's, where they became reconciled with the new Abbot. But the outbreak was not yet completely quelled. In the same year a plot was hatched by some of the fugitives to kill Guido. One of them, Columban by name, was apprehended and brought before Lanfranc. When charged with the suspected crime he confessed that he would certainly have killed the Abbot if an opportunity had occurred. Lanfranc ordered him to be stripped naked before the door of S. Augustine's and publicly flogged. After this his cowl was removed, and he was driven out of the city. No further trouble arose at S. Augustine's while Lanfranc lived.[1]

While the Archbishop's action was high-handed, the position was so difficult that he could hardly avoid giving offence to a community situated so close to the cathedral foundation. S. Augustine's was the older community, but the greater prestige was enjoyed by Christ Church. If the annual synod was an episcopal visitation, the S. Augustine's monks were bound to attend together with the other clergy of the diocese, at least in accordance with Lanfranc's policy, which submitted the monasteries to episcopal jurisdiction. But the S. Augustine's monks appear to have regarded the summons to the synod as an attempt to make their community a permanent dependency of Christ Church, and they claimed no more independence than was secured at Battle, and attempted at S. Edmund's. Moreover, their refusal to accept Guido was parallel with the case at Glastonbury and at Rouen. Their compliance with the order to attend the sermon or visitation charge at Christ Church

[1] Sax. Chron., *Latin Acta*—a good authority. The accounts are fairly consistent. The S. Augustine's writer says that Lanfranc consecrated Guido under compulsion from the King, and although Guido was in reality Lanfranc's candidate, this agrees with William's refusal to allow Lanfranc's claim to the right of election, as reported by Gervase. It is improbable that the S. Augustine's monks accepted the consecration at Christ Church as Gervase implies, so that the story of the Saxon Chronicler may be followed. But according to the S. Augustine's writer (p. 346) Guido appeared as their candidate and Lanfranc at first refused him.

suggests a willingness to submit to Lanfranc's episcopal authority.[1]

Like the account of the building of Rochester Castle, the story of the trouble at S. Augustine's illustrates the strained relations which existed between Rufus and Lanfranc shortly before the latter died. The Archbishop found it necessary to rebuke the King for a breach of the coronation oath.[2] Rufus replied that no man could keep all his promises, and from that time he could never look the Archbishop straight in the face,[3] although the influence of Lanfranc acted in some measure as a restraint upon him.[4] Doubtless Rufus regarded his old preceptor with the same kind of reverence as he had formerly felt for his father, but there is little to indicate that if Lanfranc had lived on, the King would have continued to bridle his growing self-will. On a later occasion when Anselm rebuked the wrong-doing of the Red King, Rufus replied that Lanfranc would not have dared to speak to the Conqueror as Anselm had spoken to him. But while Lanfranc would not have remained silent in the presence of the King's wrong-doing, he would have avoided some of the mistakes made by Anselm in his attitude to William. No mere theory would have taken him to Rome. He would have fought his own case, and if he had secured a victory less in dimensions than that obtained by Anselm, he would have secured one which would have been far more effective, and the English Church would not have been left for four years [5] without an Archbishop of Canterbury, at the mercy of a king who spent the Canterbury revenues on follies and vices which were a reproach not only to religion but to civilization.

[1] Lanfranc's attitude to S. Augustine's was not always unfriendly. A reeve named Brumar had enforced payment on the lands of S. Augustine's in the time of the Conqueror. The case came up before Lanfranc and Odo of Bayeux. A judgement was given for S. Augustine's, and the reeve was compelled to swear that he would not interfere with the rights of either community at Canterbury. (Freeman, *N. C.* iv. 365, n. 6, quoting an entry in Domesday.)

[2] Malmes., *G. P.*, p. 73.

[3] Eadmer, *Hist. Nov.*, p. 25.

[4] Matt. Paris, *Hist. Ang.* i, p. 38.

[5] Saxon Chron., *Lat. Act.*, 1089.

Shortly before the close of Lanfranc's life he again had to deal with correspondence from the contending Popes. A letter was received from Urban II in which the Pope announced his succession to Gregory VII. He referred to the troubles of the Roman Church and reminded Lanfranc that Canterbury had received the rudiments of faith from Rome, and should therefore set an example of loyalty to the Roman Church more conspicuous than that of other metropolitans. He also begged for the assistance of Rufus. If the payments due to Rome were made, the King would find that the Roman Church would help him to the utmost of her ability.[1]

It is not clear whether the accession of Urban II was at once recognized in England. Three letters received from the anti-pope Clement III suggest that the hesitation which marked the attitude of the Conqueror and Lanfranc to the Papacy, when Clement was in opposition to Gregory, was still maintained. Clement wrote twice to Lanfranc asking him to persuade Rufus to pay Peter's Pence, and especially urged him to visit Rome to assist the interests of Clement.[2] These requests were repeated in a third letter in which Clement commented on Lanfranc's contribution to learning,[3] and requested that certain lands which had been alienated from the Abbey of Wilton during the time of the Conqueror should be restored by Rufus. The Abbess of Wilton apparently had appealed to Clement asking him to intercede with Lanfranc on behalf of the Abbey lands.[4] She would not have taken this action unless she had known that Clement possessed some influence in England. Further evidence for the doubtful attitude of Rufus and Lanfranc towards Urban II is forthcoming in the statement of William of Malmesbury that England, owing to fear of William II, inclined to the side of Clement.[5]

[1] Urban II, Epis. IV (Migne, cli).
[2] *Eng. Hist. Rev.*, April, 1901, pp. 330–1. [3] Ibid., p. 331.
[4] Liebermann. Introduction to the three letters of Clement (*Eng. Hist. Rev.*, April, 1901). The letters are in the library of Trin. Coll., Camb., B 16, 44, pp. 406–7.
[5] Malmes., *G. P.*, p. 86.

Lanfranc's last days were passed at Canterbury.[1] Whether compelled to retire thither by infirmity or old age, or whether deliberately shutting himself up on account of the breach which existed between William and himself, we have no means of determining. The Whitsun festival had passed, and on the octave he was attacked by a malady which may have been that which annoyed him in earlier years.[2] The Infirmarian, or possibly the physician Albert, prescribed a draught, but the Archbishop postponed taking it until he had made his Communion. The physician warned him of the danger of delay, but the patient declined to comply. During the interval the contents of the cup became rancid, and when he took the draught it hastened his end,[3] which came at 1 a.m. on Monday, 28th May 1089, on the day following the octave of Whitsun.[4] He died as he wished in

[1] Longuemare, *Lanfranc*, p. 174, says that he shut himself up in his palace, saddened by the death of friends, and consoled himself with pious exercises, and corresponded frequently with Bec and especially with Anselm. Hook, *Archbishops*, ii. p. 167, says that he returned to the cloister as Abbot. But there appears to be no authority for either statement.

[2] Longuemare, p. 177, suggests that he was ill for some weeks.

[3] Malmes., *G. P.*, p. 73.

[4] Different dates in March, May and June have been fixed. Matt. Paris (*Hist. Maj.* ii, p. 29), *Flores Hist.* (ii, p. 21), Bartholomew de Cotton (Rolls, p. 53) place it on IX Kal. Aprilis (24th March). Arnold Wion, Hugh Menard and some other late writers have tertia die Junii (3rd June); cf. Migne, cl., col. 27. Most of the early writers place it in May, but on different dates. Robt. of Torigny in William of Jum. (vii. 26) gives VI Kal. Junii (27th May). Florence, Sym. of Dur. (ii, p. 217), followed by Hoveden (i, p. 142) have IX Kal. Junii, feria V (Thursday, 24th May). Johan Oxendes (p. 37) gives IX Kal. Junii (24th May). In 1089 the 20th May fell on a Sunday, so that feria V (Thursday) did fall on IX Kal. Junii (24th May). But Gervase (ii, p. 370) gives V Kal. Junii feria II (28th May, Monday), and fixes the date by saying that it was the day following the octave of Whitsun. Easter that year fell on 1st April, so that Whitsunday was the 20th May, the octave was on the 27th May, and feria II was the 28th May. Gervase is supported by Milo 52 and *Vita Gundulfi* (Migne, clix, col. 825), who have V Kal. Junii. The Sax. Chron., *Latin Acta* says that his archbishopric lasted eighteen years, nine months, and two days, which agrees more closely with Gervase than with any of the other writers. The date of Gervase is fixed finally by the

full possession of the powers of intellect and speech,[1] and was perhaps able to read a letter which may have arrived from Anselm about this time.[2] He had prayed to be carried off by dysentery or a rapid fever, and not by the ravages of old age.[3]

The scene which followed at Christ Church may be pictured from the regulations given in the Benedictine Decreta, and from the account of Herluin's death. His funeral was conducted by Thomas of York. He was buried in the minster of Christ Church, in the Chapel of the Holy Trinity on the south side of the altar.[4] When the church was rebuilt his body was transferred to a tomb at the altar of S. Martin. But no trace of it remains. At the translation a monk cut off a piece of his chasuble which exhaled a fragrant odour.[5] Although he was not canonized Lanfranc received beatification.

The day of his death was always commemorated by the Benedictines, although it occurred at the season of Pentecost. The anniversary of the Lord Archbishop Lanfranc was pronounced at the chapter. All the brothers processed into the church singing ' Verba mea ', while the bells were ringing. After supper, when the bell sounded for the vigil, everything proceeded in the accustomed manner. The vigil was observed festively. The responses, twice times three, three times six, and four times nine were sung. On the next day each priest was expected to sing a Mass for him, and those who could not sing Masses sang forty psalms. The Mass in the minster was celebrated festively with white albs, while the Cantor and two others wore copes. For the responses three brothers wore copes, and for the ' tractatus '[6] four others were similarly robed. The Treasurer was expected to give forty solidi to buy food for the poor on that day. The refectory was decorated festively, as on the

Bec calendar (which is also an obituary; cf. Longuemare, p. 180) which celebrated his anniversary on the 28th May. Gervase gives 1 a.m.

[1] Malmes., *G. P.*, p. 73. [2] Anselm, Lib. II, Epis. LIII.

[3] Malmes., *G. P.*, p. 73; Lanfranc, *Decreta pro Ordine S. Benedicti*, xxiii

[4] Gervase, i, p. 16; Ord. iv. 8 (iii, p. 309) says he was buried before the crucifix. [5] Mabillon, *Acta Ord. SS. Ben.*, vi. Pt. ii. p. 659.

[6] A piece of chanting after the Response Gradual.

feast of an apostle and the church remained prepared as on the feast of S. Augustine, until the service was completed.[1]

Thus with rites which he had helped to draw up for others, and in which he had often partaken, with the ringing of bells, and the singing of festive Masses, the memory of the great Archbishop, who was the 'father and comforter of monks',[2] was kept green, by the order whose tradition of scholarship and stately ritual, asceticism and quiet devotion he had himself so worthily upheld.

As in the case of other prominent churchmen, the records of Lanfranc's life have not been allowed to come down without some of the trappings of sainthood. But no miracles are attributed to him. This is perhaps one of the best testimonies to the impression made upon the men of his day by the practical and restrained common sense of his life and actions. But the monastic writers go as far as they can, by reporting the dreams of Lanfranc, to give him a fitting place among the saints who were honoured by the special favour of the unseen world.

The story of the assistance rendered to him by S. Dunstan during the case on Penenden Heath is suspiciously like the similar tale told of Wulfstan when the question of his deposition was discussed. Osbern, a monk of Canterbury, who was a public preacher especially appointed by Lanfranc, records that during the dispute with Odo of Bayeux, Lanfranc consulted his patron saint. He offered a Mass to S. Dunstan, and then sat down to await events, and to meditate upon what to say to his opponents. During his agitation of mind, the saint appeared, standing between two angels, with angelic dignity, and with the features of an angel, showing on his face approval of Lanfranc. The Archbishop was so inspired by the vision that he speedily overcame his adversaries.[3]

On another occasion Lanfranc was lying ill at Aldington, a benefice situated at some distance from Canterbury. His

[1] Wharton, *Ang. Sac.* i, p. 55.

[2] Sax. Chron. (Peterborough, 1089).

[3] Osbern in *Memorials of S. Dunstan* (Rolls), p. 144; Eadmer, ibid., p. 239.

case was given up by the physicians, and he sent a message to the brothers of Christ Church, who were in the neighbourhood, and especially to the senior members, telling them to take his body back to Canterbury if he died. When the brothers arrived, Lanfranc, either because of his malady or because he could not bear the sight of grief, turned his face to the wall. He saw what appeared to be an army of men clothed in white, decorated with golden ornaments which the unbelievers wear, making broad jokes, with a certain happy suavity of manner. As they passed by he looked upon them with happy eyes, and was made to understand that he was in S. Dunstan's house, and that the saint was not far away. So he began to search their faces more carefully to see if he could recognize Dunstan, because he hoped to obtain a renewal of health from him more readily than from others. Suddenly the blessed Father Dunstan appeared, surrounded by a company of reverend seniors, and clothed like them. But he was taller than all, from the shoulders upward. Lanfranc humbly approached, and going to the side of his horse, attempted to embrace his foot in the stirrup, and to draw it towards him in order to kiss it. But Dunstan, desiring to do honour to Lanfranc, drew up his knee and lifted up his foot to himself with both hands. While this contest was going on, Lanfranc was restored to health, so that not a trace of sickness remained. He called those who were kneeling close at hand, and gave them a clear account of what had happened, and asked them to have an altar prepared for him, for they would see one offering at it who a short time before could scarcely move his lips. They thought he was delirious. Then he called the seniors and ordered them to go back to Canterbury, and after closing the doors of the church, to offer a Mass of thanksgiving to S. Dunstan. He did not wish to return at once himself, lest people should think he had the power of seeing the saints of God.[1]

S. Dunstan apparently went round the monastery on that day, seeing what good he could do. A chaplain of the

[1] Osbern, *Mem. of S. Dunstan*, pp. 151–2; Eadmer, ibid., pp. 239–41.

Archbishop had been troubled for eight months by a serious visitation of fever, and was so wasted away, that his skin scarcely kept his weakened bones together. At the moment when the Archbishop was healed, his chaplain also was restored to health. In the morning, on hearing that Lanfranc had recovered, the chaplain went to him and asked who had helped him. Lanfranc told him the story, and asked after the chaplain's health. 'I am quite well,' was the reply, 'for he who rescued you from the miserable point of death last night, also healed me on account of thy favour. I was thrown down on my bed, separated from yours by only a wooden wall, when I saw the blessed Dunstan celebrating Mass in the Church of Our Saviour. I was serving him as a subdeacon, and when I had read the Epistle, I approached his feet as though I were kissing God, and sought his benediction. I departed, healed by his blessing.' The venerable father Lanfranc broke forth with joy and said, 'It was not possible that any sickness should remain in this place, which the servant of God deemed worthy to illumine by his visit.'[1]

Apart from these stories of the monastery no attempt was made by writers of succeeding times to place the Archbishop among the wonder-working saints of the Church, or among the special favourites of the unseen world. D'Achery has collected a number of tributes to him, ranging from the eleventh to the seventeenth century.[2] In these epithalamia no reference to sainthood is made. Lanfranc is handed down to posterity as the learned scholar, the man who revived religion and particularly the monastic life, the builder of churches, and the friend and counsellor of the Conqueror, who was as competent in the conduct of secular as of ecclesiastical business. If due allowance is made for the work of the other great monastic reformers of Normandy, from William of Dijon onwards, the tributes of these writers form a not exaggerated estimate of the man and his work. A churchman who achieved so much might well have been handed down by ecclesiastical writers with more adulation than we find offered to the memory of Lanfranc.

[1] Osbern, *Mem. of S. Dun.*, p. 153; Eadmer, ibid., p. 241.
[2] Migne, cl, col. 97–100.

The strongest bond maintained by Lanfranc with the men of his day was his love of learning. He has been handed down by the writers of that age as a scholar of towering accomplishment. The anti-pope Clement III uses flattering terms of his service to the study of letters and philosophy, and the revival of Latin scholarship.[1] But the keenest intellect of the age knew Lanfranc's limitations, and though after his death he defended his reputation as a scholar, yet Anselm could not regard him as his equal even in knowledge of the past.[2] The thing which he probably knew best was Roman and Lombard law, but that was laid aside when he took the cowl.[3] The testimony, oft repeated right up to modern days, that he knew Greek is based on no clear evidence.[4] He was acquainted with the Greek genitive absolute, and drew attention to it in his commentary on Romans III. But this is the only reference to Greek grammar in his writings, and may well have been learned from a Latin grammarian. A quotation from the Timaeus in the commentary on 2 Timothy ii, a passing reference to Plato in the commentary on 1 Corinthians ii, and to Aristotle in the commentary on Colossians ii, and the recognition of a quotation from Epimenides in his notes on Titus i, together with a quotation from Cicero's *Topica* in his notes on 1 Corinthians ii, comprise all the classical allusions to be found in his extant writings. But while most of these refer to Greek sources, they were probably read by Lanfranc in Latin translations.[5]

His Latin style maintained a high standard. It has been compared with that of Bede, Alcuin, Scotus Erigena and Berengar. But it contains the confusion of 'suus' with

[1] *Eng. Hist. Rev.*, April, 1901, Epis. III.

[2] Anselm, Lib. I, Epis. LXVIII.

[3] Lanfranc, Epis. XXXVI.

[4] Longuemare, p. 54, mentions an eleventh-century MS. at Avranches containing an anonymous translation of Boecius' 'On Music' in modern Greek, written in majuscules.

[5] Charma (*Notice Biographique*, p. 96), quoting Lanfranc on Gal. i, Tit. i, and Cassian, 2 Collat., finds signs of a knowledge of Greek in the use of the words 'evangelium', 'catholicus' and 'anthopomorphicus', but these words had by this time become Latinized.

'ejus' common to mediaeval writers.[1] It exerted a marked influence upon the style of his pupils and contemporaries. A peculiar play upon words, by means of which he transposed adjective and substantive in the same sentence and formed a verbal antithesis, occurs frequently in his writings. 'On reading' one of Anselm's letters he had 'pondered', and 'pondering he had read'; by his 'request' he 'commanded' Wulfstan, and by his 'command' he 'requested'.[2] But this feature was not confined to Lanfranc's Latin. It appeared in earlier writers, and was used sometimes by Anselm.[3]

Liturgiology and the history of tradition and ritual remained one of his chief interests to the end. Cases relating to Baptism, the Eucharist,[4] the use of vestments, and ceremonial rites[5] were frequently referred to him. He gave careful attention to patristics and the decrees of the councils of the Church.[6]

But his extant writings and correspondence show little beyond an acquaintance with the chief Latin fathers[7]—Augustine, Ambrose, Jerome, Gregory[8] and Hilary.[9] He does not always quote Augustine and Ambrose accurately,[10] but he appears to have possessed a lost copy of one of the works of Ambrose.[11]

His attention was especially drawn to the teaching of Hilary by the controversy with Berengar, who claimed certain passages in Hilary's works in support of his own views. In Lanfranc's reply to a joint letter from Reginald, Abbot of S. Cyprian's at Poitiers, Sentunus a monk, and Henry a canon of that city,[12] he quoted the opinions of Pope Gelasius, Augustine and Jerome on Hilary's orthodoxy, and

[1] Charma, *Notice Biographique*, p. 97.

[2] Lanfranc, Epis. XV, XLIX.

[3] Anselm, Lib. I, Epis. XLVIII.

[4] Lanfranc, Epis. XXXVI.

[5] Epis. XVI.

[6] Epis. XXVI.

[7] Possibly some of Lanfranc's books may be among the Canterbury volumes in the library of Corpus Christi College, Cambridge, which were formerly in the library of Archbishop Parker. I owe this suggestion to Sir Geoffrey Butler.

[8] Commentaries on S. Paul's epistles.

[9] Lanfranc, Epis. LVI.

[10] *Hist. Litt. de la France*, viii, p. 277.

[11] De Crozals, *Lanfranc*, p. 57.

[12] Lanfranc, Epis. LVI.

proceeded to deal at some length with Hilary's doctrine of the Trinity. He pointed out that Christ had suffered as a man, that the Godhead did not suffer, and that if God could in any sense be said to have suffered it was only on account of the unity of Christ's personality, in which the human and divine were merged at the Incarnation. Thus Lanfranc's teaching was quite free from the Patripassian heresy, and the two-nature doctrine which Cyril of Alexandria attributed to Nestorius.[1] Sufficient evidence is contained in this letter for disproving the charge brought against him after his death by Roscelin, who taught that the three Persons of the Trinity were either three angels, though united by one will and power, or else the Father and Spirit also became incarnate with the Son.[2] This was an attempt to divide the issue of the mystery of the Trinity by an arithmetical test. In reality, he taught, it must consist of either three or one. Roscelin claimed Lanfranc's authority for this teaching. But Anselm vigorously cleared the reputation of his old master.[3] In earlier years, before the controversy with Berengar broke out, Lanfranc may have had liberalizing tendencies which his secular training made almost inevitable, and which lent colour to Berengar's charge. But from the time that he took up the case against Berengar these disappeared, and his teaching remained unimpeachably orthodox. The development and strength of his thought suffered in consequence, and the Norman Church may have lost an independent thinker of more than ordinary power. From Lanfranc's method of dealing with practical abuses and the tenets of the Hildebrandine reform, it is probable that a similar independence exerted in the sphere of dogmatic theology would have thrown his teaching on to lines resembling those pursued by Berengar. But having declined this course, his mind was such that, unlike Anselm's, it remained uncreative when confined to orthodox and traditional channels.

Patristic studies formed the main part of the ordinary reading of a theologian of the day, but Lanfranc's interest

[1] Bethune-Baker, *Nestorius and his Teaching*.

[2] A theory suggested by Augustine, Epis. XI (Migne, xxxiii. col. 75).

[3] Anselm, Lib. II, Epis. XLI.

in the traditions of the past was doubtless strengthened by his earlier studies in law. The legal and ecclesiastical traditionalist have much in common. They are both bound by the authorities of bygone ages, and any development of their knowledge consists mainly in the re-interpretation or adaptation to present conditions of the judgements and rules laid down in the past. When hardened by practice this method becomes the explanation of the legalism of ecclesiastical traditionalists. Lanfranc was saved by a breadth of vision, and a practical common sense, developed by constant contact with affairs, from becoming a mere traditionalist, but the conversation with Anselm on the case of Alphege shows that there were times when the old legal instinct became too strong for him, and the lawyer and traditionalist overbalanced the philosopher and statesman. Yet when every modification has been made which is justified by the quality of his extant writings, Lanfranc still stands forth as one of the most scholarly men of his day. He was not a writer who created great works of intellectual value for posterity. But he was a great reader of books, a student who assimilated knowledge sufficiently to be able to reproduce it for the benefit of contemporaries. The man of action always had a store of knowledge ready for use, when confronted by practical points in the administration of ecclesiastical or civil business, or when consulted by his numerous correspondents. The practical nature of Lanfranc's studies is revealed in all the writings which he has left behind.[1] In earlier days the requirements of his profession as a lawyer fixed the habits of his later scholarship and study. The needs of the moment, the tendency to connect all present cases with examples from the past, urged upon him the function of a scholarly adviser or director. So he brought out of his treasures things rather old than new. His pronouncements in the courts and councils of England, like the acute legal exegesis of the days at Pavia, show that his mind was possessed of rare power and ingenuity, but so far as the written word testifies, he never rose far above the level of an ecclesiastical antiquary,

[1] Cf. Appendix III,

when he put pen to parchment. But that only causes him to stand forth pre-eminently as a man of his own day. Berengar was excommunicated just because he was original and therefore beyond his age. Though the master of Anselm, and living on long enough to read at least one of his great successor's works, the fact that Lanfranc could not fully appreciate Anselm's treatise [1] shows the dividing line established by Anselm between the school of philosophic theology founded by him, and the orthodox writers and scholars of the past. In Lanfranc's days mere book knowledge and a ready Latin style were applauded as the ripe fruits of scholarship and intellect, and if we may judge Lanfranc by the literary standards of his own age, then the plaudits of his contemporaries may be allowed to resound. He was indeed the greatest scholar in an age of bookish students, bound by the methods of their studies to the traditions of the past.

The extensive building operations at Canterbury, Rochester and S. Albans did not exhaust the munificent liberality which gave to his rule a more than usual splendour. We find Lanfranc devoting attention to the creation of parish churches and hospitals, as well as almshouses and episcopal lodges in different parts of his domains.

Outside the north gate of Canterbury he built a large stone house for poor people, containing dwelling-rooms with the necessary offices, together with a spacious court or quadrangle. The community was named after S. John the Baptist and was divided into two sections, with accommodation for men and women. Clothes were provided yearly and an allowance of food was distributed daily. Priests were appointed to attend to the spiritual welfare of the inmates, and guardians were nominated to see that the men and women were kept separate.[2]

On the other side of the road the hospital and church of S. Gregory were erected (1084),[3] in which the six canons, who

[1] Anselm, Lib. I, Epis. LXVIII, *supra*, p. 181.

[2] Eadmer, *Hist. Nov.*, p. 15; Malmes., *G. P.*, p. 72; Milo, 25. *Dugdale Monasticon*, vii, p. 763.

[3] *Dugdale Monasticon*, vii. 614–15 for date.

attended to the almshouse, were lodged. Their special duty was to baptize and to hear confessions, to bury the dead and to say Masses for their souls.[1] A school for grammar and music formed part of the foundation. The charter issued by Lanfranc grants freedom from all control save that of himself and his successors.[2]

About a mile from the western gate of the city, on the slope of a hill, wooden huts for lepers were constructed, with dwellings for men on one side, and for women on the other. The church of S. Nicholas was erected, and the spiritual ministrations were fulfilled by priests who were inmates of the community. We read that they laboured with such kindness and patience that disputes never arose.[3] In both these foundations Lanfranc was assisted by the King.[4]

Similar almshouses for the poor, made of stone, were built on many of the Canterbury manors, and were supported by annual grants commenced by Lanfranc.[5] Frequent journeys[6] were undertaken round the properties belonging to the see, and they sometimes took him great distances from Canterbury.[7] These visits may have been due to the custom which later became the regular habit of the King and lay magnates, in order to save the transport of produce from the farms to the principal seat of the owner, but they also afforded an opportunity for bringing the landowner into contact with his dependants, and for checking the administration of the manors. In order to provide accommodation for himself and his suite, Lanfranc, following the practice of Dunstan, erected lodges on many of his manors. Some were constructed with stone and some with wood,[8] and they served the needs of his successors for a long period. At Canterbury he built a palace for the

[1] Eadmer, *Hist. Nov.*, p. 16; Malmes., *G. P.*, § 44; cf. Boehmer, *Die Fälschungen*, pp. 173–5.

[2] Printed by Boehmer, *Die Fälschungen*, pp. 173–5.

[3] Eadmer, *Hist. Nov.*, p. 16; Milo, 26; Malmes., *G. P.*, p. 72; Gervase, ii, p. 368; *Dugdale Monasticon*, vii, p. 653, which names this hospital Herbaldoun.

[4] Malmes., *G. P.*, p. 72.

[5] Milo, 26.

[6] Lanfranc, Epis. XXI, XXIX.

[7] Ibid. XXXVI.

[8] Eadmer, *Hist. Nov.*, p. 16.

Archbishops,[1] and a church at Harrow, which he was prevented from consecrating by his death.[2]

The correspondence with Anselm is full of allusions to Lanfranc's liberality to his old home at Bec, and his kindly thought for old acquaintances. A courier named Gerard, who desired to become a monk, was redeemed from debt by Lanfranc at Anselm's suggestion. The procedure necessitated a journey from Bec, and Gerard was detained by his creditors. But Anselm wrote saying that he would be back again by the following Easter, and begged that Lanfranc would not be angry with Gerard on account of the delay.[3] So also, in England, in addition to endowing almshouses, he spent large sums of money on general acts of charity. This was the practice of liberal-minded dignitaries of the day, and formed one of the rules of life for the head of a Benedictine abbey, but it appeared to contemporaries to be an unusual virtue in a Lombard.[4] While maintaining simplicity of life himself, he distributed five hundred pounds yearly among the poor.[5] Almsgiving played an important part not only in his own practice, but in his exhortations to other people. At his consecration he took as a text, 'Give alms, and all things are pure to you',[6] and when those who heard him began to offer gifts for the Archbishop to distribute, he said, 'Let us contend in mutual rivalry; you give, and I will distribute.' Money was contributed from all quarters, so that on one occasion he was able to make large distributions at one of the Councils.[7] Monks who confessed sins were ordered to take alms to poor people as a penance.[8]

All kinds of people benefited from Lanfranc's liberality—monasteries in distress, needy clergy and lay folk, poor scholars, travelling pilgrims, as well as the sick and aged. According to Eadmer, no congregation of monks or canons applied to him without receiving more than they had hoped.

[1] Eadmer, *Hist. Nov.*, p. 13. [2] Ibid., p. 45.
[3] Anselm, Lib. I, Epis. XIX; cf. Epis. XIII.
[4] Milo, 48; Malmes., *G. P.*, p. 68. [5] Milo, 49.
[6] Milo, 49; Malmes., *G. P.*, p. 68.
[7] Ibid. [8] Osbern, *Mem. of S. Dun.*, p. 146.

No pauper cried to him and was refused. No pilgrim of any rank sought help and was despised.[1] Poor scholars were encouraged to earn relief by taking part in disputations and discourses. The successful competitor was rewarded with a prize, and the other received a solatium.[2]

Three leading principles guided his works of charity. He gave cheerfully, taking special care to condole with those who were distressed, refusing to allow the recipient to know whence the gift came, or to permit other people to know the nature of the gift.[3] He gave with discretion, never handing money to the poor, but bread, shoes and clothes,[4] individual cases being considered on their merits.[5] He performed acts of charitable service himself, waiting personally on poor people, girding up his robe and supplying them with meat and drink, while his face shone with gracious kindness upon the recipient like the sun at morning, which dispels the clouds, calms the winds, and purifies the atmosphere.[6]

The care of the monks and their relations occupied his special attention,[7] particularly where poverty might have compelled the monks to abandon the religious life.[8] He did not wait to be approached, but when he perceived a case of need, offered his services. The mother of one of his monks received from him thirty gold coins yearly, which were transmitted to her at the rate of five at a time. On one occasion the monk gave the money to his mother, bound up in a cloth, while talking, and she, not paying attention to what she was doing, allowed it to fall out when she had left him. When she returned and asked what had happened to the money, the monk left her with a dejected countenance, partly on account of his mother's loss, and partly because his carelessness might come to the ears of the Archbishop, and be the means of the annuity being stopped. But Lanfranc had entered the cloister as mother and son separated, and noticing the monk's dejected looks, asked

1 Eadmer, *Hist. Nov.*, p. 14; Malmes., *G. P.*, pp. 68–9.
2 Malmes., *G. P.*, p. 69.
3 Eadmer, *Hist. Nov.*, p. 14.
4 Malmes., *G. P.*, p. 69.
5 Eadmer, *Hist. Nov.*, p. 13.
6 Malmes., *G. P.*, p. 69.
7 Eadmer, *Hist. Nov.*, pp. 13–14.
8 Malmes., *G. P.*, p. 71.

the cause of the trouble. On hearing what had happened, he said, 'Why are you sad my son? God intended to give those coins to another, who perhaps needed them more than thy mother. But lest what has occurred shall in any way disturb your mind, I will order seven coins, in place of the five, to be given to your mother. But take care that no man know it.' [1]

According to the statement of a late writer,[2] Lanfranc sometimes took money, from those who came to him for confession, as a penitential offering, and on other occasions in the form of fines for breaches of the law. If we may trust this writer, he was not quite satisfied with the latter payments, and although he tolerated them, seized a suitable opportunity to talk to the King about the matter. But most of the authorities pay tribute to Lanfranc's generous charitable actions. He was completely free from the avarice which characterized the Lombard race.[3] His manner was mild and friendly.[4] His name matched his character and behaviour, his heart was large and he was big and good towards all men.[5]

Another class of sufferers who received his attention were the women who were subject to ill-treatment from the Norman settlers.[6] During the disturbed days of the Conquest, many women, both married and unmarried, had sought the protection of the convents. At one of Lanfranc's councils the question was raised whether these women were to be regarded as bound by the vows they had taken. Lanfranc's decision was that unless they voluntarily desired to remain within the cloister they were free to depart and to marry.[7]

A similar decision was given in a letter sent to Geoffrey, Bishop of Coutances: [8]

With regard to the nuns concerning whom your most sweet fraternity sent letters to me, I reply to you as follows. The

[1] Eadmer, *Hist. Nov.*, p. 14.
[2] Higden (Rolls), vii. p. 334.
[3] Malmes., *G. P.*, p. 68; Milo, 48.
[4] Milo, 52. Robt. of Torigny in Jumièges, vii. 26.
[5] 'Brevis Relatio' (Giles, *Gesta Will.* i. 9).
[6] Ord. iv. 3 (ii, p. 171).
[7] Eadmer, *Hist. Nov.*, p. 124.
[8] Lanfranc, Epis. XXXV; Freeman, *N. C.* v. 781, quotes the

nuns who have made the profession for the sake of observing the rule, or who, although they are not so far professed, have offered themselves at the altar, are to be advised, urged and constrained to keep the rule according to their customs and mode of living. Those who are neither professed nor oblates are to be regarded as free until their desire for maintaining their order shall be more carefully examined. Concerning those who, not from love of religion, but from fear of the Normans, as you say, have fled to the monastery, if they are able to prove this by the sure testimony of the more reliable nuns, liberty for withdrawing is to be granted to them. This is my counsel and the King's. May Almighty God preserve your life in welldoing.

But, within the limits imposed by him, discipline was to be enforced. He permitted no abuse of the liberal provisions of the marriage decree of 1076.[1] He was prepared to run the risk of a scandal, in order to prevent worse troubles than those caused by bringing evil to light.[2] But he always showed caution, whether engaged in charity or disciplinary action.[3]

The directions sent to Anselm for the discipline of his nephew, and his attitude to the canonization of S. Alphege, indicate an element of severity in his character. On most occasions he showed a willingness to meet special cases when applying general rules of life and conduct. In the case of S. Alphege he had not to deal with the sufferings or misdemeanour of an individual living in his own day, but with the historical evidence for canonization, and although a legal interpretation of the evidence may have caused him to lean towards too severe a test of the facts, the case can hardly be cited against him as a sign of undue severity.

Similar questions are raised by the disputes with Thomas, Odo, and William of S. Carilef. But in these cases Lanfranc had to decide upon matters of general principle or actual breaches of the law. In the York dispute the charge of unscrupulousness depends upon Lanfranc's complicity in the forgery of the evidence. But this is not proven. Odo and William of S. Carilef were charged with breaches of feudal duty, and as offenders against the legal standards of the

case of an English woman named Leagifu, whose will Lanfranc enforced.

[1] Lanfranc, Epis. XXIV.

[2] Epis. LXI.

[3] Epis. XXVII, XLII.

day they were judged by Lanfranc in his capacity as adviser to the King. The case of S. Augustine's, Canterbury, has indeed a different appearance, but under the most favourable conditions friction was bound to arise between Christ Church and S. Augustine's, and it is not clear that all the provocation lay on the side of the Cathedral monks.

If his actions sometimes bore the character of an overbearing disposition, he was never a resentful opponent, nor did he allow malice to remain after a dispute was settled. He was found on more than one occasion working in harmony with Thomas of York. During the trial of William of S. Carilef he offered to intercede for him to the King. If the advice offered to John of Rouen, after the disturbances among the monks, may also be taken as an indication of Lanfranc's own practice, we have ample evidence that he believed in burying the hatchet when the fight was over.[1] No man could carry so many different schemes to a successful conclusion, or guide the Church and advise the King during times so unsettled, without sometimes being called upon to do and to say things severely, and even with an aspect of high-handed action. If on the one hand we do not meet with the saintly humility of S. Anselm, neither do we meet with that prelate's doctrinaire stubbornness in the pursuit of a theory, and Lanfranc never indulged in ruthlessness or unscrupulousness of action, which could be compared, in any degree, with that of Odo of Bayeux. The fact that he was the Conqueror's chosen Counsellor is another point in his favour. William may have made use of violent men occasionally, when violent action had to be taken, but he seldom used them a second time if their unscrupulousness became apparent. If he resorted to extreme measures himself, it was usually only after extreme provocation. He seldom made use of capital punishment, and often forgave the clearest treason. In many respects Lanfranc resembled the King. While maintaining a firm control over all branches of the ecclesiastical administration, he did not strike hard unless principle demanded it. The utmost that Lanfranc can be charged with, apart from the

[1] Epis. XVII.

question of the forgery, is a resort to expediency in difficult cases. But that is sometimes essential if men and kings are to be judged and used on their merits, and not made the victims of principle or policy.

The York writer, while admitting that he was a good and wise man, charges him with being more desirous of glory and dignity than befitted a monk.[1] By men of Lanfranc's character such an impression might easily be created. But if he was self-assertive it was on behalf of his office as Archbishop and his order as a monk. Something, too, must be allowed to a man who lived in a foreign country amongst strangers, and who had to compel others to take him at his own valuation. This appears to have been less easy for a Lombard, who was regarded as a member of a grasping, avaricious race. In reality he was a humble man,[2] made more humble by disappointments met in early life in Italy, and in Normandy, and by adopting the life of a monk at an age when ambition must have lost its glitter. He shunned publicity. His hesitation before accepting Canterbury was more real than the behaviour of some other men in a similar position. Here and there throughout the letters are traces of a yearning for the quiet life of the student,[3] which he was never able to indulge again until perhaps the last few weeks of his life. But having been pushed into publicity he performed the duties which lay before him faithfully, laboriously and with a firm hand. Even if the necessity of fulfilling his conceptions of duty or of defending a principle made him combative, he generally realized the limitations of his own position, especially in relation to the question immediately on hand. If one feature more than another was specially characteristic of him, it was a sound and practical common sense exercised in the fulfilment of duty. When this test is applied to his actions they generally respond. No other quality could have won for him the almost unqualified tributes of the English as well as the

[1] *Historians of York*, ii, p. 100. [2] Lanfranc, Epis. III, XIX.

[3] Longuemare, *Lan.*, p. 131, says that he retired every year into one of the monasteries of his diocese for eight days, and refused to be treated more favourably than any other monk.

Norman writers. As an Italian he may have been more acceptable to the people of England than a native-born Norman would have been, but as an Italian he must have experienced more difficulty in understanding English life than any Norman. The Normanization of England, which had gone on before his arrival, assisted him, and thirty years of life in Normandy had given him a complete understanding of Norman character. But by constant journeys round his widespread domains he attempted to make himself familiar with the conditions of English life,[1] and on one occasion at least spoke of the English people and himself as 'we English'.[2] No foreigner, and one whose career presented many of the features of an adventurer, ever more completely won the approval and applause of the people among whom he lived. The Saxon Chronicle is consistent in its praise of him. His many acts of charity, and his kindly treatment of English women, show that the estimate, if exaggerated, possessed some foundation.

Without ranking among men of genius, who either in thought or action have done work which no one else could have done, and without which the progress of mankind would have been hindered, Lanfranc none the less has his place among the ablest of our administrators. It would be too much to claim that the Conqueror could not have found another man to do the work that Lanfranc did, and to do it well. The Norman monasteries sheltered in those days the ablest men of executive and administrative capacity in Europe. William of S. Carilef, although coming late in the period of the Conquest, showed that Lanfranc was not *sui generis*. But it is doubtful if any ecclesiastic of that day could have so completely won order out of the chaos of the Saxon Church, or so successfully laid the foundations of the Norman Church, or so effectively revealed such a range of usefulness to the monarch who was laying anew the foundations of England. As an adviser of the King in matters of State he was the first medieval ecclesiastic to show the power and efficiency of the Church in the sphere

[1] Lanfranc, Epis. XXI, XXIX, XXXVI.

[2] Epis. XXXIII, XXXVI.

of practical politics as distinct from ecclesiastical theory, and to foreshadow, at the dawn of our history as a nation, the high function of the English Prime Minister.[1] All was done by virtue of an innate independence of mind and habit of thought, which could not be repressed, and found constant and abundant outlet in the service of Church and State. He could be claimed by no one of the great movements, at that time working up into full momentum, and conflicting with each other. He was neither Hildebrandist nor feudalist, neither ascetic nor imperialist, in the full sense of any of these terms, but he selected the best of all their schemes, and welding together different elements which were won out of the great thoughts and great movements of his day, by his independent wisdom and practical common sense, he presented in his character and life a unity and effectiveness which neither wandering nor change, friendship nor opposition, King nor Pope, were ever able to disarrange for long.

This independence of spirit and action is illustrated by the fact that he had few friendships. Friendship depends upon community of taste and outlook, but above all of temperament and policy. The temperament of that age was governed by the community instinct. Men worshipped in confraternities. They fought in crusades. This was in itself largely the result of the unity of thought which controlled the great policies of Church and State. The papalization of the Church, the feudalization of the State, were transposed into concrete forms by the community instinct of both monk and soldier. But to neither the one nor the other did Lanfranc give way. The papal claims never enticed him from his allegiance to the King. The feudal organization never caused him to forget that he was a bishop of the Holy Roman Church. He stood alone and worked alone, even under the aegis of the Conqueror's confidence and approval, and finally he died alone, without even having won the full confidence of the chair of Peter. The death of Alexander II, years before, had made it certain that Lanfranc would not be counted among the stalwarts of the new

[1] Perhaps Dunstan preceded him in this achievement.

theocracy at Rome. In Alexander II Lanfranc lost one of the few friends of his life. The connexion with William was formed too late for it to become for either the inspiration and rejoicing that friendship can be. If both men had been twenty years younger when they met outside Rouen, the story might have been different. But those who form friendships after middle life may create relationships which influence policy and action, but seldom weave bonds that tie the heart and unite spirit.

Even the correspondence with Anselm was inspired rather by his love for Bec than for the Prior. Although an old pupil like Alexander, Anselm was too far divided in character and outlook from Lanfranc to create a tie similar to that which caused the Pope to rise at Lanfranc's approach to the apostolic see. The very excellences of their respective characters, so complete in themselves, yet so divergent in tendency, were bound to keep asunder the bookish statesman and practical man of affairs from the intellectual inquirer and Christian saint. Of friendship for Herluin there are few signs. If Lanfranc carried any one warm feeling down to the grave it was his love for Bec and the old home between the two hills by the little stream in Normandy. Not Anselm, not his nephew, but the hallowed memories of former days attracted his thoughts always across the channel, and drew from him a stream of letters for Bec, most of which have not survived.[1] His was not an uncommon nature. It was the temperament of the man who belongs to no party and is never a partisan. Possessing a few friends, formed largely under the influence of localities, and becoming fewer as the years go on, as one by one they are laid in the grave, or pass to other spheres; always making new connexions and winning satisfaction from new faces and above all from new work, but retaining an ardent love for the scenes and environment of early years—such were the experiences of Lanfranc, the product of his own

[1] Many of Lanfranc's letters were destroyed in the fire at Bec in 1624. D'Achery, Migne, cl, col. 16. An unprinted letter to a monk named Simon exists among the manuscripts of the Abbey of Dunes, which are now at Bruges, in the Bibl. de la Ville. (Cf. *Hist. Litt. de la France*, viii, p. 297.)

spirit, which lived alone, and while mingling with men of many types, was content to influence rather than to be influenced. Not that he was incapable of strong feeling, but strong-willed and perceiving more clearly than most men the defects in other people, and realizing the trouble they would cause in life, he found it impossible to win their love by that charm which pleasant people exert, though at the expense, if not of moral conviction, at least of the performance of moral duty. Lanfranc made no attempt to win men by complying whole-heartedly with their policy, if it failed to measure up to his standards of what was wise and what was expedient.

APPENDIX I

(*a*) THE PAPAL PRIVILEGES

A QUESTION of crucial importance, which is, however, independent of the claim to the primacy, hangs upon the relation of the letters, quoted by Lanfranc at the Council of 1072, to the letters inserted in the accounts of Eadmer and Malmesbury. The history of the relations between Canterbury and York was sufficient to prove Lanfranc's claim to the primacy, independently of the papal letters. But the presence of a series of forged or partly forged letters in the accounts of Eadmer and Malmesbury casts a suspicion upon the probity of Lanfranc's conduct, if these were the letters quoted by him at Winchester in 1072.[1] There is, however, reason for believing that the Eadmer-Malmesbury series were not the letters quoted at that Council. It is remarkable that the list quoted by Lanfranc in the letter to Alexander II does not agree with the Eadmer-Malmesbury series. The letters of Formosus and John are not mentioned by Lanfranc, while another letter quoted as 'item ultimi Leonis' is mentioned by him, and yet does not appear in Eadmer-Malmesbury. He also includes the original constitution of Gregory, which is omitted in the Eadmer-Malmesbury.[2]

The searching criticism of Professor Boehmer has proved beyond all doubt that the Eadmer-Malmesbury [3] letters contain among their number some which have been forged, while nearly all have been edited. But it proves no more. The result of Boehmer's inquiry is summed up in the conclusion that of the

[1] Boehmer, *Die Fälschungen Erzbischof Lanfranks von Canterbury* (Leipzig, 1902).

[2] Lanfranc, Epis. V; Boehmer, p. 171: 'Gregorii, Bonifacii, Honorii, Vitaliani, Sergii, item Gregorii, Leonis, item ultimi Leonis privilegia atque scripta, quae Dorobernensis aecclesiae praesulibus Anglorumque regibus aliis atque aliis temporibus, variis de causis sunt data aut transmissa.' There is nothing to indicate that Lanfranc knew of two letters from Boniface and two from Sergius. The absence of 'item', to indicate a second letter from Boniface and Sergius, suggests that he knew of only one from each of the other Popes, so that the discrepancy between the two lists is even greater, but cf. *infra*, *passim*.

[3] Eadmer copied an earlier recension (Boehmer, p. 16).

nine letters contained in our series, five are forgeries, three are partly forged, and one is genuine.[1] But this conclusion lays open the possibility that Lanfranc made use of the genuine letters, and other authentic documents, which Boehmer admits lay behind those letters in the series which were only partly altered. Moreover, among the partly altered letters is one, that of Leo III to Ethelhard of Canterbury, which has generally been accepted as genuine by critics who were prepared to question the validity of all the rest.[2] Even Boehmer admits that though forged in its present form, a genuine privilege lies behind it. There is therefore a probability that this letter contains the contents of the original privilege, and that together with the admittedly genuine letter of Sergius to the three English kings [3] we are in possession of the actual contents of two genuine letters, or copies of them, to which Lanfranc had access.

Moreover, it is Boehmer's opinion that we possess too little knowledge of the Chancellery of Sergius to say that his letter to all the bishops of England is a forgery,[4] and, that a true document concerning the pallium lies behind it. There is also some doubt whether Lanfranc may not have used the letter of John to Dunstan, but if so, we again have Boehmer's opinion that a real letter may lie behind our copy.[5]

Thus there are traces of no less than four letters in the Eadmer series of nine letters, which Lanfranc was in a position to quote at the Council of 1072, and therefore the prime motive for the forgery is removed, for though, while not possessing a series of authoritative papal statements which could compare with the weight and volume of the Eadmer series, if those were genuine, Lanfranc none the less had at his disposal sufficient documentary evidence to give him a presentable case, and to win, by the aid of his own powerful advocacy, the victory which he obtained in 1072.[6]

[1] Boehmer, p. 102.

[2] Cf. Haddan and Stubbs, Jaffe-Lowenfield, *passim.*

[3] Boehmer, p. 91.

[4] Ibid.: 'Aber wir haben zuwenig Nachrichten über die Kanzlei dieses Papstes als dass wir deswegen das Verdikts "gefalscht" fällen dürften.'

[5] Ibid., p. 101. But Lanfranc does not refer to this document in his letter to Alexander.

[6] Cf. p. 282 on the documents mentioned by Ralph of Canterbury in 1120.

What are the contents of these four letters in the Eadmer series ?

(1) The first epistle of Sergius I is addressed to Ethelred, King of Mercia, Ethelfrith, King of Northumbria, and Ealdwulf, King of East Anglia. The kings are urged to receive Bertwald as Archbishop of Canterbury and chief bishop of all Britain. If they declined they would show contempt not for Bertwald, but for him who sent him.[1]

Boehmer admits that the historical suppositions for this letter are sound. It mentions a journey of Bertwald to Rome, and while Bede only refers to a journey of Bertwald to Gaul,[2] the *Liber Pontificalis* says that Sergius I consecrated Bertwald. The form of the address to the three kings is a sign of authenticity, for a forger would not have disregarded the names in Bede, who mentions Wihtrad and Suabhard of Kent.[3] The absence of any reference to Ini of Mercia is to be explained by the fact that at that date he was at war with the Kings of Kent and East Anglia, and had been defeated. There is no reference to the constitution of Gregory, so that Boehmer allows that the authenticity of the letters can be accepted, and that no objection need be lodged against the use of the words ' primam pontifex ' for this title is given to Bertwald by Waldhere of London and by Eddius.[4]

(2) In the letter of Leo III to Ethelhard of Canterbury, the Pope states that he had ordered a scrutiny of the records to be made. It appeared that the primacy over all the churches of the English had been granted by Gregory to Augustine for life (in aevum [5]) and Leo conceded that all the churches of the English should be perpetually subject to Ethelhard and his successors, as they were in times past.[6]

The historical background of the letter was the question of the archbishopric of Lichfield. In 787 Higbert, the Bishop of Lichfield, was raised to metropolitan rank, through the influence of Offa of Mercia. Higbert received the pall from Hadrian I, and in 794 took precedence over Jaenbert of Canter-

[1] Eadmer, *Hist. Nov.*, p. 266 ; Malmes., *G. P.*, § 34 ; Boehmer, p. 151.

[2] Bede, v. 8.

[3] Ibid. : ' regnantibus in Cantia Uictredo et Suaebhardo.'

[4] Boehmer, pp. 89–91.

[5] Unless ' in aevum ' is to be interpreted to mean ' for ever ', which seems scarcely possible.

[6] Eadmer, *Hist. Nov.*, p. 270 ; Malmes., *G. P.*, § 37 ; Boehmer, p. 155.

bury on signing a charter.[1] The question of the archbishopric of Lichfield was reopened by Kenwulf, King of Mercia, in a letter to Leo III (798). The King stated that the bishops and learned men had informed him that the province of Canterbury had been divided contrary to the canons and the constitution of Gregory I. On account of enmity to Jaenbert, Offa had persuaded Hadrian I to sanction the new archbishopric of the Mercians. Kenwulf asked for instructions, and directed the Pope's attention to a letter sent already by Ethelhard of Canterbury to Rome, concerning Canterbury and the affairs of the whole of Britain.[2]

We have the reply of Leo III in an indubitably genuine letter, which is not included in the Eadmer series. The Pope stated that the see of Lichfield had been elevated to archi-episcopal rank, because of the unwieldy nature of the province of Canterbury. He avoided the question of Gregory's constitution. He replied as though Kenwulf had asked whether Canterbury or London should be the metropolitan seat. He would not dare, he said, to suggest that it should be London, but as the primacy (*primatum*) was fixed at Canterbury he agreed that this should be the primatial see (*primam sedem* [3]). The Pope's letter is certainly guarded and non-committal. There is nothing to show that the term 'primacy' was used of the whole island or merely of the southern province. The letter might have been quoted in support of either view. But the correspondence of Alcuin proves that the question of the primacy was in men's minds at the time, and that the Archbishop of Canterbury was regarded, by some, and occasionally even by Alcuin, as the chief bishop in England.[4] Thus the Lichfield question, the existence of Leo's letter to Kenwulf, and the attitude of Alcuin create a valid historical setting for the letter of Leo III to Ethelhard, especially as the terms of that letter are more guarded than those used in the letters which were pure forgeries. Even Boehmer, who places this epistle among those of the series which are only partly forged, adopts a distinctly wavering attitude. He regards it as forged in its present form. He points to the forced explanation of the constitution of Gregory, and to the use of 'anglia', which is, he alleges, a sign of forgery at that date. But then he proceeds to admit that there are also signs of genuineness.

[1] Haddan and Stubbs, iii. p. 446.
[2] Ibid., pp. 521–3.
[3] Ibid., p. 523.
[4] Cf. *supra*, pp. 745.

The date (802) appears to be in order with the exception of the absence of the imperial year and the indiction. He thinks it was based upon an authentic document of Leo, who undoubtedly gave Ethelhard a privilege in connexion with Lichfield.[1]

(3) Just as the letter of Leo III to Kenwulf creates a presumption in favour of the letter of the same Pope to Ethelhard, so the letter of Sergius I to the three kings lends a valid presupposition to the letter of Sergius I to the English bishops. In this epistle Sergius commends to the English bishops Bertwald, who had been elected to succeed Theodore, according to an ancient custom, which had been retained by his Church from the time of Gregory until the present. He had been invested with the primacy by the Pope, and indeed, by the blessed Peter, when he had asked for it, by means of the sacred usage of the pallium and the holy dalmatic. The bishops were therefore exhorted to render obedience to him as to the chief bishop who possessed the primacy. All ranks of the clergy were admonished not to disobey the injunction of the apostolic see, either then or in the future.[2]

In his criticism of this letter Boehmer again wavers. He points to the use made of the constitution of Gregory. He rejects the passages in which the primacy is expressly mentioned. He finds fault with the construction and the style. But he confesses that we know too little of the Chancellery of Sergius I to pronounce it a forgery. He says that it may have been the work of some scribe who is unknown to us, and owns that its style is no worse than that of the *Liber Diurnus*. He asks why Ethelhard did not refer to it and concludes that a pallium document may lie behind it, which would have been useless to Ethelhard.[3] Haddan and Stubbs, while regarding it as doubtful, admit that there is nothing to cause suspicion in the letter itself.[4]

We may certainly admit that the manner in which the primacy is alluded to in this letter is suspicious. The forger of our series may have strengthened the terms of the papal original. But it is to be noted that during the period between Theodore and Egbert of York, the claims of Canterbury were most likely to be asserted, and to be sanctioned by the Papacy. The English

[1] Boehmer, pp. 97–8.

[2] Eadmer, *Hist. Nov.*, p. 267; Malmes., *G. P.*, § 35; Boehmer, p. 152.

[3] Boehmer, pp. 91–3.

[4] Haddan and Stubbs, iii. p. 231, n.

Church had made a new beginning under Theodore. Its organization was based upon the *de facto* if not the *de jure* recognition of the primacy of Canterbury under him. As the papal nominee, his pretensions were supported. It is improbable that any of his successors would have relaxed the authority of Canterbury, and the fact that the Lichfield archbishopric, although created by a papal decree, was challenged, is an illustration *ad rem*. It is to be observed that if Ethelhard did not appeal to the letter of Sergius, neither did he appeal to the pre-eminence of Theodore.

(4) With the tenth letter of the Eadmer series, that of John XII to Dunstan, we are scarcely concerned. It is not mentioned in the list contained in Lanfranc's letter to Alexander II. But it is allowed by Boehmer to be only partly forged. It is not discredited by historical considerations. The style is that of a well-known scribe of the Chancellery of John XII. There is a small error in the date, but this can easily be accounted for by a scribal blunder. The indiction is a sign of genuineness. The only suspicious features are the passages which refer to the primacy and the constitution of Augustine. A genuine pallium document, issued by John XII to Dunstan on 1st October 960, probably lies behind it. The text is trustworthy, with the exception of the passage which refers to the primacy.[1]

But the primacy is spoken of in distinctly guarded terms. Permission is given to Dunstan to exercise the primacy with full powers, in the manner in which his predecessors had done, and as the representative of the holy see, as Augustine and his successors had held it. The pallium for celebrating the Mass was sent, but it was only to be used in the manner sanctioned by John's predecessors. The privileges of Canterbury were to remain in *suo statu*.[2] We may admit that the reference to the primacy has perhaps been strengthened, but if invented *de novo* it is curious that it does not possess the more definite character of other forged documents in the series. The archbishopric of Dunstan was a period when some such pronouncement was extremely likely to have been made. The English Church was again in a state of disorganization, and, in pursuance of its old

[1] Boehmer, pp. 100–2.

[2] Eadmer, *Hist. Nov.*, p. 274; Malmes., *G. P.*, § 39; Boehmer, p. 159.

policy, there is no reason why the Papacy should not have proceeded to assist with its reconstruction by again centring full authority in the chair of Canterbury.

The other five letters of the Eadmer series may be passed over.[1] Boehmer's case against them appears to be complete. But while proving that they were forged *de novo*, he admits that authentic documents lie behind each of them.[2] The passages which bear indubitably the character of forgeries are those referring to the primacy. With the exception of the Bede letters, lying behind the first two letters of the series, we have no means of determining to what extent the original sources bore upon the question of the primacy. The sources of the forged letters of Vitalian, Gregory III and Formosus are entirely problematical. But that certain letters of Vitalian to Theodore, of Gregory III to the British bishops concerning Tatwin of Canterbury, and of Formosus, lie behind the forgeries, and were therefore at Lanfranc's disposal, is a very possible contingency,[3] and that these, for the sake of quoting all available privileges, whether directly bearing upon the primacy question or not, may have been quoted by Lanfranc is also possible. It is even possible that, in fairness to Thomas, Lanfranc may have quoted the two genuine letters of Bede. In that case he would have been making use of a well-known dialectical device, whereby through giving a little rope, his larger claims became more readily admitted. At any rate, in spite of Boehmer's elaborate attack upon the Archbishop, it appears that Lanfranc had access to a large amount of documentary evidence of a genuine character, sufficient to enable him to present a good case, and to win a forensic victory, without being under the necessity of resorting to forgery.

When the pages of Bede are turned over, we find no copies

[1] Eadmer, *Hist. Nov.*, pp. 262, 263, 265, 268, 273; Malmes., *G. P.*, §§ 31, 32, 33, 36, 38. Boehmer, pp. 147, 148, 149, 153, 157. Boniface to Justus, Honorius to Honorius, Vitalian to Theodore, Gregory III to the bishops, Formosus to the bishops. But a letter of Hon. I was in the papal Chancellery. Cf. *infra*, pp. 281–2.

[2] Boehmer, *passim*. He also admits that we know so little of affairs in the end of the ninth and beginning of the tenth centuries that silence about the letter of Formosus is not surprising (p. 51).

[3] Boehmer, p. 99, admits that an historical note ('memorabile factum') included by Eadmer (p. 271–2) as an introduction to the letter of Formosus was quoted by Dunstan, but claims that this only proves that it was in existence before 980, and that it is a legendary account of the sub-division of the Wessex diocese.

of any documents which would have been useful to Lanfranc at the council of 1072, with the exception of the two letters of Boniface and Honorius used by the forger. The silence of Bede therefore is regarded as weighty evidence against the existence of any genuine documents in 1072. But the silence of Bede is an argument of doubtful cogency. Of the genuineness of what he records there can be no question. But he is silent upon other matters for which we have ample authority in other quarters. He makes no reference to S. Patrick,[1] or to the deposition of Wilfred by Theodore.[2]

It has been suggested that Bede's silence on S. Patrick was due to the fact that he had no interest in Irish matters.[3] It is possible that his silence on any document bearing upon the primacy of Canterbury, or upon any claim to it, was due to his prejudice, as a northern churchman, in favour of the Archbishopric of York. In his letter to Egbert of York (734) he showed the keenest interest in the affairs of York. He thought that Egbert should have the pallium. His complete silence on the deposition of Wilfred by Theodore is a striking indication of his prejudice in favour of York. Moreover, he was supplied with information about Canterbury mainly by Albinus, Abbot of S. Augustine's,[4] the rival house to Christ Church, which was the archi-episcopal chair. Between 590 and 672 Bede quotes no papal letters or privileges. Boehmer suggests that either he did not think the relations with the Papacy of sufficient importance during that period, or that Albinus sent no copies,[5] but as he has just referred to Bede's reverence for the papal see as a reason for Bede's quotation of letters in the earlier part of his history, the first of these suggestions is weakened. If Albinus knew of copies of letters which were not forwarded to Bede, then the argument from silence goes at once. There are signs even in Bede's record that this was the case, unless we may argue that Bede did not include a copy of every letter which was sent to him. He mentions a letter sent by Boniface IV to

[1] This has been used as an argument by those who question the historicity of S. Patrick, but Prof. Bury has established the traditional S. Patrick as an historical personage.

[2] In iv. 16 and 17, Bede mentions the expulsion of Wilfred, but he makes no reference to Theodore's part in the deposition.

[3] J. H. Maude, *The Foundations of the English Church*, p. 23.

[4] Boehmer, p. 48.

[5] Ibid., p. 49.

Ethelbert of Kent (610),[1] but does not quote it. He mentions another letter of Boniface IV to Laurence (610),[2] and a third from Boniface V to Mellitus and Justus (619–24),[3] and again does not quote them. So Bede inserted no complete record of correspondence in his work, and we are thus aware, on his own authority, of two if not three letters which he did not quote. If the letter from Boniface IV to Ethelbert is the first letter in the Eadmer series, then Bede omitted it either because Albinus sent no copy, in view of its authority for Christ Church claims, or, if he did send one, then he suppressed it on account of northern prejudice.

Another argument from silence has been drawn from the absence of any reference to our letters in the epistle of the English bishops to Leo.[4] But it is not clear that the bishops could have made much use of any of the documents which were at Lanfranc's disposal, save pallium documents. They were protesting against the journey of the Archbishop of Canterbury to Rome for the pallium, and they quoted pallium documents. But this was not a matter dealt with by the authorities quoted by Lanfranc. Moreover, it is not clear that they had any access to the archives of Christ Church. Their letter, which is only a fragment, is based almost entirely upon the history of Bede.

(*b*) PERIOD OF THE FORGERIES

Lanfranc's failure to secure a written recognition of the settlement of 1072 from Rome left the way open for a renewal of the dispute. The relations between Canterbury and Rome became strained when William declined to do homage, and when Lanfranc failed to visit Gregory in Rome. The undecided attitude of the Archbishop during the dispute between Urban II and the anti-pope Clement III created a resentment against Canterbury which became active after the death of Lanfranc. Urban sent

[1] Bede, ii. 4. May not this be the first letter in the Eadmer series ?

[2] Ibid.

[3] Ibid. ii. 7; cf. Haddan and Stubbs for dates of these letters.

[4] Haddan and Stubbs, iii. p. 559, who date the letter 805 (though on p. 66 they give 801) in the pontificate of Leo III, at the appointment of Wilfred. Boehmer, p. 94, assigns it to the pontificate of Leo IX at the appointment of Stigand (1050–2).

a letter to Thomas of York, summoning that Archbishop to appear at Rome to answer for having broken the constitution of Gregory, by promising obedience to Lanfranc.[1] But Thomas had already taken steps to undo the settlement of 1072. At the consecration of Anselm he had refused to recognize Anselm as primate, and only when the words *in metropolitan Cantuariensem* were inserted in the deed of consecration, in place of the words *in primatem*, did he complete the rite.[2]

Urban II's successor Pascal II at first supported the claims of Canterbury, especially during the investiture contest, when it was to the papal interest to have the support of Canterbury. Anselm was recognized as primate of Britain, and Pascal ordered Archbishop Gerard, the successor of Thomas I at York, to swear obedience to him (1101). Hugh alleges that the question was raised by Gerard at Rome, and that the only privilege on behalf of Canterbury forthcoming there was the constitution of Gregory.[3] But this does not prove that our forged documents were already at Rome. It only proves that copies of whatever documents Lanfranc had submitted were not regarded as having settled the primacy question finally. Moreover, as Pascal's later attitude showed, it did not suit the papal policy now, any more than in the time of Hildebrand, to surrender the question entirely to Canterbury. Again, the privilege of Honorius I, which the papal Chancellery produced on a later occasion, was not forthcoming, so that the scrutiny was incomplete.

At the consecration of Thomas II to York (1108) the new Archbishop refused to take an oath of obedience to Anselm.[4] In 1109 Cardinal Ulric landed in England with orders from Pascal to settle the question on the basis of the constitution of Gregory. This is the statement of Hugh.[5] Eadmer does not mention that Ulric took part in the proceedings of the Council of Westminster held at Whitsun, when the Canterbury privileges were read, and Thomas was compelled by Henry I to read an oath of submission.[6] But at York, in July, when the pallium was handed to Thomas II, Ulric took the York side, and, according to Hugh, settled the dispute on the basis of Gregory's constitution.[7] The English investiture question was now over.

[1] *Historians of York*, ii., p. 103.
[2] Ibid., p. 105.
[3] Ibid., p. 114.
[4] Ibid., p. 112.
[5] Ibid., p. 119.
[6] Eadmer, *Hist. Nov.*, pp. 207–10.
[7] *Historians of York*, ii. p. 126 f.

Anselm was at peace with Henry, and Pascal II could safely modify his previous attitude to Canterbury.

But no mere attempt to settle the dispute by smoothing over the feelings of both parties could be successful for long. After the accession of Thurstan II at York (1114), Pascal II was again working in the York interest. In January 1116 he sent a letter to the York chapter in which he referred to Urban II's rebuke of Thomas I, and again announced the independence of York on the ground of Gregory's constitution.[1] He then proceeded in characteristic manner to try to appease Ralph of Canterbury by sending to him, to the King, and to the bishops and abbots of England, a letter in which he stated that he had no desire to belittle the authentic privileges of Canterbury, and referred again to the constitution of Gregory and the letter of Honorius I.[2] Boehmer points out that Pascal makes no allusion to our forged documents or to the settlement of 1072. But were our documents at this time in the possession of the papal Chancellery? On the other hand, Pascal mentions authentic Canterbury documents, which may easily refer to the documents used by Lanfranc, and may or may not have been in Pascal's possession at Rome. If Pascal refers to the genuine documents used by Lanfranc it need cause no surprise that he does not regard them as final proofs of the Canterbury case. The primacy dispute had long passed the stage when it was a mere question of precedence of Canterbury over York. The York chapter was contending for the complete and final independence of their metropolitan from the influence of Canterbury. The dispute had become a York case. Throughout this period the York party were the appellants on nearly every occasion. Thus the Canterbury documents, apart from our forgeries, were gradually losing their relevancy to the question at issue, and the constitution of Gregory and the letter of Honorius I appeared to be increasingly relevant. It became obvious that Canterbury needed more documents, especially as the York documents were growing in volume. At the Council of Salisbury (1116) Thurstan quoted the letter of Urban II to Thomas I, in addition to the constitution of Gregory and the letters of Honorius I.[3] In 1120 he produced the letters of Pascal II and Gelasius II.[4] The Papacy had completely

[1] Ibid., p. 134 ff., but the letter is not registered by Jaffé-Lowenfeld.

[2] Jaffé-Lowenfeld, 6547.

[3] *Historians of York*, ii., p. 136.

[4] Ibid., pp. 205–6.

turned against Canterbury and was issuing letter after letter in favour of York.[1] Calixtus II apparently placed Ralph of Canterbury and the Church in England under an interdict until justice was done to Thurstan.[2]

A determined effort was made by Ralph to regain the papal support by means of a letter sent to Calixtus II [3] (after January 1120).[4] This letter contains a lengthy and cogent historical argument, based upon the early history of Canterbury, such as Lanfranc might well have used in 1072. It made no reference to the letters of the Eadmer series, but quoted only the constitution of Gregory, the letter of Honorius I, the letter of Leo III to Kenwulf, and a letter of Alcuin to Ethelhard. There is thus a remarkable agreement between the documents mentioned by Ralph and those which we have seen were at Lanfranc's disposal in 1072.[5] Why were not more of these documents quoted? Possibly because they were already in the hands of the forger of the Eadmer series, or had been destroyed by him. The letter is an extremely valuable specimen of the strong case which the Canterbury advocates could put forward, without any reference to the Eadmer series. Such a case in the hands of Lanfranc, supported by his forensic ability in court, was quite capable of securing the victory of 1072.

Professor Boehmer suggests that Ralph did not quote the Eadmer series because those letters were now suspect, and had been suspected since 1102.[6] But if so, why did the Yorkist writer make no allusion to the suspicion of forgery? The only charge of forgery brought by him against the Canterbury party, until the forged documents were produced at Rome in 1120, relates to the alleged forgery of the written submission of Thomas I in 1072.[7]

Some time after the consecration of David, Bishop of Bangor, in the spring of 1120, another Council met to discuss the dispute between Ralph and Thurstan. At this Council the York party produced its most lengthy collection of documents,[8] and at this

[1] *Historians of York*, ii., pp. 138, 148, 149.

[2] Ibid., pp. 193–4. But Hugh's account is to be received with caution. Some of the letters quoted by him are suspicious, especially those sent by Calixtus II; cf. Boehmer, pp. 40–1 n.

[3] Ibid., pp. 228–51.

[4] Boehmer, p. 41 n.

[5] Cf. *supra*, p. 272.

[6] Boehmer, p. 41.

[7] *Historians of York*, ii., p. 101; cf. *supra*, p. 93.

[8] Cf. *supra*, p. 281.

Council for the first time appeared the full series of our forgeries.[1] Eadmer states that a search was made in the Chancellery of Canterbury, and our letters were discovered. He transcribes them in full. But if the letters were known at Canterbury since the time of Lanfranc, why did not Eadmer, like Malmesbury later, insert them into his account of Lanfranc, and why did he hold them back until describing the events of 1120, and then write in such terms as to indicate that they were discovered in 1120 for the first time? It may be replied that he wished to cover the reputation of Lanfranc, but the obvious method of covering Lanfranc was not to insert the letters at all. There is a suspicion that Eadmer knew more about the origin of the letters than he has admitted.

The letters were shown to Cardinal Pierleoni in 1121, and he pronounced in their favour.[2] We have no means of ascertaining Ralph's opinion, but his successor, William, ventured to take the letters to Rome, when he went to receive the pallium. One of the cardinals asked if the privileges had bulls attached to them. The reply was that the originals with bulls attached were at Canterbury, and that only copies had been brought. The cardinals asked the Canterbury envoys if they were ready to swear to their statement. They discussed the point among themselves, and one of them urged that the oath should be taken. But the others declined. The envoys replied that the bulls had been destroyed or lost through the passage of time. One of the cardinals laughed, another put his finger beside his nose, a third laughed aloud, and said that it was remarkable that parchment should survive while lead had been destroyed, the story was a fable, and he who presented it was a liar. The Canterbury envoys suggested that perhaps bulls were not used by the Papacy in early days. The cardinals replied that bulls had been in use since the time of Gregory the Great, and that privileges, with bulls attached to them by him, were in the archives of the Roman Church. So the envoys departed in confusion.[3]

As Boehmer remarks, the story about the collocation between the Canterbury envoys concerning the reply they should make

[1] Eadmer, *Hist. Nov.*, pp. 261 ff.; Hugh, *Historians of York*, ii. pp. 203–6. Malmesbury has improved the text of the Eadmer series. Cf. Boehmer, p. 5.

[2] Eadmer, *Hist. Nov.*, p. 296.

[3] Hugh, *Historians of York*, ii, pp. 204 ff.

may be put down to Yorkist spite. But it is clear that our forgeries were produced at Rome in 1123, and that this attempt to secure fresh documents to strengthen the Canterbury case against the growing victory of the Yorkist party failed. During the rest of the story we hear no more about our documents.

Why did not the Canterbury party fall back upon the documents mentioned by Ralph in the letter to Calixtus? Because these had already failed to make the requisite impression at Rome. The Papacy was asking for more evidence. Why was no reference made to other documents which appear to have been known to Lanfranc? Because the forger had destroyed them in the interests of his own series, so that William and his envoys may not have been acquainted with them. At some time in the first two decades of the twelfth century, probably between the dispatch of Ralph's letter to Calixtus II (after January 1120) and the meeting between Ralph and Thurstan (after April 1120), the Eadmer series was forged by the Canterbury monks or by one of their number. The originals used by Lanfranc in 1072 were destroyed.

Have we any palaeographical evidence to support this contention? Among the British Museum manuscripts are two collections of documents, each containing the ten letters transcribed by Eadmer and Malmesbury. The MS. Faustina B. VI contains nine of our documents in a twelfth-century hand, with the exception of the first—the letter of Boniface to Ethelbert, which is in an eleventh-century hand.[1] The missing letter has been bound up in a third collection, Claudius A. III.[2] We have seen that the privilege of Boniface to Ethelbert is not concerned with the primacy question. It was bound up in the collection Faustina B. VI as a privilege concerned with the pontificate of Lanfranc.

Thus the palaeographical evidence agrees with the history of the documents. They date only from the beginning of the twelfth century. If they were in existence in the eleventh century and were produced in 1072, fifty years before the date of Eadmer's discovery of them at Canterbury, why has not a single copy come down in an eleventh-century hand, with the exception of the first letter which is not concerned with the primacy question?[3] We have therefore reason for believing that the Eadmer series II–X are a twelfth-century forgery. The

[1] Boehmer, p. 7. [2] Ibid. [3] Cf. *infra*, pp. 287–91.

forger made use of genuine documents which can be traced in Nos. V, VI, VIII, and X of the series. They were forged at a period when the conflict had reached its height, and when fresh documents were essential to the Canterbury party.

Who was the forger? We do not know. But Boehmer gives reasons for the contention that the other early twelfth-century collection of our documents, Cleopatra E. I, was made by Eadmer, apparently during 1120–1,[1] the period of the discovery of the documents in the archives at Canterbury. Eadmer's interest in the dispute is undeniable. No one at Canterbury was better qualified than he to make the collection. But although Boehmer is not prepared to go farther than the suggestion that Eadmer may have been the transcriber of the collection Cleopatra E. I, may we not go farther and suggest that he was responsible for the forgery? Is it possible that he was the "schriftkundiger, belesener, und gebildeter Mann",[2] who 'wrote and wrote',[3] not during the spring of 1072, but during that of 1120, the man acquainted with the history of Bede, and with the customs of the papal Chancellery? If Eadmer knew less of the papal Chancellery than Lanfranc, he certainly knew more of the history of the English Church, and of the see of Canterbury. The forgeries are the work of an historical scholar, not a man of affairs. It is doubtful whether Lanfranc possessed the necessary historical knowledge for the work, and even if this assumption is questionable, it is difficult to supply time for the elaborate studies which the forgeries must have entailed. Boehmer pins the forgery down, on the basis of a doubtful paragraph, to the seven weeks between Easter and Whitsun 1072. But the documents must have been produced at Winchester, even if an adjourned meeting was held at Windsor[4] to

[1] Boehmer, p. 14. [2] Ibid., p. 110. [3] Ibid.

[4] *Die Fälschungen*, pp. 29, 143, 169. But the evidence for an adjourned meeting at Whitsun does not appear in four of our chief authorities. It is not mentioned by Cotton Nero, A, VII (Brit. Mus.); Sheppard, *Litt. Cant.* (Rolls), iii, App. I; Malmes, *G. P.*, § 27; Milo, 33. The doubtful passage (cf. *Die Fälschungen*, p. 169) appears in Cleopatra E. I, and Domitian, A, V (Brit. Mus.); Cant., A, 5, 6 (Wilkins, *Concilia*, i, p. 324); Eadmer, *Hist. Nov.*, p. 253; Diceto, i, p. 206. Even if the passage is authentic, it contains nothing to prove that the documents were not produced until the meeting at Windsor. 'Ventilata autem est haec causa prius apud Wentanam civitatem in Pascali solempnitate in capella regia, quae

sanction the terms of the settlement, otherwise the case would have gone against Lanfranc, and of this we do not read, even in the Yorkist writer's account. Moreover, the knowledge of the forger of our documents was not gained in seven weeks. Lanfranc did not come to England until August 1070. Early in 1071 he made his journey to Rome. The York dispute did not become a serious question for him until after the papal court had referred the matter back to an English council. That leaves the winter of 1071–2. But during that period Lanfranc was fully occupied with getting into touch with the general business of Church and State; he had very little leisure for historical research. He came to England most unwillingly, and it is improbable that he had spent some of the time at Caen working up a detailed knowledge of the history of England. Lanfranc regarded scholarship from the point of view of the business of life immediately at hand,[1] and at Bec and Caen his business was the teaching of theology and the organization of the monastic life. His studies were therefore theological and liturgical, and were devoted especially to the text of S. Paul's epistles and the constitutions of the abbeys of Normandy. They were not historical or concerned with matters across the Channel.

But in the case of Eadmer, the history of the English Church, and especially of Canterbury, was the passion and work of his life. In his seclusion at Canterbury he had ample time and opportunity to equip himself with the qualifications of the forger. Moreover, he possessed an incentive which was absent in Lanfranc's case. The needs of the situation in 1072 were not documents, but a skilful use of documents already existing. But in 1120 the Canterbury claims to the primacy depended entirely upon the production of fresh documents stamped through and through with the marks of papal authority and papal sanction. It was a more probable date for the forgeries than 1072.

If Lanfranc had been disposed to forge, a far simpler method lay before him. He based his case originally upon a supposed historical precedent for demanding a written oath of obedience

ita est in castello, postea in villa regia, quae vocatur Windlesor, ubi et finem accepit in praesentia regis, episcoporum, abbatum, diversorum ordinum, qui congregati erant apud curiam in festivitate Pentecostes.' The debate took place at Winchester, and the terms of the settlement were finally agreed upon at Windsor—that is all that this passage alleges.

[1] Epis. XXXVI.

from Thomas. A search among the records must have revealed the fact that such was not forthcoming. But it would have been an easy matter to have forged a written confession, and to have attributed it to a former Archbishop of York. Several copies of the submissions of suffragans, dating from the time of Ethelhard (790–805), were in the archives. There also existed a letter of submission in which the name of an Archbishop of York had been spuriously inserted,[1] but this was not even quoted by Lanfranc. If forgery had been the course decided upon, this would have been a far safer as well as a far easier method, for it could not have been checked by the papal archives.

APPENDIX II

THE FIRST PRIVILEGE IN THE EADMER–MALMESBURY SERIES

This professes to be a copy of the original letter sent by Boniface to Ethelbert.[2] But certain clauses in the opening of the Eadmer-Malmesbury privilege are repeated verbally in the letter of Honorius to Edwin, copied by Bede,[3] and the impression is created that the Eadmer-Malmesbury privilege is a forgery, based upon the record of Bede, and that therefore the quotation in Alexander's letter to Lanfranc is a forgery. Professor Boehmer's theory of the forgery is very ingenious. The Eadmer-Malmesbury privilege was forged by Lanfranc,[4] who made use of the letter of Honorius to Edwin quoted by Bede. It dates from the period Easter to Whitsun (1072); it was produced at the Council of 1072, and then sent on to the Curia where the papal secretary copied part of it into the epistle of Alexander II which was sent back to Lanfranc.[5]

We are mainly concerned with the passage quoted in the letter of Alexander.[6] The Pope states definitely that a scrutiny

[1] Haddan and Stubbs, iii, p. 506.

[2] Eadmer, *Hist. Nov.*, p. 261; Malmes., *G. P.*, § 30; Boehmer, p. 145.

[3] Bede, ii. 17.

[4] Or by one of his supporters (ibid., p. 60).

[5] Boehmer, *Die Fälschungen*, pp. 31 ff. and 52 ff.

[6] 'Gloriose filii . . . emendationem.'

of the records had been made, that the privilege of Gregory the Great to Augustine had come to hand, and that from the same source the letter of Boniface to Ethelbert and Laurence had appeared. According to Boehmer, we cannot accept the Pope's statement as a proof that a search was made. He claims that it was not the custom of the medieval Papacy to order a scrutiny unless the petitioner appeared in person ; that the words ' hinc habetur ' do not prove that Alexander had the letter of Boniface before him ; and that we have therefore direct proofs that Lanfranc sent both documents to the Pope.[1]

But no evidence is forthcoming for the dispatch of these documents by Lanfranc to the Papacy.[2] On the other hand, we have the express statement that a scrutiny of the papal records was made. We know certainly that a copy of Gregory's letter to Augustine was at Rome at the time,[3] and we have evidence in Bede for the dispatch of a letter by Boniface IV to Archbishop Laurence and Ethelbert of Kent.[4] It is remarkable that Alexander does not refer to a letter addressed solely to Ethelbert, but to Laurence and Ethelbert. He is supported therefore by Bede, and not by Eadmer-Malmesbury.[5] This important point is ignored by Boehmer.

Professor Boehmer develops his ingenious theory by pointing out that the absence of any reference to the receipt of copies of the documents from Lanfranc was due to the fact that both he and the Papacy wished his application to Rome to be kept secret. Lanfranc was afraid of William's attitude if the petition

[1] Boehmer, p. 33.

[2] With his letter to Alexander at the close of the York dispute Lanfranc sent a copy of the written statement which was sent to all the churches of England, and also other documents (Lanfranc, Epis. V ; Boehmer, p. 172 : ' Cujus exemplar . . . ex hoc atque aliis quae transmissa sunt '), but he does not say what these were. If they were the letters or copies quoted at Winchester, which he carefully mentions, it is curious that he does not draw attention to the fact. But even if they were, it does not prove that the letter of Boniface to Ethelbert contained in Eadmer-Malmesbury was included. He only mentions a letter of Boniface, which may have been the letter referred to in Bede, ii. 4, but not transcribed by Bede.

[3] *Greg. Epis.* xi. 65 (Migne, LXXVII).

[4] Bede, ii. 4.

[5] The Eadmer-Malmesbury privilege is addressed to Ethelbert only.

became known, and the Pope supported his cautious measures. But the suggestion is based solely upon the well-known attitude of the King to Rome when purely political issues were at stake. It seems entirely contrary to the equally well-known attitude of the King towards ecclesiastical questions. This was peculiarly the kind of question upon which the King would give support to Lanfranc. William and his lay lords may have been persuaded at first by the arguments of Walkelin,[1] just as he was persuaded at the opening of the York case by the arguments of Thomas, but there is no reason to suppose that Lanfranc failed to convince the King on this point any more than upon the question of the primacy, which was more closely related to political considerations.

There is no conclusive evidence that Lanfranc appealed to the Papacy on the Winchester question. We have the general statements of Malmesbury and Eadmer that in order to prevent trouble on any future occasion the Archbishop secured the assistance of the Pope. But no reference is made to the dispatch of an embassy for this purpose, still less to the dispatch of any documents. The letter of Alexander says that the Pope heard only indirectly of the trouble in England, and independently forwarded his opinion. There is, on the other hand, sufficient reason for believing that Lanfranc settled the dispute himself, both on the ground of Eadmer's and Malmesbury's statements, and in view of the general movement towards monasticism which was going on at the time. If an embassy was sent by Lanfranc, it carried verbal messages only.[2]

It is suggested [3] that the clause ' metropolis totius Britanniae ' was also copied by the papal secretary into Alexander's reply from Lanfranc's letter on this occasion. But even Boehmer admits that this suggestion is a mere assumption, and on this flimsy hypothesis he alleges an attempt on the part of Lanfranc to secure further sanction for the primacy of Canterbury. But on Boehmer's own evidence, that was a verdict which the Papacy consistently refused to issue at Lanfranc's request. If his assumption is correct, we are driven to the conclusion that the letter which bore Alexander's name was dispatched without being seen by the Pope, or by Hildebrand, who was even less anxious

[1] Eadmer, *Hist. Nov.*, p. 18.
[2] Cf. Epis. of Alexander to Lanfranc, *supra*, p. 149
[3] Boehmer, *Die Fälschungen*, p. 33.

to give a charter for the primacy, and less likely to permit correspondence to leave the Chancellery without being seen by himself. The clause is not really inconsistent with the guarded attitude of the Papacy on the primacy question. It supplies no approval of Lanfranc's claim. It merely refers to the historic fact of Canterbury as the mother-Church of England.

With regard to the letter of Boniface to Ethelbert of Kent, Lanfranc may well have produced a copy at the Council of 1072. But our evidence beyond the Eadmer-Malmesbury series is the statement in his own letter to Alexander II at the close of the York dispute, that a letter of Boniface was then produced. We are not told in that epistle to whom the letter of Boniface was sent, but we have seen that a letter was sent by that Pope to Ethelbert,[1] and this may have been the letter quoted by Lanfranc in 1072.

How, then, are we to account for the first privilege in the Eadmer-Malmesbury series? It is, as Boehmer has proved, a forgery. The first half of the privilege is based upon the letter of Honorius to Edwin quoted by Bede,[2] with the exception of certain details in the date, and certain words, which do not affect the tenor of other parts of the letter.[3]

The second half of the letter, commencing 'Qua propter gloriose filii', is based upon the genuine letter quoted by Alexander II,[4] and like the letter of Sergius and Leo III contains authentic matter from the Pope whose inscription it bears.

Eadmer-Malmesbury I was forged by an eleventh-century monk at Canterbury, with the object of strengthening the claim of Christ Church to precedence over S. Augustine's. The original at Canterbury was destroyed, like the originals of the letters of Sergius and Leo III. The eleventh-century manuscript in our possession,[5] written on a page torn from a copy of S. Luke's gospel, filled with erasures and corrections, may be the forger's original copy or a transcription made by a novice during his daily exercise in the scriptorium. The forgery is that of an unlearned monk. Lanfranc would not have made the clumsy plagiarism from Bede, nor, if the copy in Claudius A. III represents the true copy, would he have left his handiwork so badly exposed.

[1] Bede, ii. 4. [2] ii. 17. [3] Boehmer, pp. 52 ff.
[4] Possibly the letter referred to in Bede, ii. 4.
[5] Cotton Claudius A. III (Brit. Mus.).

The historical argument against the issue of a privilege by Boniface to Ethelbert for a monastic foundation at Canterbury is also unconvincing. Boehmer maintains that it was not possible for a bishop's house to be organized on monastic lines in Augustine's time, and that Augustine did not live in a cloister, but in a house arranged on cloister lines.[1] But this is merely to read the conditions of the sixth century through the spectacles of the eleventh. The early bishops of England, whether Roman or Celtic, were all monks, and they lived in monastic communities, whether Benedictine or Celtic. The clergy who assisted them in the work of preaching and organizing were also monks. Moreover, we have the express injunction of Gregory that Augustine was to live among his clergy, who were to be monks.[2] We have evidence that Ethelbert was zealous for the foundation of religious communities.[3] If Bede does not quote the letter of Boniface to Ethelbert,[4] that may be due to the fact that Albinus, Abbot of S. Augustine's, who supplied him with information about Canterbury, omitted to send a copy of this letter because it was concerned with the rival house. The fact that both S. Augustine and King Ethelbert were buried at S. Augustine's only proves that house to have possessed more prestige at that date, as the older and more powerful community.

APPENDIX III

(*a*) DOUBTFUL WRITINGS

A small work entitled 'De Celanda Confessione' has been handed down on the authority of two manuscripts under the authorship of Lanfranc.[5] The subject-matter reveals the same breadth of view and common sense characteristic of all his writings and utterances. If priests were so scarce that a penitent could find no one to whom he might make his confession, he should confess to a layman of pure life, and if such a one could not be found, he should not worry, but rest contented with

[1] *Die Fälschungen*, p. 53.
[2] *Greg. Epis.* xi. 64.
[3] Cf. Haddan and Stubbs, iii, p. 52, for Ethelbert's genuine charter to Rochester, and (pp. 53–60) for the doubtful charters to S. Augustine's and S. Paul's. Even if spurious these charters testify to the King's interest in the monks.
[4] Bede, ii. 4.
[5] *Hist. Litt. de la France*, viii, p. 292, printed in Giles, ii, pp. 303–11.

having made his confession to God. The secrets of the confession were on no account to be revealed by the priest, nor might he or the penitent seek or give information about others which had been obtained through the confessional. Confession, as a renunciation of sin, is compared with Baptism.

A fragment containing eight short rules for the monastic life has survived. The cloister must not be left without permission. The rules of silence, poverty and obedience are laid down. Murmuring is to be avoided, and the love of God maintained. The services of the Church must be strictly performed and confessions properly made. The fragment closes with an injunction that the Eucharist is not to be withheld from any of the faithful.[1]

Other writings attributed to Lanfranc's editorship are an edition of Cassian with the words 'Huc usque correxi', and his own name attached, in a twelfth-century hand;[2] the Hexameron, the Apology of David, a treatise on the Sacraments, all by Ambrose;[3] and the *Elucidarium*. The writer in the *Histoire Littéraire de la France* maintains that the *Elucidarium* is the commentary on the epistles of S. Paul under another name.[4] But it appears anonymously in the twelfth-century catalogue of Bec, and the subject-matter is so entirely different and the teaching often so puerile, that it is doubtful whether Lanfranc would have written such a work. It consists of a dialogue between a teacher and his pupils, on the religious sensibility of material elements, on creation, the mystical body of Christ, seculars and regulars, laymen, miracles and pilgrimages.[5] Three copies of the work are in the library of Trinity College, Dublin, under Lanfranc's name, but a larger number of copies, elsewhere, attribute it to Anselm. The work is not included by D'Achery in his collection of Lanfranc's writings. Giles suggests that it could not have been written by the sedate Anselm, and that if it is not by Lanfranc, it may have been written by one of his pupils.[6] There seems to be little reason for attributing it to Lanfranc.

[1] Cf. Giles, ii, pp. 301–2. Two copies exist, one in the library at Alençon and the other at Mans. Delisle thinks the latter is the original (Chron. Robt. Torigny, i, p. 74). Cf. Porée, *Hist. de l'Abbaye du Bec*, i, p. 92.

[2] De Crozals, *Lanfranc*, p. 65.

[3] *Hist. Litt. de la France*, viii, p. 287.

[4] Ibid., p. 297.

[5] Cf. Hook, *Archbishops*, ii, pp. 98–105, and H. W. C. Davis, *Eng. under the Normans and Angevins*, pp. 49–50, for a précis of the work.

[6] Giles, *Opera Lanfranci*, vol. ii, p. vii. I am informed that the

A copy of a work on the Apocalypse and the Song of Songs has been assigned to him. Three other short works—De Diversis Casibus Missae, De Sacramentis Excommunicatorum, De Consuetudinariis Ecclesiae, which are also attributed to him, were probably written by Osmund, Bishop of Salisbury.[1]

A better tradition assigns to him a lost history of the Church in his own times.[2] This work may have been used by Malmesbury for his *De Gesta Pontificum*. Siegbert of Magdeburg says that he wrote a history of William the Conqueror.[3] A short account of the Canterbury and York dispute, together with the minute of the Council of 1072, are assigned to him.[4] A written account of the settlement was certainly distributed among the churches of England, but his authorship of these writings and of the minutes of the Councils of 1075 and 1076[5] remains uncertain. Other lost writings attributed to him are a commentary on the Psalms and a collection of decretals.[6] The only writings which can with confidence be assigned to him during this period are his last works on the text of the Bible, the *Benedictine Decrees*,[7] and parts of the *De Corpore et Sangüine Domini*. But the history of the Saxon Church appears to have become one of his studies after his arrival in England. At the Council of 1072 he quoted the authority of Bede generally in support of his case, and although, apart from the letters which are alleged to have been produced on that occasion, the reports of the Council do not necessitate an intimate knowledge of Bede, there can be little doubt that the history of the Saxon church and institutions formed one of his studies during the following years. There is evidence of this in his discussion with Anselm concerning S. Alphege, and his interest in Saxon saints generally.

Elucidarium is a work of Honorius, so-called Augustodunensis, a German solitary near Regensburg, who lived in the twelth century.

[1] *Hist. Litt. de la France*, viii. pp. 298–9.

[2] Eadmer, p. 13.

[3] *Hist. Litt. de la France*, viii, p. 295. The Sax. Chron., *Latin Acta*, says that he caused an account of the proceedings of the Council of 1075 to be written, ' at the request of many.'

[4] Boehmer, *De Fälshungen*, pp. 141–3.

[5] *Hist. Litt. de la France*, viii, p. 293.

[6] Longuemare, p. 208.

[7] The inclusion of Alphege in the calendar fixes the spring of 1079, the time of Anselm's visit, as one of the limits for the date of the Decreta, unless it was added later.

(b) SPURIA. THE THREE CANONS

An attempt has been made to attribute to Lanfranc three canons which appear in a Trinity manuscript.[1] The first and the third authorize the monks to exercise the functions of parochial priests; to preach, to baptize, to give the communion, to impose penance and to absolve from sin. The second authorizes them to receive tithes.[2] They were quoted at the Council of Nismes (1096),[3] where Urban II presided. Canon I is included in the collection of Ivo of Chartres (c. 1092), and in that of Anselm of Lucca (c. 1080). Canon II only appears in the Trinity manuscript,[4] and they are all absent from the collection of Burchard of Worms.[5] Yet with this history behind them, they have been attributed by Boehmer to the Archbishop, on the slender evidence that they are to be found in the Trinity manuscript and in three other manuscripts which also issued from Canterbury.[6] Boehmer associates them with the attack of Walkelin on the privileges of the monks in 1072,[7] and suggests that they were forwarded by Lanfranc to Alexander II, together with a forged copy of the letter of Boniface to Ethelbert,[8] and so came into the hands of Urban II.[9]

Boehmer's starting-point is a note in the Trinity manuscript which says that Lanfranc ordered the book to be brought from Bec.[10] But this copy, which is the oldest complete version of the canons in existence,[11] is written in one or perhaps two twelfth-century hands.[12] It does not therefore contain Lanfranc's handwriting. The three canons, which are followed by three letters of the anti-pope Clement addressed to Lanfranc, appear after the note attributed to him, which clearly ended the archetype of the book, and they were entered either by a different scribe or by the same copyist at a later date. The handwriting is smaller, and is written with better ink than that of the main

[1] Trin. Coll., Camb., B. 16, 44, pp. 405–7.

[2] Boehmer, *Die Fälschungen*, pp. 161–4.

[3] Ibid., p. 69.

[4] Ibid., pp. 67, 69, 73.

[5] Ibid., p. 73.

[6] Ibid., p. 74.

[7] Ibid., pp. 76–7.

[8] Cf. *supra*, pp. 287 ff.

[9] Boehmer, p. 82.

[10] 'Hunc librum dato precio emptum ego Lanfrancus archiepiscopus de Beccensi cenobio in Anglicam terram deferri feci et ecclesie Christi dedi.'

[11] Boehmer, pp. 62, n. 2, 65.

[12] James, *Trin. Coll. Camb. Catalogue of Western MSS.* i. 540 f.

body of the book, which comes before Lanfranc's note. But the resemblance between the two hands is sufficiently marked not to militate against the possibility of the same authorship. In medieval handwriting especially, if the scribe commenced a paragraph with smaller letters than the previous script, the symmetry of the penmanship necessitated its continuance. The large hand in which Lanfranc's note is copied is clearly a concluding flourish to the main work.

The original collection was completed before the three canons were added by some one else, who copied the concluding note, like the scribe of the Corpus manuscript; and although the original came from Bec, there is only presumptive evidence, based upon the note, that Lanfranc compiled it. The note only says that he ordered it to be brought to England after he became Archbishop. He bought it as a precious gift for Christ Church. If he himself compiled it, why was it necessary to buy it? Why did he not send for it as for the Commentaries on S. Paul? [1] The book may have been compiled after he left Bec. Whatever its date may be, it may have been originally compiled by Ivo of Chartres, Lanfranc's own pupil at Bec, the great canonist and collector of ecclesiastical privileges, and if so, one of the three canons may have originated from him. In this case their popularity in France and their recurrent appearance at the French councils are explained.

Boehmer suggests that the forgery of the canons dates from the same period as the forgery of the first privilege in the Eadmer-Malmesbury series, and was produced at the Council of 1072.[2] But the question of the privileges of the monks was not raised at that Council. Moreover, his contention that the first canon was an attempt to prove that regular monks were superior to secular canons is not borne out by its contents, and so was not relevant to the dispute with Walkelin. Furthermore, the contents of the three canons are not supported by the rigid rules drawn up by Lanfranc for the community of Christ Church, in which the Almoner alone was permitted to carry out pastoral functions. They are not supported by references in his writings which ordered the monks to remain within the cloister.[3] Again, if, as the canons claim, the monks were free to exercise parochial

[1] Anselm, Lib. I, Epis. LVII. [2] Boehmer, pp. 79–80.

[3] Lanfranc, Epis. LXIII, LXVI, and *Sermo sive Sententiae*, Giles, ii, p. 299.

functions, it is curious that Lanfranc did not enforce them at the Council of 1076 when the laxity of the clergy was discussed. A better opportunity for emphasizing the contrast between the strictness of the monastic and the slackness of the parochial clergy could not have occurred.

We may admit that the three canons are forgeries. The first does not belong to Boniface IV. The second only appears in the Trinity manuscript, although it is attributed to a Parisian Council. The third, which is copied from the forged decretal of Nicaea, does not belong to Gregory, and Gratian dissociated it from that pontiff in his collection.[1] They are contrary to the orders of Alexander II issued to the Church in Florence, and to the Roman decrees of 1078.[2] Their previous history clearly associates them with the Norman and French clergy, and they harmonize better with the extravagant claims put forward at the end of the eleventh century in Normandy and France, on behalf of the monks, than with Lanfranc's system in England, where the monastic organization was not allowed to interfere with parochial arrangements.

[1] Boehmer, p. 68.

[2] Ibid., p. 73.

INDEX

M

N

Y